THE BRITISH GRAND PRIX

NEXT PAGE
'Golden Boy', Stirling Moss, first British winner of the British Grand Prix, in the Mercedes-Benz W196 at Aintree, 1955.

B.T. BATSFORD LTD   LONDON

The BRITISH GRAND PRIX

1926-1976

Doug Nye

*The start of the first Donington GP with Sommer's
Alfa Romeo, Farina's V8 Maserati and Maclure's Riley on
the front row. The Belisha Beacon had no legal
significance.*

First Published 1977
Copyright © 1977 Doug Nye

ISBN *0 7134 3283 7*

Filmset in 10 on 11pt. Monophoto Apollo by
Servis Filmsetting Ltd, Manchester
Printed in Great Britain by
The Anchor Press, Tiptree, Essex
for the publishers
B.T. Batsford Ltd
4 Fitzhardinge Street
London W1H 0AH

Contents

Acknowledgment

Compiling this history of Britain's major motor race has been a long and often confusing task. Reading contemporary race reports has sometimes made one feel that there were two or three different British GPs run each year, for the pressure of a weekly schedule must tell on those who have to work to it. Unravelling the mysteries, contradictions, claims and counter-claims has been a difficult but fascinating business.

Many people helped considerably in putting the record straight, and although it was a shock to discover that the RAC themselves have kept no complete record of their premier motor race I am sincerely grateful to Dean Delamont, Neil Eason-Gibson and Phil Drackett of the Club for their assistance.

Others, like Bob Gerard, Tony Brooks, Bernie Ecclestone, Tony Rudd of BRM, Rodney Clarke of Connaught and an enormous list of other drivers and entrants have all contributed useful British GP detail, perhaps unwittingly, while talking in general about 'the old days'.

Eric Bellamy of the National Motor Museum Library at Beaulieu has been extremely helpful in unearthing contemporary reports of the earliest races, while Geoff Goddard did much more than provide the bulk of the photographs which illustrate this volume. Access to his comprehensive collection of programmes was invaluable, and I must also thank Charles Mortimer for loaning 1926–27 Brooklands programmes, including one which has 'Wonderful, Wonderful, Wonderful Campbell' pencilled all over it! Cyril Posthumus provided most of the pre-war GP photographs from his collection, and with Denis Jenkinson was an ever-helpful mine of information on the pre-Doug Nye period events, particularly when it came to unravelling which type of Maserati was driven by whom, and which ERA did what. 'Autosport' kindly loaned prints of the 1973 Silverstone pile-up taken by David Oliver, while further information was drawn from contemporary copies of 'Motor Sport', 'Motor', 'Autocar', 'Speed', 'Motoring News' and the annuals 'Autocourse' and 'Motor Racing Year'. I have also dipped into innumerable driver and entrant biographies and marque histories, plus such classics as George Monkhouse's 'Motor Racing with Mercedes-Benz' to gain added perspective. Chassis number detail has been checked and discussed with Duncan Rabagliati of the Formula 1 Register, and his patient response to my late-night telephone calls has been much appreciated. After all this research, any errors which appear are the fault of my compilation – not that of my sources, and for those I apologise in advance.

Finally, thanks to my wife Valerie for enduring too many days of home-shaking typewriting when things were going right, and many more of grizzly-bear soreheadedness when they were going wrong. I have assured her that somebody else will be recording the story of the next fifty years of the British Grand Prix . . . if the purest form of motor racing is allowed to survive that long . . .

Doug Nye
Lower Bourne, Farnham
September 1976

Introduction

If the story told in these pages confined itself strictly to 'The British Grand Prix', it would begin in 1949 and would grind to an abrupt halt after 1971. This would not be an accurate picture of Grand Prix racing in Britain, and so I have included the Royal Automobile Club Grand Prix races of 1926–7 and 1948, the great Donington Park events of the 'thirties, and this country's Formula 1 World Championship-qualifying rounds run in 1972–6, from which the perfectly honourable (and accurate) 'British' title had been removed.

Two names put Britain on the Grand Prix map during the 'twenties: Segrave and Sunbeam. This duo won the classic *Grand Prix de l'ACF* at Tours in 1923, and in the following season they won the first-class Spanish race at San Sebastian. While cynics pointed out that the driver was an Irish-American, and his car an Italian-designed Fiat copy prompted by a French-born chief executive, Segrave was as English as they came and his car proudly carried British Racing Green before Continental audiences.

These successes prompted the AIACR, which was the sport's international controlling body at the time, to offer a Grand Prix date to the Royal Automobile Club for 1925. Unfortunately they had no suitable circuit, for a special Act of Parliament would be required to close public roads on the mainland, and most politicians were still trenchantly horse-orientated. The RAC's Tourist Trophy course in the Isle of Man was considered unsuitable for Grand Prix racing, and so while officials hesitated in Pall Mall the 1925 calendar was published without a British Grand Prix.

Meanwhile, thoughts turned towards Brooklands, where H.F. Locke-King had built the world's first properly-designed artificial motor course in 1906–7. It had been intended as a centre where the British motor industry could test and develop its products free from the legal restrictions of the public road, and where motor racing and speed events could be run before a properly-policed (and paying) public.

Brooklands was a bland, blank expanse of dished concrete, but it had its history and its character. The possibility of reproducing 'road-like' features on the Weybridge track had been suggested in *The Autocar* as early as 1914, when H. Massac Buist discussed a suggestion by Gordon Watney – one of the Track's well-known drivers – in the July 18 issue. The idea was that zigzag sandbanks should be introduced along the finishing straight, before the cars '. . . issue onto the Home Banking'.

Buist continued: 'This in effect would be undergoing the equivalent of traversing a circuitous road such as is often used for part of the Continental courses'. The idea was dismissed after the war as being too expensive 'for the cartage of sand alone', but in 1922 Buist resurrected the idea in preparation for a projected 500-Mile race along Indianapolis lines, to be organized by the Brooklands Automobile Racing Club that September.

This great venture failed due to lack of entries, and it was left to the enthusiastic and energetic Junior Car Club to turn to something like Watney's eleven-year-old sandbank chicane idea for their 1925 200-Mile race. Their course took cars down the finishing straight, through 180 degrees round a marker barrel, and then back onto the outer circuit. This event, won by Segrave in an STD Darracq at 78.89 mph proved that such a circuit was not a car-breaker, and that it could be *very* entertaining for the crowds.

So the sandbank idea came to be revived, almost as first devised, for the 1926 RAC Grand Prix, when the AIACR introduced the *Grand Prix d'Angleterre* to their calendar for August 2. This 'First RAC Grand Prix' was the penultimate round in the slipshod 'World Championship' then running, but the San Sebastian race on July 25 left only a week for preparation, and so the date was changed to August 7.

Two weeks before the great day, RAC and Brooklands officials supervised installation of the sandbanks in the finishing straight. Garish builders' sand was used, positioned and repositioned during tests made by Paul Dutoit – Segrave's riding mechanic at Tours – driving an old Alvis racer. A line of covered race pits had been built, more sandbanks at their rear keeping the public at bay, and new scoring boards were erected opposite the main spectator areas. A temporary bridge was erected across the finishing straight, supported on the track itself. Prophetically, J. Smith & Co of Albemarle Street, London's Delage agents, bought the bridge's advertizing space. The Grand Prix attracted considerable interest with this new 'road-like' 2.616-mile course, and yet the Brooklands motto of 'The Right Crowd and No Crowding' was enforced by expensive admission charges of 5s per head and 10s per car. Entry to the paddock and special enclosure nearby would cost the real enthusiast £1 per head and 10s per car, but 'special catering arrangements' *were* promised.

It was in these surroundings that Britain had her first taste of Grand Prix racing, but when the 1927 race saw the 1½-litre Formula creep out on a depressingly low note, the RAC lost interest. They were offered the *Grand Prix d'Europe* title for 1928, but their money and enthusiasm were both too low. The Tourist Trophy sports car race in Ireland became their national *Grande Epreuve* – indeed it had a right to that title as one of the oldest races in the world, dating back to 1905. The ideal of Grand Prix racing for single-seater cars over an internationally-recognized distance lived on in some enthusiasts' hearts, and in Derbyshire lived a man with the dynamism to make that ideal a reality.

Fred G. Craner was a tough, bluff Midlander, involved in the motor business. One could hardly imagine someone more different from the RAC establishment in Pall Mall. He was Secretary of the modest Derby and District Motor Club, and in 1931 he managed to persuade a local land-owner, John Gillies Shields, to allow the Club to run motor-cycle races around the paths and tracks of his estate just outside Castle Donington.

Thus Donington Park became established as England's first mainland road-racing course, and in the winter of 1932–3 the Derby Club drummed together £12,000 to widen and develop the woodland circuit to accommodate cars. Sir George Beaumont opened the 2¼-mile course on March 25, 1933, and Colonel Lindsay Lloyd, on behalf of the RAC, 'spoke with satisfaction about the sporting nature of the track and hoped it would meet with the support it deserved'.

In fact Donington went from strength to strength, its combination car and motor-cycle meetings proving very popular. The course was lengthened and improved, growing from 2 miles 327 yards to 2 miles 971 yards after the first season. Pits and grandstands were erected, a proper paddock laid down, and a public address system installed. By 1935 Fred Craner's circuit was gaining in importance. He lived there, in Coppice Lodge, and *Motor Sport* commented in their report on the August meeting: 'The energy of the Donington authorities was now a byword, and one never failed to see some improvements and innovations which owe their execution to the enterprizing Mr Fred Craner . . . We greatly admired the alterations at Coppice Corner, where the "no-passing" section (between farm buildings) has been eliminated, the new permanent circuit completed, and a block of fine new garages erected on the lines of those at Nurburgring.'

This was all in preparation for the realization of Craner's ambition: a full-length 300-mile race under contemporary Grand Prix rules. Naturally he called it the Donington Grand Prix; only the races at Brooklands had been called 'British Grand Prix', and this was the RAC's title – he had a good one of his own.

That first Grand Prix proved a great success, and although less exciting its successor in 1936 established the event as a minor classic. William L. Bemrose, the Derby Club's President, wrote in the programme for the 1937 Grand Prix: '. . . when Donington was in its early stages . . . the Derby and District Motor Club organized their first Grand Prix race. It was . . . a great success, and was followed by a still more successful Grand Prix meeting in 1936. Both these races . . . were lacking in one important feature, and that was the participation on a large scale of the best Continental teams . . .'.

For that 1937 race Craner had put matters right and had won the support of the great German teams, who made that race and the 1938 event true classics in every sense of this much-misused term. For these races, and for the RAC's TT which accompanied them in the Donington season, the circuit was further lengthened to 'three-mile an' a furlong' (3 miles 220 yards). In the winter of 1937–8 the gradients on the new loop's twin Melbourne Hills were eased, the pit area redesigned and the road substantially widened between McLean's and Coppice Corners. Then came the war, Donington Park's requisition by the military, and its demise as a racing circuit. Until 1956 the Park formed the biggest military transport depot in this country, but today it houses the world's biggest racing car museum, and is being rebuilt to modern circuit standards. Perhaps one day a *British* Grand Prix will run there.

After the war Britain had no motor racing circuits. Brooklands had been wrecked and sold to Vickers Aircraft. Donington Park was devastated and choked with rusting military surplus vehicles, and Crystal Palace was choked with weeds and brambles.

Only one motor race meeting was held on English soil in 1946, and that was a virtually clandestine affair organized by the Cambridge University Motor Club on the disused airfield at nearby Gransden Lodge. It was very successful, airfield racing was proved to be feasible, and in 1947 the Cambridge Club combined with the Vintage Sports Car Club to run a repeat meeting – quietly – at Gransden. Dennis Poore won the main event in the Alfa Romeo 8C–35 which had won the Donington Grand Prix eleven years and a World War before. There were 15,000 spectators, and now the RAC were looking seriously at airfield sites as a suitable stop-gap measure to bring British motor racing back to life.

While Colonel F. Stanley Barnes and his RAC

Three of the most important of the British Grand Prix trophies: the Mervyn O'Gorman which dates back to Brooklands days, the Fred G. Craner Memorial Car Trophy in memory of the man behind the Donington races which were never 'British' Grands Prix as such, and the Royal Automobile Club Trophy.

Competition Committee began looking around various abandoned airfields and made official contacts with the War Office and relevant ministries, some amateur enthusiasts found the perfect venue. On the evening of the September 1947 Shelsley Walsh hill-climb, a Midland hostelry was packed with revelling 'motorists'. Next day saw eleven chain-drive Frazer Nashes, a Bugatti, and – so the story goes – a spectating Tiger Moth – arriving at the bleak aerodrome above Silverstone village for an impromptu race around its runways and perimeter tracks. Maurice Geoghegan, one of the 'organizers' lived in the village and had used the airfield to test a racing car he had renovated the previous winter.

When the RAC representatives saw the place it had instant appeal. It was situated almost at England's geographical centre, within easy reach of London, the Midlands and the North, East and West. Most of the site was cultivated, and its cavernous hangars were used by the Rootes Group for the concentration of Hillman cars before export.

Barnes formed an RAC Sub-Committee to clear Silverstone's use with the interested Ministries (of War, Air, Town and Country Planning, Agriculture, Supply, Transport, Fuel, Works *and* the Board of Trade!), and to set about organizing an RAC Grand Prix there for 1948.

Earl Howe was Chairman, presiding over Lord Waleran, T.A.S.O. Mathieson, Major-General A.H. Loughborough, John Morgan of the JCC (soon to be re-styled BARC), Fred Craner, S.C.H. Davis, Rodney Walkerley, Desmond Scannell of the BRDC, Col. Barnes, Captain A.W. Phillips and Major John Upton.

Their intensive work bore fruit, and while racing began at the Duke of Richmond & Gordon's Goodwood estate on September 18, around the perimeter of the old Westhampnett fighter-base, the RAC Grand Prix circuit at Silverstone was being prepared for its great day on October 2 . . . a date granted at short notice by the FIA.

The circuit was laid out to give 'the maximum possible frontage' to spectators, and to 'simulate a true road circuit in reproducing corners of varying severity and of right- and left-hand type'. Pits, paddock and start-area were arranged where the perimeter track passed closest to an access road, and this 55-feet wide roadway was combined with an hour-glass infield section up the 150-feet wide main runways, suitably marked with barrels and strawbales.

The start was opposite Luffield Abbey Farm, founded near the site of that ancient Abbey suppressed by Henry VIII, which gave its name to the sweeping curve before the pits. Other corners were named after the local Maggotts Moor, the ruins of Thomas á Beckett's Chapel, nearby Stowe School

and the reserved Club enclosure, while Segrave and Seaman gave their names to the infield runway sections. Lap length was 3 miles 1,180 yards, and canvas barriers were erected at the runway intersection to spare drivers the unnerving sight of other competitors approaching head-on.

For 1949 the FIA granted the race *Grande Epreuve* status, and the RAC celebrated by christening it The British Grand Prix. They abandoned the runway sections of the 1948 course, from which spectators had been prohibited due to intensive cultivation on the intervening strips of land. The pits were moved further away from Abbey Curve for safety's sake, and a tight chicane introduced at Club Corner to force 'the use of second gear', and to give a length of exactly 3 miles.

Later that year the BRDC ran their first, very successful, International Trophy meeting there for Formula 1 cars, in conjunction with *The Daily Express*.

For the 1950 *Grand Prix d'Europe*, the Club Chicane was suppressed, corners eased, and lap-length cut back to 2 miles 1,564 yards. This was hailed as 'The Second British Grand Prix', the 1948 race and those of the 'twenties being conveniently forgotten, but in 1951 the public were suddenly presented with 'The Fourth British Grand Prix' as at least the post-war race was retrospectively renamed by the organizing club! In his foreword to the programme the RAC Chairman, Wilfrid Andrews, wrote: 'Silverstone itself was an expedient, a place on which competitions of all kinds could be run and it has fulfilled that need. The lease will not be renewed by the RAC after 1951 because of the immense volume of work entailed by the control of the many events which form the year's calendar . . . the Club desires to help any organization which can take over the course in the future so that something more permanent may arise from what originally was a temporary expedient.'

The BRDC under Desmond Scannell's direction won support from *The Daily Express*, and that aggressively promotion-minded journal made Silverstone the home of the British Grand Prix until 1955, when it began its few years' flirtation with Aintree. With backing from the *Express*, the BRDC remodelled Silverstone for 1952, when they moved the start area to beyond Woodcote Corner, and erected permanent pits, paddock, race control buildings and enormous scaffolding grandstands.

Silverstone survived little-changed until the 1963 Grand Prix meeting, when a car spun out of Woodcote in the last race of the day and killed scrutineer Harry Cree in the pits. A similar fatality had occurred earlier in the season, and that winter saw the pits totally rebuilt, with an elevated pit-road reached by a ramp in front of the race control building, and Woodcote Corner slightly re-aligned. This facility survived until the winter of 1974–5, when it was demolished and an all-new pits and paddock area constructed. Together with miles of catch-fencing and other safety measures, this represented an investment of £140,000 by the BRDC and their subsidiary Silverstone Circuits Ltd, and then for the 1975 Grand Prix it was all spoiled as the spine-chilling sweep of Woodcote itself – one of the most exciting corners in the world of Formula 1 racing – had to be castrated by the installation of a chicane.

Aintree, amid the industrial suburbs of Liverpool, was of course world-famous for its Grand National horse race when the owner, Mrs Mirabel Topham, formed the Aintree Automobile Racing Company and built an interesting, if very flat, 3-mile road circuit around her stadium for 1954. The first meeting was run anti-clockwise, but from the start of the 1955 season they began to race the conventional way. The paddock was outside the circuit for 1955, behind the Aintree, County and Tatts Grandstands, while these huge permanent structures themselves gave a fine view out across the whole course with its tight infield loop and fast return Railway Straight, parallel to the embankment with British Rail tracks on top. Melling Crossing, where the Railway Straight ended in a flick left, then right, across the old Melling Road, was a demanding and petrifying 'S' which formed the circuit's best feature.

The first Aintree Grand Prix races were sponsored by *The Daily Telegraph*, the last, in 1962, by *The Daily Mirror*, and then in 1964 the RAC decided to organize their own race once more, and did so in conjunction with Motor Circuit Developments (the company which owned and administered Brands Hatch) and *The Daily Mail* and *Evening News* newspapers.

Brands Hatch itself had been used as a motor-cycle grass track between the wars, and was revived in 1949. A tiny, kidney-shaped loop was surfaced here in Brands' narrow valley in 1950, and the circuit became the home of the 500 Club, which later grew into the large and influential British Racing and Sports Car Club.

Their 500-cc meetings were always good fun, often with more 'tumble' than 'rough' about them, and in 1954 Druid's Hill loop was added, and spectator amenities improved. This 1.24-mile course was very successful, and remains so today for club events, while in 1960 another extension was made out into the backwoods to form a 2.65-mile Grand Prix circuit.

With continual development, Brands Hatch has remained the alternate home of the British Grand Prix to this day, but its severely restricted infield, tightly-packed pits, inadequate pit-lane and remote, steeply shelved paddock presented all kinds of problems at such major meetings until a £300,000 rebuild in 1976.

Since 1972 Britain's World Championship-qualifying Formula 1 race has lost its national title so far as officialdom is concerned. To everyone apart from the RAC and their commercial sponsors, the race is still 'the British', but the sponsoring tobacco company has a decidedly parochial view of sharing its corporate title in promotional activities such as this. The company concerned has done a magnificent job of supporting the Lotus team through some of their most successful seasons, and then thoughtlessly destroyed their good image by this stunningly small-minded attitude to a race which had become a national institution. Perhaps the race's desperately chaotic story in recent years has given its sponsor their just desserts – but for the whole story, from 1926, read on.

Britain's first Grand Prix start was a ragged affair, with Campbell's wire-wheeled Bugatti (No 7) leading Eyston's Aston Martin (3), Moriceau's Talbot (6), Benoist's Delage (2), the Halford Special (5) and Senechal's winning Delage (14) away from the line in pursuit of the leaders.

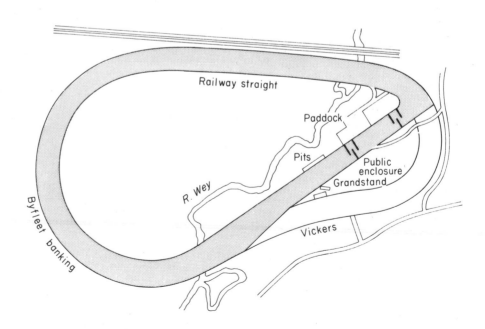

1926 Brooklands

August 7, Brooklands, 110 laps of 2.616-mile circuit
approximately 287.76 miles

The RAC's first British Grand Prix rejoiced in what was, for the time, an outstanding entry of no less than thirteen cars.

The STD combine reserved three entries for the debut of their brand-new Italian-designed, French-built straight-eight Talbots, and opted for a coat of green paint in this 'home' event. A fourth Talbot, an old 4-cylinder model, was entered by Captain Malcolm Campbell. Louis Delage promised three of his exciting new straight-eight cars; J.G. Parry Thomas was hastily completing his two 'Flat-Iron Specials' in his Brooklands workshop; Alvis entered their sophisticated new straight-eight front-drive; and two private entries came from Captain George Eyston – for his Anzani side-valve-engined Aston Martin with Powerplus supercharger – and from Major Frank Halford, whose Halford Special featured his own 6-cylinder engine mounted in an ancient Aston Martin chassis. Campbell managed to buy a new Bugatti Type 39A during the summer, and substituted it for his Talbot entry, which was then listed for Alastair Miller but which did not run.

In the week preceding race-day the brand-new Talbots arrived from Suresnes, together with the Delages freshly rebuilt at Courbevoie following their torrid debut in the European Grand Prix at San Sebastian, three weeks previously.

Up in Coventry the Alvis was behind schedule and the entry was withdrawn, while Parry Thomas was also forced to scratch his cars for Clive Gallop and 'Scrap' Thistlethwayte due to gearbox machining errors.

This left only nine cars to line-up for A.V. Ebblewhite's famous red starting flag, yet that was three more than had run in Spain and six more than had started in the French Grand Prix 'classic' which had opened the World Championship season.

The rakish, wicked-looking Talbots had been tested briefly at Montlhéry before crossing the Channel to England, but drivers Albert Divo, Henry Segrave and ex-riding mechanic Jean Moriceau were horrified to find desperate braking problems during their first practice laps. As they swept off the Byfleet Banking and down to the first sandbank chicane, the Talbots' front axles blurred into a savage chattering judder the instant the brakes were applied. Segrave said: '. . . one saw the front wheels bouncing up and down about a foot from the ground and the car

swaying about in an alarming manner'. While the Talbots could storm away along the straights and round the bankings, the Delages held them easily just under braking into the chicanes.

Nothing could be done to rectify the problem without returning to Suresnes, so the new Talbots went into their first race at a distinct disadvantage.

This was lost upon the large crowd which gathered that dull but warm Saturday morning. They had two home heroes to cheer – Campbell and Segrave – both of whom had made their names by breaking the World's Land Speed Record within the previous eighteen months, while the latter had the notable distinction of having won the French Grand Prix itself for Sunbeam in 1923. The Delages were to be handled by Robert Benoist, the veteran Louis Wagner and Robert Senechal, with the wealthy enthusiast André Dubonnet present as reserve.

The field formed-up in line abreast at the end of the Finishing Straight, beneath the loom of the Home Banking. Senechal was on the inside, flanked by Benoist, Divo, Eyston, Halford, Moriceau, Campbell, Segrave and Wagner, and as 'Ebby' dropped his flag it was Divo's Talbot which rapped away crisply into an immediate lead with Campbell, Moriceau and Eyston next away round the foot of the Banking. Both Senechal and Wagner were slow off the line, and trailed badly as Divo led his Talbot team-mates, Moriceau and Segrave, through the mile-long sweep of the Byfleet Banking.

As they dived down towards the gaping mouth of the Finishing Straight, Moriceau felt his car lurch and watched thunderstruck as its front wheels leaned drunkenly towards each other. The Talbot weaved wildly, slowed, then juddered to a halt on the left of the track. Its badly-machined front axle had broken just like the V12 Formule Libre car's in Spain, two weeks previously. One down, eight to go . . . and one hundred and nine laps remaining.

For the first six of those laps Divo towed Segrave at an average of 82 mph with Benoist's pale blue Delage sitting contentedly in their joint slipstream. Senechal was firing the crowd with lurid cornering in the chicanes, and had passed Eyston, but Wagner was in deep trouble with his Delage misfiring. He stopped and changed plugs, stopped and changed again, but still the car popped and banged, and what was worse his foot-pedals and the cockpit panelling

13

were being scorched by the exhaust. After four stops in six laps the veteran Frenchman stopped for good, hopped out in enraged agony and hobbled to the pit counter in disgust.

Segrave's second-place Talbot began spitting flame from its exhaust on the over-run, '. . . and his brakes were a calamity . . .', and only seven laps had been run when Divo's leading car began misfiring and he swept into the pits. This allowed the grim-faced Segrave into the lead, while Benoist sat back in second place, '. . . a slightly satirical smile on his face'.

Segrave's lead lasted six laps until a stop to change rear wheels and tyres dropped him behind Benoist. Senechal had punched his Delage up into third place, and three leaders in the opening thirteen laps was almost unbearably exciting for the spectacle-starved crowd. Halford's snarling Special was sounding very healthy in fourth place, and Divo was back in the race and rushing round to make up lost time.

At twenty-five laps Benoist led Segrave, Senechal, Halford, Campbell, Eyston and Divo — the seven survivors. The sun shone out from an overcast sky as Segrave's brakes deteriorated, and desperate downchanging took the edge off his engine's vivid exhaust note. While he, Divo and Benoist flashed low around the bankings, the theatrical Senechal swooped high around the lip. Divo's car was trailing blue oil smoke from its forward oil cooler, which had split over the Brooklands bumps.

On lap 35 Benoist dived into his pit, changing rear wheels and rejoining before Segrave's ailing Talbot could catch him. Segrave stopped and the Talbot's rear-hinged one-piece engine cowl was flipped back to investigate 'carburettor trouble'. He rejoined, but four more stops followed in the next seven laps. His brakes were entirely shot, and on one occasion the Talbot slithered straight past the first chicane, and Segrave had to snatch reverse to take another bite at the cherry.

Eyston went out with a blown gasket, but Segrave's problems had given the gallant Halford Special third place behind the leading Delages of Benoist and Senechal, and Campbell was chiselling away at his lap times in the wire-wheeled Bugatti.

Divo was still hurtling round in his delayed Talbot, and after fifty laps Benoist began to suffer. His car's exhaust system had split, and as the fractured edges began to glow and crumble so twinkling little flames played on the dash-panel and pedals. Senechal had made his stop and was throwing his car around with Gallic abandon, and when Halford made a slow stop for fuel and tyres on his fifty-fifth lap he gave third place to Campbell until that little martinet of a man made his own call at the pits. This promoted Halford once more, but he was passed almost immediately by Divo whose superb fight-back was gaining him four seconds a lap on Senechal.

Segrave's time had come. In a stop to change plugs spirit had spilled on the track beneath the car and caught fire, and once that was smothered the Talbot refused to start. Driver and mechanic 'achieved unheard-of revolutions with the starting handle and pushed until exhausted', when the straight-eight suddenly fired, and Segrave stuttered away for one final lap before retiring with the supercharger casing split.

During this drama Benoist stopped for fuel and tyres, and for an attempted exhaust repair. The Delage refused to restart, plugs were changed and it fired only after a lengthy push. Despite this delay Benoist still led at seventy-five laps, from Senechal, Divo, Halford and Campbell. The second-place Delage had now blown its exhaust box, and holes had burned in Senechal's shoes! Benoist's car was slowing as its driver was in acute discomfort, and Divo's Talbot sounded flat but was lapping much faster than the Delage.

Divo stopped on his eightieth lap, and Senechal came in simultaneously, handing his car to the redundant Wagner and plunging his burned feet gratefully into a tray of cold water. As the bearded Frenchman recovered, Wagner led Divo's recalcitrant Talbot away through the second chicane and out onto the broad oil-soaked concrete of the Home Banking.

Halford's steady and impressive drive stumbled as his gearchanging seemed reluctant, and on the eighty-third lap the Major couldn't find a gear at all into the first chicane, then found one, the engine revved, but there was no drive. The front prop-shaft UJ had parted, and as the Special rolled to a stop Wagner dodged by through the centre bridge arch. Campbell was fourth.

On lap 88 the fast-moving blue speck which should have been Benoist's Delage swooping off the Byfleet Banking resolved into detail as Wagner's car, and then Benoist was spotted touring in trailing smoke. He stopped amid a flurry of excitement then rejoined, chased, caught and passed his team-mate for two laps, then stopped again. Wagner regained the lead briefly, then he too stopped, plunged his feet into the water trough, then restarted!

While his feet were still steaming, Divo's Talbot at last refused to restart after a long pit-stop, and was retired with the supercharger casing ruptured and probable internal engine damage from oil loss. Dubonnet — wearing a lounge suit — relieved Benoist in the Delage which had led for so long, and drove gaily away without benefit of practice.

Both surviving Delages were in a sorry state, and the Benoist/Dubonnet car was now back on the same lap as Campbell, in third place with the Bugatti. Campbell was cheered every time he rasped down the short straight between the chicanes, weaved through the sandbanks below the Home Banking and then bucketed away after the Delage towards the Hennebique Bridge over the Wey. Dubonnet was having to learn the circuit as he drove, and this gave Campbell the chance he wanted. Into lap 102 the Bugatti and Delage were closing along the Railway Straight, and out of sight behind the aerodrome buildings. Up on the Members' Hill spectators strained to see the outcome of this last-minute battle, and as the two cars drew together on the Byfleet Banking and the taller machine drew ahead a great cheer told the Campbell pit that their man was second.

Wagner made a quick final stop at this time, and he toured the last uncomfortable, anxious laps in the smouldering Senechal Delage to pass under 'Ebby's' flag and win the first British Grand Prix, the car having averaged 71.61 mph for a merciless four hours' racing. The Bugatti came home second to a joyous reception for its famous English driver, having made only two stops in the entire distance, and Dubonnet enjoyed his third place hugely in the Benoist car.

The Delages had been lucky winners in many respects, for the Talbots had the legs of them early on, and Campbell's Bugatti was certainly the

The wickedly beautiful but fragile Talbots sweep through the first of the Finishing Straight's sandbank chicanes, Segrave in crash helmet leading Divo in cap. The Delage which outlived them both to win is just entering the turn.

healthiest finisher. Segrave had the consolation of fastest lap, at 85.99 mph, and he won Sir Arthur Stanley's special trophy for that performance. When he had cleaned off his coating of oil and grime, Segrave went to a champagne lunch laid on by STD manager Alan Fenn to revive the team's spirits. He arrived late, and was amazed to see a terrific row in progress, with everyone bawling out Bertarione, the designer. Divo and Moriceau were loud in their opinion of the Italian's parentage and a suitable demise for his new car, and eventually Segrave drove them all back to London where he deposited them – still cursing in voluble French – on the pavement in St James's Street. Much the same scene could have greeted Lory of Delage, but for the fortitude of his drivers and the problems of his opposition, and as night fell over the Weybridge track the first British Grand Prix was hailed as 'a magnificent battle . . . a memorable motor race'.

Results

1 R. Senechal/L. Wagner (Delage No 14) 110 laps in 4 hrs 0 mins 56 secs, 71.61 mph; **2** M. Campbell (Bugatti No 7) 4 hrs 10 mins 44 secs, 68.82 mph; **3** R. Benoist/A. Dubonnet (Delage No 2) 4 hrs 18 mins 8 secs, 68.12 mph.

FASTEST LAP H.O.D. Segrave (Talbot) 85.99 mph.

RETIREMENTS J. Moriceau (Talbot) front axle failure; G. Eyston (Aston Martin Anzani) blown gasket; F. Halford (Halford Special) broken forward prop-shaft universal joint; L. Wagner (Delage) persistent misfiring and exhaust heat damage; A. Divo (Talbot) split supercharger casing and incurable oil leaks; H.O.D. Segrave (Talbot) split supercharger casing.

1927 Brooklands

October 2, Brooklands, 125 laps of 2.616-mile circuit
approximately 327 miles

After the encouraging success of 1926, the RAC accepted an October date for the British Grand Prix's return to Brooklands in 1927. They received sixteen entries, including three works Delages, six Bugattis which included three officially entered by the Molsheim factory, three new Fiats, the pair of Thomas Specials which had scratched the previous year, a single front-drive Alvis – much modified for the new season – and, from America, Indianapolis winner George Souders' single-seater Duesenberg.

After the 1926 race, Delage had rushed their cars straight to Courbevoie for major revision, leaving the Italian Grand Prix, and the obscure World Championship of the time to Bugatti. Lory redesigned the engine to place its exhaust valves and that devilish exhaust system on the nearside, away from the driver, and then shuffled the entire engine and transmission line four inches to the left to give his drivers even more room. The revized engine gave 170 bhp and swept all before it during 1927. With typical cocksurety, Louis Delage sent just a single car to Monza for the Italian Grand Prix, where Benoist won by 22 minutes from an OM and an Indy Miller. Brooklands followed, the last race of the two-year 1½-litre Formula, with an in-strength Delage turnout for the benefit of potential British customers.

During the Monza meeting Fiat fielded their incredibly potent Tipo 806 with twin-six 12-cylinder engine. Bordino won the supporting Milan Grand Prix with it, but this was the last outing for a Grand Prix car from Fiat, the management concentrated on their Schneider Trophy aero-engine programme, and the Brooklands entries were cancelled – indeed it is very doubtful if more than the one Monza car were ever built.

At Brooklands itself, tragedy had smothered the promising Thomas Specials' development as Parry Thomas had been killed in March while attempting to retake the Land Speed Record on Pendine Sands. The Alvis, with conventional twin-overhead camshafts replacing the unusual opposed-valve, side camshaft system of the 1926 car, appeared for Grand Prix practice, introducing all-independent suspension to this class of racing, but poor Harvey had to withdraw with a defective oil pump – said to have been rendered so by an errant piece of piston! Souders' Duesenberg burst its gearbox at Monza, and so only eleven cars remained to do battle, including the under-developed

BENOIST

Thomas Specials.

The start was at noon on an overcast, grey day, the track wet from drizzle carried on a cold, gnawing breeze. 'Ebby' lined-up the cars at the start on the Railway Straight. Bourlier's Delage refused to fire as the rest of the pack barked into life, and his mechanics hastily push-started it before the red starting flag dropped. As he rolled forward, Bourlier de-clutched, waited for the pack to surge alongside, and then took off, wheel-spinning in their wake.

Materassi punched his Bugatti into the lead, spray pluming from its narrow tyres as it howled away past the sewage farm. He led to the first chicane, past the pits, the second chicane, then out onto the Home Banking and back past the start-line where 'a long blue Delage went by in one confident rush'. It was Divo, lapping at 88 mph in the wet, and two laps later Bourlier and Benoist were through in the sister cars. They pulled out as much as three full lengths just between the two chicanes, were faster still on the rest of the course, and the race was already firmly pocketed.

The works Bugattis were driven hard to keep the Delages just in sight, Materassi leading Conelli and Chiron. Campbell was on their tail, Eyston stopped early with plugs oiling-up, Scott's hopeless, unsupercharged Thomas went out very early with clutch

Benoist's remodelled Delage, with exhaust moved to the nearside, after its 1927 Brooklands British Grand Prix victory. On the dais with the victor are Col. Lindsay Lloyd of Brooklands, left, and – looking like a Feydeau farce villain – Louis Delage in the scarf.

slip, and Purdy's car frightened him by getting into a wild skid, was beset by continual plug trouble and was soon retired with transmission failure . . . the end of the last British car in the race. Materassi was forced to stop when his Bugatti began gushing water.

Divo made the first scheduled Delage stop just after quarter-distance, refuelling and changing one wheel and tyre in a leisurely 2 minutes 18 seconds to show the team's disdain for their 'opposition'. It set the tone of the race.

Eyston lost a lot of time in another enforced plug change, and Prince Ghika retired his Bugatti as its inlet manifolding came adrift, venting his disgust on the pit counter with a large and heavy hammer.

The drizzle blew away on the wind, and by half-distance the track was dry. Bourlier was leading team-mates Benoist and Divo at an average of 87.05 mph, Conelli was fourth in the best Bugatti, and then the second round of scheduled Delage stops saw Bourlier dropping 2 minutes for fuel, tyres and oil, and Benoist 2 minutes 14 seconds for the same service, and a top-up with water. This allowed Divo to inherit the lead, while down in the field Campbell was unhappy with his Bugatti's engine and handicapped by the small brakes he was forced to fit by his unaccountable preference for wire wheels. Conelli had run out of fuel at the foot of the Byfleet Banking, and pushed more than a mile to the pits where the enigmatic 'Williams' took his place.

Davis took over from Eyston at half-distance, following a poor pit-stop in which the driver was soaked in fuel, but already the Delage pit-staff were signalling 'SLOW' to their drivers and any recognizable element of competition had drained from the race. Conelli's massive time-loss had allowed Chiron

into fourth place by three-quarter distance, and with seventy miles to run Benoist strode forward, displacing Bourlier for second place and then inheriting the lead when Divo slowed, apparently because his car's exhaust system was coming adrift. He made a very leisurely pit-stop, complained to officials of the heat, did a solitary lap before another long stop, then watched contentedly as Benoist and Bourlier toured by. He then rejoined, to complete a carefully pre-arranged 1–2–3 victory in race-number order for Automobiles Delage.

Benoist drew into his pit, undisputed Champion of Europe, his compatriots swarmed over the counter to engulf their beaming victor and M. Delage himself produced a huge bouquet and a crate of champagne. His cars had never been extended, the drivers using only 6,800 of the available 7,500 rpm rev limit, and the only undue exertion to which the cars had been subjected came when the drivers sought to inject some fun into this moribund race by 'skidding' the chicanes. The second British Grand Prix had been a one-make dominated 327-mile bore, and on this low note the $1\frac{1}{2}$-litre Grand Prix Formula, which had promised so much, crept out of existence not with a bang, but with a long drawn-out whimper.

Results

1 R. Benoist (Delage No 2) 3 hrs 49 mins $14\frac{3}{5}$ secs, 85.59 mph; **2** E. Bourlier (Delage No 3) 3 hrs 49 mins $21\frac{3}{5}$ secs, 85.58 mph; **3** A. Divo (Delage No 4) 3 hrs 52 mins 20 secs, 84.46 mph; **4** L. Chiron (Bugatti No 12) 76.03 mph.
FLAGGED-OFF/RETIRED: C. Conelli/'Williams' (Bugatti), G. Eyston/S.C.H. Davis (Bugatti), M. Campbell (Bugatti); W.B. Scott (Thomas), clutch failure; H. Purdy (Thomas), transmission failure; E. Materassi (Bugatti), water leaks; Prince Ghika (Bugatti), manifold failure.

1935 Donington Park

October 6, Donington Park, 125 laps of 2.551-mile circuit
approximately 318 miles

Fred Craner and his Derby and District Motor Club attracted an interesting, if not sensational, entry for their first Donington Grand Prix. The field included three Europeans: Dr Giuseppe Farina (at that time a promising 31-year old driver), Gino Rovere, and Raymond Sommer. The Italian Scuderia SubAlpina brought over Maserati cars, an all-independent suspension 4.5-litre V8/R1 for Farina and a 3.7-litre Tipo 34 (reputedly Nuvolari's late-'34 car) for Rovere, the Maidenhead-domiciled team sponsor. Sommer had his ex-works Alfa Romeo 2.9 *Monoposto*, finished in French blue, and this trio faced twelve 'home' entries.

They were led by three 3.3-litre Bugatti Type 59s for Earl Howe, C.E.C. 'Charlie' Martin and A.H. Lindsay Eccles. Richard Shuttleworth, the dashing young Bedfordshire squire renowned as 'Mad Jack' for his reckless driving, had a similar ex-Scuderia Ferrari Alfa *Monoposto* to Sommer's, and Harry Rose drove an older 2.3-litre two-seat *Monza* model. Two 2.9-litre Maseratis were to be handled by 'Buddy'

Featherstonhaugh (8CM) and Austin Dobson (8C), while last but not least of the supercharged runners was the young Siamese Cambridge undergraduate Prince Birabongse Bhanubandh, enjoying his first racing season in a brand-new 1½-litre ERA. The car had been given to him as a twenty-first birthday present by his cousin, Prince Chula Chakrabongse, who ran their team.

Completing the field were four Rileys; two entered by Freddy Dixon and driven jointly by the Hon. Brian Lewis with Cyril Paul, and Pat Driscoll with Wal Handley, while Percy Maclure had his 500-mile car and Hector Dobbs his offset single-seater.

Farina dominated practice with his remarkably quiet Maserati V8, whuffling around the undulating woodland glades in 2 minutes 8 seconds, which was a clear second below Eccles' contemporary record. Sommer was 6 seconds per lap slower, while Maclure astounded everyone by equalling the *Monoposto*'s time in his fleet Riley. Rovere found his Maserati a real handful on this narrow, twisting course, and he

---

1935 Grid

6 Maclure (Riley) 2:14.0		**16** Farina (Maserati V8/RI) 2:08.4		**8** Sommer (Alfa Romeo Tipo B) 2:14.0	
12 Featherstonhaugh (Maserati 8CM) 2:17.0		**1** Howe (Bugatti Type 59) 2:16.0		**9** Shuttleworth (Alfa Romeo Tipo B) 2:19.0	
2 Martin (Bugatti Type 59) 2:21.8		**10** Rose (Alfa Romeo 'Monza') 2:23.0		**14** 'B. Bira' (ERA R2B) 2:23.0	
4 Lewis (Riley) 2:24.0		**5** Handley (Riley) 2:17.0		**18** Dobson (Maserati 8C) 2:27.0	
7 Dobbs (Riley) 2:23.0		**11** Everitt (Maserati Tipo 34) 2:23.0		**3** Eccles (Bugatti Type 59) 	

Reserve drivers: 2 C. Brackenbury, 3 P.G. Fairfield, 4 C. Paul, 5 L.P. Driscoll, 6 E. Maclure, 7 A.W.K. Von Der Becke, 11 G. Rovere, 16 G. Bertocchi

Non-starter (reserve entry): L. Fontes (Alfa Romeo) 2:28.0

took on W.G. 'Bill' Everitt to co-drive in this long race. Farina nominated Guerrino Bertocchi (to become very famous as Maserati's Chief Mechanic) as his reserve driver, Pat Fairfield joined Eccles, Charles Brackenbury stood by for Martin and Edgar Maclure for his brother, Percy. Reserve entry Luis Fontes practised his Alfa Romeo, but was not to start the race.

The Saturday dawned wet and windy, but the rain showers blew away fifteen minutes before the scheduled start time, rain covers were pulled off the cars and they lined up three-by-three on the broad grid. After a frustrating delay while wandering spectators were cleared from the course, the first Donington Grand Prix was flagged away (with a Union Jack) fifteen minutes late, and it was Farina who led the initial sprint into the ninety-left at Red Gate Corner, with Shuttleworth barging through alongside Sommer for second place.

As the noise of the pack echoed away through the woods, the startline grandstand buzzed with excited chatter, and after two minutes the deep engine note of Farina's Maserati, 'just like a Ford V8', was heard returning along the Starkey Straight. Hard on the brakes behind the pits, down through the gearbox, then sliding neatly round the Starkey's Corner hairpin to accelerate back past the startline, it was Farina

with 80-yards lead from Sommer. Shuttleworth was 50-yards adrift, with Featherstonhaugh, Howe, Martin, 'Bira', Maclure, Rose, Dobson, Lewis and Everitt in hot pursuit, the latter having just passed Eccles at Starkey's. Dobbs and Lewis straggled by, the latter finding the cockpit of Dixon's Riley just too small for comfort.

Farina tore away into an ever-increasing lead. Sommer could not hold him, but in turn was leaving Shuttleworth, while Martin was making ground and passed Howe's similar Bugatti to steal fifth place.

Farina lapped Lewis after only seven laps, and two more circuits saw him doubling Dobbs. Martin was charging hard after Featherstonhaugh's fourth place, but he spun onto the grass at Starkey's, caught the big Bugatti as it nosed round in the right direction, and continued. 'Bira' revolved into the mud at Red Gate, and lost two laps extricating the ERA.

Light showers of rain still blew across the circuit, but Farina's 10-lap average was 64.55 mph, and at twenty laps he had pushed it up to 66.61 mph as he settled into a rhythm and his Maserati's fuel load lightened.

Featherstonhaugh let Martin through into fourth place by slewing onto the grass in avoiding a backmarker, and Martin was hauling in Shuttleworth's Alfa for third when he overdid his braking into

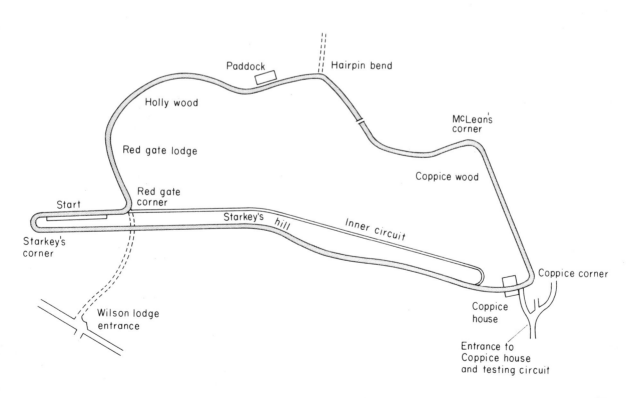

Starkey's, and spun. Undaunted, he gathered it up once more, and remounted the chase.

Eccles' face had been cut by a stone, and he handed over to Pat Fairfield, and on lap 35 'Bira' and Shuttleworth came boring over the brow into Starkey's side-by-side, the Siamese holding the inside line with such determination that 'Mad Jack' found himself barged off onto the wet grass and slithering to a halt only just short of the safety bank. He rejoined visibly shaken, and after two thoughtful laps he stopped at his pit to enter a protest, which did little but allow Martin through into third.

Farina burbled through the forty-lap mark at an average of 65.47 mph, but immediately the Maserati revved wildly at The Hairpin then rolled under the Stone Bridge and on up the incline towards McLean's where Farina abandoned it with a broken halfshaft. Almost simultaneously, on the other side of the circuit, Rose coasted into retirement at the pits with engine trouble.

Sommer inherited the lead, and at fifty laps he was 1 minute 40 seconds clear of Martin, with Howe third, 10 seconds behind. Shuttleworth had rejoined fourth, but he saw Sommer closing up to lap him, took heart and began to race once more. He pulled away from the Frenchman's similar car on the road, and this developing dice kept the crowd interested until

Richard 'Mad Jack' Shuttleworth corrects a wild power slide in his Monoposto *Alfa Romeo on the way to victory in the first Donington Grand Prix. C.E.C. Martin looks on apprehensively in the Bugatti Type 59 which performed so well.*

Shuttleworth slid wildly at The Hairpin and did a lurid wall-of-death act around the retaining bank!

Sommer slammed by to lap him before he could rejoin, and on lap 59 the Frenchman swept into the pits to refuel and change plugs. This work cost 3 minutes, during which Martin shot by to lead at the sixty-lap mark, at an average of 66.04 mph. Howe then made his stop, Shuttleworth crackled by second, and Sommer rejoined on the Englishman's tail to resume their battle.

He regained second place on lap 65 as Shuttleworth slithered into the pits for a record 70-second stop to refuel and adjust his brakes. He accelerated out again down in fourth place, behind Everitt who was working wonders in the tricky Rovere car and had stolen by into third.

Sommer was set to catch Martin's Bugatti when his RAC regulation bonnet strap broke and he was flagged into the pits to remove it. Rejoining without a strap he was flagged in again to replace it. These petty delays so infuriated Sommer that he lost his head, and began hurling his Alfa around the Park in a frenzy, and on lap 70 it was all over, and the blue *Monoposto* was out with another broken halfshaft.

Martin was left with an apparently secure lead from Everitt whose handling of the Maserati had persuaded the Italian owner to leave him be. He had made one swift stop without losing his place to Shuttleworth, now running third ahead of Howe touring round carefully in fourth place. But the Park circuit was proving very hard on brakes, and both Everitt and Driscoll spun at Starkey's as their brakes grabbed. Dobson slithered off into the bank at The Hairpin, retiring unhurt, and Featherstonhaugh lost sixth place when his Maserati's transmission failed at Coppice. Dobbs had lost second gear and handed over to Von Der Becke, while Eccles was having an unhappy drive with constant brake problems.

Everitt had at last had enough of the big Maserati, and handed over to Rovere, staggering across to the pit counter on feet numbed by the car's terrific vibration.

After one hundred laps Martin was still leading from Shuttleworth, Howe, and the Everitt/Rovere car, with a lap between each of them and 'Bira', and Eccles sixth on ninety-three laps. On lap 104 Kensington-Moir, running the Martin pit, brought in his driver for a precautionary eight gallons of fuel. 'You've got two-minutes' lead', he cried, and Martin ripped away after 34 seconds, disappearing left-handed round Red Gate, away past the Lodge, right-handed over the brow through Holly Wood and down to The Hairpin and the Stone Bridge. He did not reappear.

Shuttleworth rushed by the pits, then Howe and the rest, and they came by again before the PA system crackled with the news that Martin was off the road at McLean's and could not restart. Officials finally succeeded in push-starting the travel-stained Bugatti, but with just ten laps left even the irrepressible Martin had no chance.

Shuttleworth sat back and toured those closing laps, conserving what little brakes his *Monoposto* had left, and doing enough to hold off a late charge by Earl Howe with 45 seconds in hand. Driscoll and Dobbs had a wild few laps, one sans brakes the other sans second gear which was embarassing in the slow corners, and the unfortunate Martin boomed home third to a generous reception. It was an exciting finale to a long and gruelling race, not one of the immortal Alfa Romeo *Monoposto*'s more memorable victories, but a worthy successor to the true British Grands Prix which preceded it.

Results

1 R.O. Shuttleworth (2.9 Alfa Romeo) 4 hrs 47 mins 12 secs, 63.97 mph; **2** Earl Howe (3.3 Bugatti) 4 hrs 47 mins 57.8 secs, 63.80 mph; **3** C.E.C. Martin (3.3 Bugatti) 4 hrs 49 mins 47.4 secs, 63.39 mph; **4** W.G. Everitt/Tipo G. Rovere (3.7 Maserati 34) 4 hrs 53 mins 59 secs, 62.49 mph; **5** 'Bira' (1.5 ERA) 4 hrs 58 mins 16 secs, 61.59 mph; **6** A.H.L. Eccles/P.G. Fairfield (3.3 Bugatti) 4 hrs 59 mins 33 secs, 61.33 mph.

RUNNING AT FINISH, BUT FLAGGED-OFF AT TIME LIMIT Hon. B. Lewis/C. Paul (1.8 Riley), 117 laps; W.L. Handley/L.P. Driscoll (2.0 Riley), 115 laps; H.G. Dobbs/A.W.K. Von Der Becke (1.8 Riley), 119 laps.

RETIRED G. Farina (4.5 Maserati V8/RI) half-shaft; H. Rose (2.3 Alfa Romeo) engine; R. Sommer (2.9 Alfa Romeo) half-shaft; A. Dobson (2.9 Maserati 8C) crashed; R.E.L. Featherstonhaugh (2.9 Maserati 8CM) transmission.

1936 Donington Park

October 3, Donington Park, 120 laps of 2.551-mile circuit
approximately 306 miles

No less than twenty-four entries came in for the second Donington Grand Prix which closed the Park's 1936 season, and all but one – a Salmson entered by the enigmatic Pablo Curtis – came to the starting line.

The Continental entry was stronger than the preceding year's and was headed by the Swiss amateur Hans Ruesch, who fielded a 3.8-litre independently-suspended Alfa Romeo 8C–35 in which Nuvolari had won that season's Coppa Ciano race at Leghorn. Ruesch agreed to share this potent machine with Dick Seaman, the 23-year-old Englishman who had enjoyed a superb season in his muchmodified nine-year-old Delage of Brooklands British Grand Prix fame. He was trailing behind 'Bira' in a tense battle for the BRDC's Gold Star award at that time, and Donington was the penultimate qualifying meeting. Seaman wanted the fastest possible car for this race, and he had written to Daimler-Benz in Germany asking for the loan of a Mercedes! They politely refused, and then Seaman found Ruesch.

Another wealthy Swiss amateur, Christian Kautz, entered a Maserati 6C, and four stripped 3.6-litre 6-cylinder Delahaye 135 *Competitions* were entered through their British concessionaire, Selborne Garage.

The cars were stopping off for this race on their way home from the Ards TT in Ulster. Drivers were René Carriere, Tommy Clarke, Maurice Falkner, Laurie Schell and Selborne himself, and the very good Frenchman René LeBegue who was sharing with Britain's famous Kaye Don. The former Brooklands and World Water Speed Record star was making a brief return to racing after serving a prison sentence for the manslaughter of his riding mechanic in a racing accident.

Five ERAs were to be driven by the Peters Whitehead and Walker (in the former's R10B); by Douglas Briault/Dennis Evans (R6B); Hector Dobbs/D.H. Scribbans (R9B), and single-handed by Reggie Tongue (R11B) and Arthur Dobson (R7B). Private Alfa Romeos included two *Monoposti*, one Charlie Martin's latest acquisition, and the other the Nuvolari German Grand Prix winner recently bought by Austin Dobson, who was to share it with Andrew Leitch. Wide-bodied Alfa Romeo *Monzas* were down for Anthony Powys-Lybbe, and Ian Connell/Kenneth Evans. Maserati 8CMs came from 'Bira' (the potent ex-Whitney Straight car) and T.P. Cholmondeley-Tapper (ex-Howe); Arthur Baron/D. Taylor and C. Mervyn

2 Tapper (Maserati 8CM	**11** Clarke (Delahaye 135)*	**5** Maclure (Riley)	**6** Parnell (MG)
1 Taylor (Bugatti Type 51)	**23** Carriere (Delahaye 135)*	**4** Jucker (Alta)	**16** Dobson (ERA R7B)
18 'B. Bira' (Maserati 8CM)	**3** Powys-Lybbe (Alfa Romeo 'Monza')	**12** Ruesch (Alfa Romeo 8C-35)	**7** Scribbans (ERA R9B)
8 Whitehead (ERA R10B)	**17** Connell (Alfa Romeo 'Monza')	**14** Briault (ERA R6B)	**10** Martin (Alfa Romeo Tipo B)
22 Schell (Delahaye 135)*	**21** Le Begue (Delahaye 135)*	**24** Kautz (Maserati 6C)	**15** Tongue (ERA R11B)
	9 White (Bugatti Type 51)	**19** Dobson (Alfa Romeo Tipo B)	

*Denotes unsupercharged engines

Reserve drivers: 12 R.J.B. Seaman – 8 P.D.C. Walker – 1 A. Baron – 4 'B. Alder' – 6 W.E. Wilkinson – 11 M. Falkner – 21 K. Don – 22 A. Selborne – 23 G. Field – 19 A. Leitch – 5 C.J.P. Dodson – 7 H.G. Dobbs – 14 D.G. Evans.

White ran Bugattis; Philip Jucker had his Alta; Percy Maclure his Riley and a local man named Reg Parnell was having a go in an MG.

Grid positions were decided by ballot, but practice saw Seaman rocketing around the Park to record an astonishing 2 minutes 2 seconds lap in the big Alfa, '. . . probably the fastest car ever to have raced in England'. Ruesch's best was 4 seconds slower, and 'Bira' was next quickest with a 2 minutes $6\frac{3}{5}$ seconds lap in his Maserati.

Race day was blessed with crystal skies, and a brilliant sun beating down through the bronzed Autumn foliage. Tapper had drawn a front-row starting position while Ruesch was buried in the middle of the grid, and promptly at 12.15 the flag fell and Tapper catapulted into an immediate lead before 15,000 spectators. 'Bira' stalled in his anxiety, and lost $1\frac{1}{2}$-laps before getting away.

Ruesch took his time building on this handicap to his closest rival, and Tapper led for four laps until the big Alfa got into its stride, wafted past and left the opposition for dead. The white-cowled red Alfa pulverized all ten-lap increment records, averaged over 69 mph for the full distance but was never pushed hard enough to break Fairfield's 72.45 mph outright lap record.

After just six laps the Swiss was 14 seconds ahead of a tight trio consisting of Tapper, Whitehead and Martin, and as the race progressed so the latter forced his *Monoposto* through into second place at twenty laps, though 54 seconds behind Ruesch who had averaged 70.55 mph to this point.

Lap 23 saw Jucker's oil pressure zero in the Alta, and White's Bugatti chewed up a prop-shaft UJ. Arthur Dobson was progressing after a steady start in fifth place, and at forty laps he had taken both Whitehead and Tapper to run third. Whitehead stopped to hand over to Walker, refuel and change plugs, allowing Austin Dobson into fifth place. Then Arthur Dobson made a long stop in his ERA, and disappeared from the leader board.

The Swiss Alfa was booming round in an imperious lead, but Ruesch had a fright when he cut in too close after lapping 'Bira' into Red Gate Corner and was shunted smartly in the tail for his pains. The Alfa was barged off onto the grass, but Ruesch recovered the road without spinning, and continued with a dented tail.

By fifty laps Ruesch was 2 minutes 9 seconds ahead of Martin, and had averaged 70.93 mph. 'Skid'

Dick Seaman going comfortably in Hans Ruesch's big Alfa Romeo 8C–35 during their easy winning drive at Donington in 1936.

Walker was hurling the Whitehead ERA around in third place, 'Bira' had recovered after his delayed start to run fourth and Tongue was fifth. Tapper had gone out on lap 42 when he spun on oil at McLean's and bent his Maserati's front axle, while Kautz followed him into retirement after fifty-five laps when a piston collapsed. Three laps later it was Parnell's turn, as the MG sheared a half-shaft.

At seventy laps Ruesch motored into his pit to refuel and hand over to Seaman, who rejoined after losing 65 seconds of the owner's three-minute lead. All he had to do was keep the Alfa running to the finish, and this he did, touring round to hold a consistent lead and seldom changing down from top gear!

The Dobbs/Scribbans ERA went out with engine trouble at sixty-seven laps, after a wild spin by Dobbs at McLean's Corner. Whitehead drove up the left-hand bank in avoidance, and Dobson's ERA was blamed for spilling oil as its filler-cap was flapping loose. Evans took over Briault's ERA and had a big fright through Holly Wood as he hit an oil slick and revolved twice at very high speed, just missing the trees.

The race had long-sunk into tedium, and Seaman came home to a polite and rather awed reception, winning the race for Ruesch and valuable Gold Star points for himself. Martin was second for the second year running, and the Walker/Whitehead and Tongue ERAs were third and fourth ahead of 'Bira'. Dobson's troubled ERA in sixth place, nearly ten minutes behind the winner, clinched the Team Award for the Bourne cars. Seaman's success brought him within one point of 'Bira's' Gold Star total, but he didn't bother to go to Brooklands for the final rounds of the competition. After his Donington win he had a telegram from Neubauer of Mercedes-Benz inviting him to a driver test at Nurburgring. He could afford to forget the Gold Star – he was destined for bigger things.

Results

1 H. Ruesch/R.J.B. Seaman (3.8 Alfa Romeo) 4 hrs 25 mins 22 secs, 69.23 mph; **2** C.E.C. Martin (3.16 Alfa Romeo) 4 hrs 28 mins 28 secs, 68.43 mph; **3** P.N. Whitehead/P.D. Walker (1.48 ERA) 4 hrs 31 mins 35 secs, 67.64 mph; **4** R.E. Tongue (1.48 ERA) 4 hrs 32 mins 29 secs, 67.41 mph; **5** 'Bira' (2.9 Maserati) 4 hrs 33 mins 19 secs, 67.21 mph; **6** A.C. Dobson (1.48 ERA) 4 hrs 25 mins 6 secs.

FLAGGED OFF AT TIME LIMIT A. Powys-Lybbe (2.36 Alfa (Romeo), 118 laps; R. Carriere/G. Field (3.55 Delahaye), 118 laps; I.F. Connell/K.D. Evans (2.55 Alfa Romeo), 115 laps; A. Dobson/A. Leitch (2.9 Alfa Romeo), 115 laps; T.G. Clarke/M.F.L. Falkner (3.55 Delahaye), 114 laps; L.S. Schell/A. Selborne (3.55 Delahaye), 114 laps; D.L. Briault/ D.G. Evans (1.48 ERA), 113 laps; Capt. D. Taylor/A. Baron (2.3 Bugatti), 112 laps; R. Le Begue/K. Don (3.55 Delahaye), 100 laps.

TEAM PRIZE Whitehead/Walker, Tongue, Dobson (ERAs).

RETIREMENTS P. Maclure/C.J.P. Dodson (1.98 Riley) 1 lap, big-end; C. Mervyn White (2.3 Bugatti) 23 laps, propeller-shaft coupling; P.F. Jucker/'B. Alder' (1.99 Alta) 23 laps, oil pressure; T.P. Cholmondeley-Tapper (2.9 Maserati) 42 laps, damaged steering; C. Kautz (1.49 Maserati) 55 laps, piston; R. Parnell/W. Wilkinson (1.49 MG) 58 laps, axleshaft; H.G. Dobbs/D.H. Scribbans (1.48 ERA) 67 laps, engine.

1937 Donington Park

October 2, Donington Park, 80 laps of 3.125-mile circuit
approximately 250 miles

Donington Park achieved full International stature during 1937, when the British Empire Trophy race, a Coronation Day meeting, the Nuffield Trophy and a 12-Hour sports car race were joined by the RAC's International Tourist Trophy, and by the third Donington Grand Prix, which had at last attracted 'the cream'.

The German Mercedes-Benz and Auto Union teams had dominated the contemporary 750-Kilogramme Grand Prix Formula with few lapses since its introduction in 1934, and Mercedes had shown interest in the Donington race as early as 1935. Now, for the 1937 Grand Prix, Fred Craner achieved the sensational coup of attracting works entries from both Mercedes and Auto Union, and for the first time in ten years British crowds were to see what *real* Grand Prix racing was about. In fact they were going to see more than that, they were going to see some of the most spectacular Grand Prix racing of all time.

Four 5.66-litre supercharged straight-eight Mercedes-Benz W125s were entered, for Caracciola, Manfred von Brauchitsch, Hermann Lang and Seaman, with the Swiss driver Kautz listed as reserve. They were faced by three 6-litre supercharged V16-cylinder Auto Unions, which were unusual in having their monster engines midmounted, between a far-forward cockpit and the rear wheels. Rudolf Hasse and two ex-motor-cyclists from the DKW works team, Bernd Rosemeyer and H.P. Muller, were their drivers.

Against this demonstration of National Socialist might, the 'home' entry was limited to eight cars by the confines of the circuit, although it had been specially lengthened to 3.125 miles by the addition of a loop running past Starkey's Corner over an abrupt brow and down to a 180-degree hairpin close to Melbourne village.

Raymond Mays had his famous works ERA (R4D), accompanied by the sister Humphrey Cook-entered cars of Earl Howe (R8B) and Arthur Dobson (R7B). Charlie Martin (R3A) was anxious to repeat his successes of earlier seasons, and Peter Whitehead had his R10B. 'Bira' was in his Maserati 8CM once more, Robin Hanson had a smaller 1.5-litre 6C model, and Percy Maclure was also running his fleet Riley.

During practice, spectators stood stunned as the silver German cars were fired into life by white-overalled mechanics wielding portable battery starters. As the cars set off through the woods, shattering new sounds battered through the foliage. Donington habitués were used to watching British, French and Italian cars flickering along the Starkey Straight at up to 140 mph, while those at the Grand Prix in '36 recalled the big Alfa booming along at 150 mph. But even these old hands gulped and stepped back as they saw real *Grand Prix* cars for the first time, exploding out of Coppice Farmyard with their rear tyres virtually alight and bucketing along the curving, undulating 'straight' towards 170 mph. These cars went faster on the quaint little roadways of the Park than anything yet seen on the 100-foot wide concrete speedbowl of Brooklands!

Rushing back up the hill towards the start-line from the new Melbourne Hairpin, both Mercedes and Auto Unions were jumping high into the air over the brow, and press and radio coverage boomed in an unprecedented manner, attracting some 50,000 spectators to Donington Park that October Saturday for the motor racing experience of a lifetime.

'Donington weather' applied once more with a low sun warming crisp Autumn air, and an excited buzz of voices was dulled as the English cars were started. With just seconds to go before the flag, the German mechanics fingered starter buttons, and their charges first crackled, then thundered into life in a shattering blast of noise which drowned all conversation, together with the paltry exhaust notes of their meagre opposition.

The flag fell and Lang burst away into Red Gate, pursued by Seaman, Caracciola – barging past Rosemeyer's Auto Union – and a jostling mass of other silver cars. The multi-coloured 'home' contingent were already floundering as the Germans flashed down through Holly Wood into the valley in front of Donington Hall, and away round that opening lap. Soon the silver cars flew by behind the pits and away over the brow to Melbourne Corner, then jounced back into sight, heavy with fuel, Lang leading Caracciola, Brauchitsch and Seaman in the four Mercedes, with Rosemeyer, Muller and Hasse behind in the Auto Unions. They had all disappeared by the time 'Bira' arrived, trailed by Martin and Mays in the first ERAs, with Hanson and Maclure bringing up the tail. Already that noise could be heard drumming back along the Starkey Straight.

Rosemeyer really went racing, picking off Seaman who was promptly thumped in the tail by Muller

1937 Grid

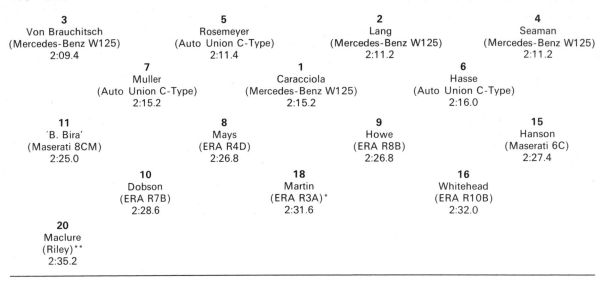

3 Von Brauchitsch (Mercedes-Benz W125) 2:09.4	**5** Rosemeyer (Auto Union C-Type) 2:11.4	**2** Lang (Mercedes-Benz W125) 2:11.2	**4** Seaman (Mercedes-Benz W125) 2:11.2

7 Muller (Auto Union C-Type) 2:15.2	**1** Caracciola (Mercedes-Benz W125) 2:15.2	**6** Hasse (Auto Union C-Type) 2:16.0

11 'B. Bira' (Maserati 8CM) 2:25.0	**8** Mays (ERA R4D) 2:26.8	**9** Howe (ERA R8B) 2:26.8	**15** Hanson (Maserati 6C) 2:27.4

10 Dobson (ERA R7B) 2:28.6	**18** Martin (ERA R3A)* 2:31.6	**16** Whitehead (ERA R10B) 2:32.0

20 Maclure (Riley)** 2:35.2

*Time set with 1500 Maserati. **Time set with 1500 Riley, 1750 engine for race.

Non-starters: A.B. Hyde, 12 (Maserati) 2:34.8 – 6 A. Varzi, replaced by Hasse – 17 R.E. Tongue (ERA) – 19 A.C. Dobson (ERA).

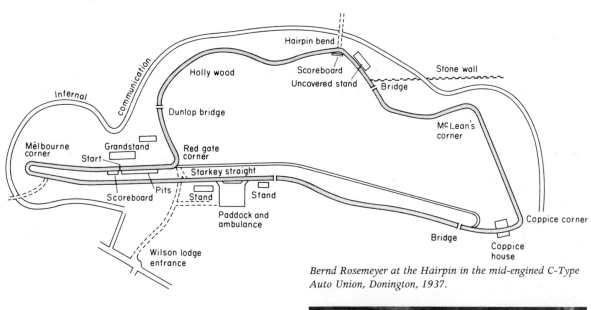

Bernd Rosemeyer at the Hairpin in the mid-engined C-Type Auto Union, Donington, 1937.

under braking at Coppice. Both cars continued, but Seaman had been up the escape road and his car's offside rear suspension was damaged. Caracciola disliked the confined circuit, and as he fell back, first Brauchitsch, then Rosemeyer rushed by. Whitehead's ERA stopped at Starkey's Corner, restarted feebly, and retired in a cloud of oil smoke after only eleven laps. Lang was averaging 83 mph, in the lead by 3 seconds from Brauchitsch who led Rosemeyer by 4.5 seconds. Caracciola was trailed by Muller and Seaman, 'Bira' was still seventh and in his wake Martin and Dobson had drawn away from the other ERAs.

Brauchitsch closed on Lang, stole the lead on lap 14, and Rosemeyer was catching them both in the Auto Union which shivered and juddered wildly under the enormous braking and cornering stresses which he imposed.

The first scheduled stops began, Brauchitsch's red-numbered W125 losing only 30 seconds while mechanics changed its rear wheels and refuelled. Lang was in next, stopping at Neubauer's black-and-red marker flag, but his stop was slower as the offside front suspension was examined. These stops put Rosemeyer in the lead, and after twenty-five laps he was 30.8 seconds ahead of Caracciola, having averaged a staggering 83.27 mph. Caracciola was signalled in for his stop, but he decided to press on until Brauchitsch was close enough to take up Rosemeyer's challenge.

Lang had dropped to seventh after his stop, and he retired on the next lap with a broken front damper. Muller was fourth behind 'Browk', Seaman had repassed Hasse for fifth but ending the twenty-ninth lap he retired his car alongside Lang's at the pits. The damaged rear damper had broken away from its mounting. Martin's gallant drive in the 1.5-litre

Manfred von Brauchitsch was trying hard, aviating over the brow up from Melbourne Corner and powering out of Coppice Wood with the Mercedes W125's rear tyres almost alight!

ERA ended with a broken piston and detached carburettor, 'Bira' inherited sixth place on Seaman's retirement ahead of Dobson, while Mays caused excitement by bouncing off the bank at Stone Bridge. The dust had hardly settled when Rosemeyer bounced his Auto Union's wildly sliding tail off the same bank and rushed away undaunted!

Rosemeyer stopped for 31 seconds on lap 32, refuelling and changing rear wheels, and this let Caracciola and Brauchitsch by, the red-helmeted aristocrat driving very quickly and setting the fastest lap of the race on his thirty-fourth tour, at 2 minutes 11 seconds. Two laps later he displaced Caracciola, and at half-distance – forty laps – the latter swept into his pit, refuelled and had tyres changed in 26.6 seconds. Rosemeyer thus inherited second place, and was driving hard after Brauchitsch.

Dobson's drive faltered on lap 42 when he had a long stop to replace a faulty magneto with one borrowed from Martin's dead ERA. In comparison to the Germans, the English stops were pitiful; Howe taking 65 seconds for fuel alone, Dobson 41 seconds for oil and water, 'Bira' approaching respectability with 37 seconds for fuel, and Mays 50 seconds for oil and fuel. The ERA founder had a fright at Melbourne on one lap as R4D's brakes failed.

The battle for the lead between Brauchitsch and

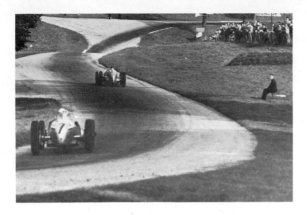

The majesty that was Donington, with Auto Union pursuing Mercedes-Benz down into the valley before Donington Hall and into the so-called 'Hairpin' at the bottom. Note the official on his shooting stick – they don't make men like him any more . . .

Rosemeyer with his bouquet congratulates Brauchitsch on his second place. Hasse looks on. Within three months Rosemeyer was dead in a record attempt, Hasse died on the Russian front during the war, and Brauchitsch is today an official in the East German sports commission.

Rosemeyer was a desperate affair, both cars blasting round from Red Gate to Coppice in a series of full-power slides. Brauchitsch had 26 seconds in hand as he stopped on lap 52, and as he charged back into the race Rosemeyer was 11 seconds away in the lead.

Rosemeyer had a second tyre stop coming up, and he carved himself a 20-second time cushion by lap 60 when Dr Feuereissen had the jacks prepared and signalled him in. Just at that moment Brauchitsch's hard-pressed left-front tyre exploded at around 170 mph along the Starkey Straight, and he clattered into his pit where a new wheel and tyre were fitted in 28 seconds. Rosemeyer was now able to make his stop and rejoin with a 31-second lead, and with eighteen laps to go only misfortune could rob him of the race.

Caracciola was tiring badly and falling away behind his team-mate, Muller and Hasse were driving quickly but unsensationally fourth and fifth, 'Bira' was miles behind in sixth place, with Howe seventh followed by Maclure whose homeric drive with the Riley ended abruptly in back axle failure on lap 67.

Rosemeyer thundered home easily, cheered to the echo by the packed and spellbound, not to say deafened crowd. He looked exhausted, grimed with dirt and oil, his overalls soaked in perspiration and worn clean through at the seat. After the regulation 15 minutes had elapsed the remaining runners were flagged-off, which meant that 'Bira' – sixth on the road and leading the English-based contingent – was too far behind even to be classified as a finisher! The circuit bookies had given long-odds against the 'unknown' Germans, and as the team mechanics and knowing punters flocked around to collect their winnings they found scattered boards and ticket stubs. The bookies had fled!

It was that kind of race, a day which put a true perspective on England's parochial form of motor racing, and a day which planted a seed in English hearts which was to bear fruit twenty years later.

Results

1 B. Rosemeyer (6.0 Auto Union – Auto Union AG) 3 hrs 1 min 2.2 secs, 82.86 mph; **2** M. Von Brauchitsch (5.66 Mercedes-Benz/Daimler-Benz AG) 3 hrs 1 min 40 secs, 82.57 mph; **3** R. Caracciola (5.66 Mercedes-Benz/Daimler-Benz AG) 3 hrs 2 mins 18.8 secs, 82.28 mph; **4** H.P. Muller (6.0 Auto Union) 3 hrs 4 mins 50 secs, 81.16 mph; **5** R. Hasse (6.0 Auto Union) 3 hrs 9 mins 50 secs, 79.58 mph; **6** 'Bira' (2.9 Maserati – Prince Chula of Siam) 78 laps; **7** Earl Howe (1.48 ERA – Humphrey Cook) 77 laps; **8** A.C. Dobson (1.48 ERA) 74 laps; **9** R. Hanson (1.5 Maserati – Mrs Hall Smith) 67 laps.

FASTEST LAP Rosemeyer and Von Brauchitsch 2 mins 11.4 secs, 85.62 mph, joint £100 award. £25 awards to leader at 15 laps – Brauchitsch; 30 laps – Rosemeyer; 45 laps – Brauchitsch; 60 laps – Rosemeyer. £100 first British-entered and British-driven car – 'B. Bira'. Team-Prize: Auto Union AG – Rosemeyer, Hasse, Muller.

RETIREMENTS P.N. Whitehead (1.48 ERA – driver) 11 laps, engine; C.E.C. Martin (1.48 ERA – driver)   laps, piston; H. Lang (5.66 Mercedes-Benz/Daimler-Benz AG) 26 laps, broken damper; R.J.B. Seaman (5.66 Mercedes-Benz) 29 laps, broken damper and collision damage; R. Mays (1.48 ERA – Humphrey Cook) 51 laps, brakes; P. Maclure (1.75 Riley) 67 laps, back-axle.

1938 Donington Park

October 22, Donington Park, 80 laps of 3.125-mile circuit
approximately 250 miles

The new year saw a new Formula, demanding capacity limits of 3-litres if supercharged or $4\frac{1}{2}$-litres unsupercharged. Fred Craner had been promised more German entries after his 1937 success, and October 2 was granted as race date until larger issues clouded the scene. The two German teams arrived at Donington more than a week before race-day to prepare, but as what became known as The Munich Crisis deepened and war seemed imminent between Britain and Germany, they hastily packed their cars, spares and tools, and drove through the night to Harwich for the boat home. The French entries were also in doubt, and on the day practice was scheduled to begin, Craner regretfully cancelled his race.

Then Chamberlain returned from Munich with his piece of paper and the last Donington Grand Prix was on again, for October 22. Mercedes returned with four W154 cars for three of their 1937 drivers; Caracciola, who had injured his foot, and who did not care for Donington anyway, was replaced by cadet driver Walter Baumer.

Auto Union had been stricken by tragedy in January, when Rosemeyer's record car had been blown off the Frankfurt-Darmstadt Autobahn, killing the Donington Grand Prix winner. It had been his last race victory, but Feuereissen had managed to sign the great Nuvolari in his place, joining the faithful Hasse and Muller, and the Swiss Chris Kautz. Ulrich Bigalke was reserve driver.

Laurie Schell's Ecurie Bleu sent across two of their 4.5-litre unsupercharged V12 Delahayes for René Dreyfus (a single-seater *Monoplace*) and 'Bodoignet Raph', while Luigi Villoresi appeared in the latest 3-litre straight-eight Maserati 8CTF. ERAs were fielded optimistically by Dobson, Ian Connell and band-leader Billy Cotton, Cuddon-Fletcher ran his ex-Parnell MG, Percy Maclure his Riley and Robin Hanson an Alta, borrowed from R.R. Jackson.

Nuvolari had won the preceding Italian Grand Prix for his first Auto Union success three weeks previously, and Monday practice saw him getting down to 2 minutes 11.2 seconds before hitting and killing a stag which leapt into his path from the woods near McLean's. The Italian ace damaged his ribs in this incident and had them firmly strapped-up for the remaining practice sessions and the race. Lang was quickest on Tuesday, at 2 minutes 11 seconds, from Brauchitsch (2:11.4) and Seaman (2:12.2). Kautz was

slowest of the German works drivers, but was suffering a heavy cold.

Once again more than 50,000 spectators packed into the Park on the misty, chill morning of October 22, but the sun quickly appeared, dispelling the mist and that Saturday developed into a warm mellow day. The Duke of Kent, President-in-Chief of the BRDC, flew up from London to watch the race, and was driven to the course in a V12 Lagonda saloon in which Seaman gave him two quick laps of the circuit. At flag-fall Nuvolari made a superb start to hammer his way into Red Gate ahead of Brauchitsch, Seaman and Lang. Villoresi hashed his start in the Maserati, and as the field streamed by to complete that opening lap it was Nuvolari's distinctive red helmet and yellow jumper in the leading silver Auto Union, with Muller, Brauchitsch, Seaman, Lang, Baumer, Hasse and Kautz on his tail. Dreyfus was ninth from Dobson, Villoresi, Connell, Fletcher, Raph, Cotton, Hanson and Maclure. The Maserati, Dobson, Cotton, and Raph all gained places next time round, but poor Kautz found his Auto Union's throttle sticking open down the hill into Melbourne Corner and rammed the earth bank heavily. He walked back to the pits, shaken but unhurt.

At ten laps Nuvolari had averaged 81.57 mph, and led by 14.6 seconds from Muller, Brauchitsch, Seaman, Lang and Baumer, but Villoresi was charging hard to atone for his poor start and the bright-red car carved its way into fifth place by lap 18 only to retire when a piston shattered. Maclure stopped on the grass after Melbourne with his Riley's back-axle broken yet again, and Dreyfus' Delahaye *Monoplace* had an oil-line part to put him out. Fletcher's MG was off the road, and on lap 26 Nuvolari stammered into his pit for a 53-second stop to change plugs. Muller, Seaman and Lang went by before 'Nivola' could rejoin, crouched forward over the steering wheel, head back, chin out and *charging*!

There followed a sensational incident on the downhill swerves to The Hairpin before Donington Hall, as Hanson's Alta threw a rod and gushed oil round this tricky section. Nuvolari broadsided off to the right, caught his car and rejoined the track at The Hairpin, Brauchitsch spun round twice and gathered up his Mercedes at the bottom of the hill, Hasse skated wildly off to the right, then back across the track and slammed into the safety bank, just missing a hut in

1938 Grid

7
Lang
(Mercedes-Benz W154)
2:11.0

4
Nuvolari
(Auto Union D-Type)
2:11.2

6
Brauchitsch
(Mercedes-Benz W154)
2:11.4

8
Seaman
(Mercedes-Benz W154)
2:12.2

1
Muller
(Auto Union D-Type)
2:12.6

5
Baumer
(Mercedes-Benz W154)
2:13.8

2
Hasse
(Auto Union D-Type)
2:15.4

3
Kautz
(Auto Union D-Type)
2:18.6

11
Villoresi
(Maserati 8CTF)
2:21.0

19
Dobson
(ERA R7B)
2:24.6

9
Dreyfus
(Delahaye V12 'Monoplace')*
2:25.4

15
Connell
(ERA R6B)

18
Cotton
(ERA R1B)

17
Cuddon-Fletcher
(MG)

12
Maclure
(Riley)

14
Hanson
(Alta)

10
'Raph'
(Delahaye V12)*
2:36.4

*Denotes unsupercharged engines

Reserve drivers: 1, 2 and 3 U. Bigalke – 9 and 10 L. Schell – 14 G.P. Harvey-Noble – 15 P.R. Monkhouse –
18 W.E. Wilkinson

which Mrs Craner was sitting. He vaulted the bank, shook off ambulance men and stamped back to the pits. Seaman then appeared, spun round close to Hasse's wreck and lost valuable time before marshals pushed him away again.

All this left Muller with a 5-second lead from Lang, with Nuvolari, Brauchitsch (peeved) and Baumer next up. Then Lang stopped to refuel in 33 seconds, flinging clear the splash cover as he howled back into the race. Brauchitsch hustled in and out in 30 seconds, then Connell brought in his ERA and handed over to Peter Monkhouse.

Muller came in at half-distance, refuelled and had the rear wheels changed in 40 seconds, which gave Lang the lead. Baumer stopped for fuel and plugs in 79 seconds, while Seaman spent 44 seconds refuelling. Then Nuvolari bulleted into the pits to change all four wheels and refuel in just 35 seconds, and he flurried out again in a cloud of dust, still third behind his team-mate.

One lap later Baumer's Mercedes crept over the Melbourne brow with its V12 engine stammering, and as he turned towards the pits a glow grew around the engine bay and flames began licking through bonnet louvres. Baumer jumped clear as the car rolled to a stop, the blaze was smothered but he was out of the race.

At the fifty lap mark Lang led Muller by 21 seconds and Nuvolari was nearly 37 seconds behind in third place, but closing fast. Just ten laps later he had taken second place with his Auto Union twitching and dancing around the Park as his dark brown arms pistoned away at the wheel. His fifty-sixth lap was covered at 82.96 mph, and his sixty-third at 83.71 which was the fastest lap of the race and which won the Italian the Craner Trophy and £100. He was within 12 seconds of Lang at sixty-three laps, and the German ace was handicapped by a shattered aero-screen which exposed him to a 165 mph airstream along the main straight. On lap sixty-four the gap was 10 seconds; lap sixty-five, 6 seconds; lap sixty-six, 3 seconds, and on lap sixty-seven the bulbous Auto Union blared past Lang's long-nosed Mercedes on the Starkey Straight.

Now there was no denying the wiry little forty-six-years old veteran, and he drove on and on in his own supremely individual and exciting style to win the second consecutive Donington Grand Prix for Auto Union at 80.49 mph, 1 minute 38 seconds ahead of Lang, and Seaman who had managed to displace little Muller. As *Deutschland Uber Alles* and the *Giovinezza* rang out over the loudspeakers in honour of the victors, Arthur Dobson came home sixth, only six laps behind the winner in his works-backed ERA. It was not obvious at the time, but this was the last Donington Grand Prix race, for within eleven months the Third Reich had begun its disastrous war, and Britain was to wait ten years to see another Grand Prix race.

Results

1 T. Nuvolari (2.98 Auto Union – Auto Union AG) 3 hrs 6 mins 22 secs, 80.49 mph; **2** H. Lang (2.96 Mercedes-Benz/Daimler-Benz AG) 3 hrs 8 mins 0 secs, 79.79 mph; **3** R.J.B. Seaman (2.96 Mercedes-Benz) 79 laps; **4** H.P. Muller (2.98 Auto Union) 79 laps; **5** M. Von Brauchitsch (2.96 Mercedes-Benz) 79 laps; **6** A.C. Dobson (1.48 ERA – driver) 74 laps; 7 W.E. Cotton/W.E. Wilkinson (1.48 ERA – W.E. Cotton) 74 laps; **8** I.F. Connell/P.R. Monkhouse (1.48 ERA – I.F. Connell) 74 laps.

FASTEST LAP Nuvolari 2 mins 14.4 secs, 83.71 mph, £100 award and Craner Trophy. £50 award for leader at 40 laps, Muller. Uttoxeter Trophy Team Award: Connell, Cotton and Dobson (ERAs). £100 and President's Trophy for first British car and driver to finish: Dobson (ERA).

RETIREMENTS C. Kautz (2.98 Auto Union – Auto Union AG) 2 laps, accident; Raph (4.49 Delahaye – Ecurie Bleu) 10 laps, oil pressure; L. Villoresi (3.0 Maserati – Maserati SA) 18 laps, piston; P. Maclure (2.0 Riley – P.W. Maclure) 12 laps, drive-shaft; R. Dreyfus (4.49 Delahaye – Ecurie Bleue) 23 laps, broken oil-pipe; A. Cuddon-Fletcher (1.39 MG – driver) 17 laps, brake rod; R. Hanson (1.49 Alta – Mrs Hall Smith) 25 laps, broken engine; R. Hasse (2.98 Auto Union) 29 laps, accident; W. Baumer (2.96 Mercedes-Benz) 43 laps, engine fire.

The start of the 1938 race, with the Auto Union and Mercedes-Benz teams the only ones in sight. The reaction of the photographers and officials illustrates the sheer noise and fury emanated by these cars.

1948 Silverstone

October 2, Silverstone, 65 laps of 3.67-mile circuit
approximately 238.5 miles

Thursday, September 30, 1948 saw Grand Prix cars being driven in anger for the first time around the perimeter track and runways of the RAC's new Silverstone airfield circuit.

Colonel Barnes' race committee had not succeeded in attracting the all-conquering Alfa Corse works team, and Farina's promised Ferrari was withdrawn, but taking his place was Alberto Ascari, who joined his friend and mentor Luigi Villoresi in a pair of the very latest Maserati 4CLT/48s, entered by the works-backed Scuderia Ambrosiana. 'Bira' had a third sister car, and Reg Parnell a fourth, while older Maseratis were to be handled by the Swiss Baron Emmanuel de Graffenried, and by Roy Salvadori, Bob Ansell/George Bainbridge, Sid Gilbey/Dudley Folland, and by Duncan Hamilton.

Paul Vallée of Ecurie France presided over the entry of four 4½-litre Lago-Talbot Type 26Cs, to be driven by forty-eight-year-old Louis Chiron (a veteran of the 1927 Brooklands Grand Prix), Louis Rosier, Phillippe Etancelin and the Italian Franco Comotti, winner of the 1937 TT at Donington.

A horde of pre-war 1½-litre ERAs were to run, with Bob Gerard in his ex-Wakefield R14B, John Bolster in Peter Bell's ex-'Bira' R5B *Remus*, David Hampshire and Philip Fotheringham-Parker sharing Parnell's prototype R1A, George Nixon's recently-acquired (from Parnell) R2A, Peter Walker in Whitehead's R10B, Cuth Harrison's re-profiled ex-Howe R8B/C, Geoffrey Ansell's R9B which he was to share with Brian Shawe-Taylor, and Raymond Mays himself with his famous R4D. In addition Leslie Johnson was to try his hand after a lengthy preparation period in the 1939 E-Type ERA GP2, and Geoff Richardson

1948 Grid

15 Johnson (ERA E-Type GP2) 2:58.6	**16** Gerard (ERA R14B/C) 2:58.2	**4** Etancelin (Lago-Talbot 26C)* 2:58.0	**20** De Graffenried (Maserati 4CL) 2:57.0	**1** Chiron (Lago-Talbot 26C)* 2:56.0

29 Rolt (Alfa-Aitken)* 3:0.2	**14** Walker (ERA R10B) 2:59.8	**6** Parnell (Maserati 4CLT/48) 2:59.8	**19** 'Bira' (Maserati 4CLT/48) 2:58.6

31 Richardson (R) (ERA-RILEY)	**25** Bolster (R) (ERA R5B)	**3** Rosier (Lago-Talbot 26C)*	**2** Comotti (Lago-Talbot 26C)*	**23** Harrison (ERA R8B/C)

8 Hamilton (Maserati 6C)	**12** Mays (ERA R4D)	**17** Watson (R) (Alta) 3:13.8	**22** G. Ansell (ERA R9B)

26 Gilbey (Maserati 6C) 3:20.0	**27** Salvadori (Maserati 4C) 3:11.0	**9** R.E. Ansell (Maserati 4CL)	**30** Nixon (R) (ERA R2A)	**24** Hampshire (ERA R1A)

11 Ascari (Maserati 4CLT/48/1597) Unofficial 2:56.4	**18** Villoresi (Maserati 4CLT/48 1594) Unofficial 2:54.6

*Denotes unsupercharged engines   (R) Denotes reserve entry

Non-starters/non-arrivals: 5 Lord Selsdon/Lord Waleran (Talbot) R – 7 Ashmore/Murray (Maserati 4CL) R –10 Sommer (Ferrari) – 11 Farina (Ferrari) – 21 Baring (Maserati 4C) R – 28 Brooke (Maserati 4CLT/48) – 32 Baird/Emery (Emeryson-Duesenberg)

fielded his ERA-engined ex-Maclure Riley. Tony Rolt was running the Alfa-Aitken, all that remained of the smaller of the two fearsome pre-war *Bimotore* Alfas which Nuvolari and Chiron had campaigned so bravely. Gordon Watson had his Alta, and the Belfast newspaper proprietor Bobby Baird the Emeryson Special which sported a $4\frac{1}{2}$-litre Duesenberg straight-eight engine from the slim Indy car which was raced in the early-thirties by the Scuderia Ferrari and by Whitney Straight and George Duller at Brooklands.

Johnson raised home hopes in the Thursday practice sessions by lapping in 2 minutes 58.6 seconds, quicker than 'Bira' on 59.6 and Parnell and Walker on 59.8. Comotti was the quickest Continental, at 3 minutes 1 second, with Etancelin 1.4 seconds slower.

'Bira's' car was sprayed blue overnight, and with more arrivals Friday practice saw Chiron getting down to 2 minutes 56.0 seconds, De Graffenreid 2 minutes 57.0 seconds and Etancelin 2 minutes 58.0 seconds.

While the 500s began practising for their supporting race the Scuderia Ambrosiana Dodge lorry arrived with its two Maseratis after a hectic three-day journey, and after a light rain shower they were taken out by Villoresi and Ascari to explore the circuit. They immediately returned times of 2 minutes 54.6 seconds and 2 minutes 56.4 seconds respectively.

Race-day dawned sunny, and the spectacle-starved British public flocked to Silverstone in their tens of thousands. Miles of traffic jams choked every approach road as an enormous six-figure crowd assembled.

Baird's Emeryson was refused a start by scrutineer Hudlass as its eight Amal carburettors proved too prone to flooding and fire during practice, and of the reserves Watson, Bolster, Richardson and Nixon were allowed to start. John Cobb, holder of the Land Speed Record, went off in a Healey to open the course, escorted by motor-cycle TT winners Artie Bell,

Lady Howe places the victor's wreath over Luigi Villoresi's shoulders after his winning drive in the first postwar RAC Grand Prix, Silverstone, 1948.

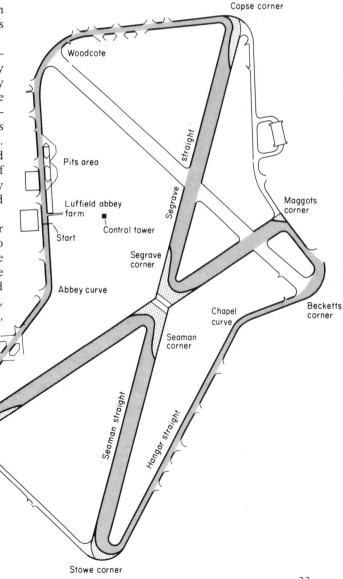

Silverstone Airfield as it appeared in 1948, showing the combination perimeter track and runway circuit used that year.

Freddie Frith and Maurice Cann, and then the supporting 500 cc race fell to the Coopers of 'Spike' Rhiando and John Cooper himself, after a slim youth named Stirling Moss had retired. After a briefing from Earl Howe the drivers clambered into their cars, with the two bright red works Maseratis on the back row, having had no official practice.

As the flag fell Villoresi and Ascari were already carving through the pack, and they quickly caught and passed De Graffenried, Chiron and Johnson the early leaders. The E-Type ERA confirmed its jinx on that opening lap as Johnson thumped a marker tub at Maggotts and snapped a half-shaft. Mays had stalled at the start, Salvadori oiled a plug and on lap two Parnell spluttered to a halt with a massive fuel tank leak after a left-over runway light had apparently punched in the drain plug!

The Ambrosiana Maseratis quickly made the race their own, while Comotti's brakes misbehaved, Rolt's 3.4 Alfa stopped with misfiring and Hamilton spun his Maserati. Mays was suffering pre-ignition which eventually destroyed a piston, and at quarter-distance Ascari led firmly from Villoresi, with Chiron, 'Bira' and Etancelin in their exhaust fumes.

Villoresi lost the shadowing Talbot as Chiron's cockpit filled with blue oil smoke and he retired at the pits with gearbox failure. Comotti's sister car's braking problems were incurable and he retired, as did Rolt, while Richardson pushed his hybrid into the pits after its back-axle broke. Etancelin was a third Talbot retirement as overheating caused the cylinder head to crack, and so much mechanical mayhem had made the circuit slick and slippery.

Both Italians found their fast Maseratis in high-speed slides, and Villoresi charged the straw bales at one point, but drove on unharmed. Geoffrey Ansell was less lucky, for his ERA slithered into the bales, tripped, and somersaulted luridly, throwing out its driver who was picked up with nothing worse than cuts and shock. Walker spun his ERA and continued, and Hamilton switched-off his Maserati when its oil-pressure zeroed.

The scheduled pit-stops were like a Fred Karno routine in most British pits, and several drivers were soaked in fuel, rejoining with car cockpits flooded and tail paintwork blistered. The Ambrosiana stops were flustered, but Ascari's 1:27 stop was mercurial by comparison, and 'Bira's' crew under Stan Holgate took 1:35. Then it was Bob Gerard's turn, and his crew loaded 30 gallons of fuel, topped-up the oil and put 'Mr Bob' back in the race in just 43 seconds which won a terrific cheer from the packed spectator enclosures.

Gerard was fifth behind Rosier, 'Bira' and the Ambrosiana cars, as De Graffenried was nursing his overheating car. Ascari's exhaust pipe had fractured, and the Ansell/Bainbridge Maserati made a string of officially-enforced stops in a hopeless attempt to cure a massive oil leak. The Gilbey/Folland car dropped out with gearbox trouble, and 'Bira' lost more and more ground as his Maserati's brakes deteriorated. Spilled oil had made the course dangerously greasy, Villoresi's rev. counter had popped out of the dash-panel and lodged under his clutch pedal to force clutchless gear changes, and he eased off considerably, as 'Bira' fell back and Gerard displaced Rosier at fifty-five laps for third place.

When Ascari took 10 seconds longer than Villoresi for a fuel stop, the result was settled, and it was left to the older man to tour home to win the first post-war British Grand Prix race from his team-mate. Gerard plodded reliably into third place ahead of Rosier, the last man to complete the full distance, while De Graffenried created eleventh-hour sensation by spinning into a potato field just before the finish, and rejoining with a commentator's microphone cable caught around his car!

As soon as the chequered flag appeared, the vast crowd spilled onto the course from behind their rope and straw-bale barriers, and the scheduled prize-giving was impossible. It had not been much of a race, but all who saw it were wildly enthusiastic – and it was at least a start.

Results

1 L. Villoresi (1.49 Maserati – Scuderia Ambrosiana) 3 hrs 18 mins 3 secs, 72.28 mph; **2** A. Ascari (1.49 Maserati – Scuderia Ambrosiana) 3 hrs 18 mins 17 secs, 72.19 mph; **3** F.R. Gerard (1.48 ERA – driver) 3 hrs 20 mins 6 secs, 71.54 mph; **4** L. Rosier (4.5 Lago-Talbot – driver) 3 hrs 22 mins 38.6 secs, 70.65 mph; **5** 'Bira' (1.49 Maserati – HRH Prince Chula) 64 laps; **6** J.V. Bolster (1.48 ERA – P.H. Bell) 63 laps; **7** D.A. Hampshire (1.48 ERA – driver) 60 laps; **8** R.F. Salvadori (1.49 Maserati – Rowland Motors Ltd) 60 laps; **9** Baron E. De Graffenried (1.49 Maserati – E. Plate) 59 laps; **10** G. Nixon (1.48 ERA – driver) 58 laps.

FASTEST LAP Villoresi 2 mins 52.0 secs, 77.73 mph.

FLAGGED OFF AT TIME-LIMIT P.D.C. Walker (1.48 ERA – driver) 53 laps; R.E. Ansell/G.H. Bainbridge (1.49 Maserati – R.E. Ansell) 50 laps.

RETIRED R. Parnell (1.49 Maserati – driver) 0 laps, fuel tank leak; L. Johnson (1.48 ERA – driver) 0 laps, drive-shaft; G. Comotti (4.5 Lago-Talbot – driver) 3 laps, brakes; A.P.R. Rolt (3.44 Alfa Romeo – driver) 6 laps, engine; D. Hamilton (1.49 Maserati – driver) 8 laps, oil-pressure; G. Watson (1.49 Alta – driver) 8 laps, sheared camshaft drive; G. Richardson (1.48 ERA-Riley – driver) 12 laps, differential; G. Ansell/B. Shawe-Taylor (1.48 ERA – G. Ansell) 22 laps, accident; P. Etancelin (4.5 Lago-Talbot – driver) 22 laps, cracked cylinder head; R. Mays (1.48 ERA – driver) 35 laps, piston; S.J. Gilbey/D. Folland (1.49 Maserati – driver) 36 laps, gearbox; L. Chiron (4.5 Lago-Talbot – Ecurie France) 37 laps, gearbox; T.C. Harrison (1.48 ERA – driver) 41 laps, valve.

1949 Silverstone

May 14, Silverstone, 100 laps of 3-mile circuit
approximately 300 miles

Only seven months elapsed before the second British Grand Prix race at Silverstone. This time round, the RAC were granted *Grande Epreuve* status to put their race on a par with such classics as the French and Italian Grands Prix, and they adopted 'British Grand Prix' as its official title, but although twenty-nine entries poured in, representing eight nations, there were no proper factory cars.

Practice began on the preceding Thursday as a squad of labourers slaved away to complete scaffolding stands on time for the great day. The circuit had been modified, dispensing with the hour-glass configuration of 1948. Now it was all perimeter road and no runway, with a tight straw-bale chicane at Club 'to force the use of low gear'.

Villoresi arrived grimy and tired direct from a race at Perpignan, and he was second quickest, 1.2 seconds behind Walker's FTD of 2 minutes 13.2 seconds.

Parnell managed a 14.7, Rolt 15.8 and Harrison 16.4, while Claes spun slowly in the chicane. On the Friday Billy Cotton announced that he would share with Hampshire, and Roy Parnell (Reg's nephew) was appointed to share Murray's car. 'Bira' arrived from Perpignan, and Claes 'who had a beauteous blonde in his pit' spun wildly out of Abbey Curve towards the pits! Best times were a 2 minutes 9.8 seconds for Villoresi (an average of 83.2 mph) with a 10.2 for 'Bira', 13.6 for De Graffenried and 14.4 for the ever-consistent Gerard.

Once again a staggering crowd packed into Silverstone, estimated at anything up to 120,000, and after the 500 cc curtain-raiser had been won by nineteen-year-old Stirling Moss, the Grand Prix began.

Compared to the enraged woodpecker noise of the 500s, the blare of sound from twenty-five Grand Prix cars was stupefying, regardless of their wide-

1949 Grid

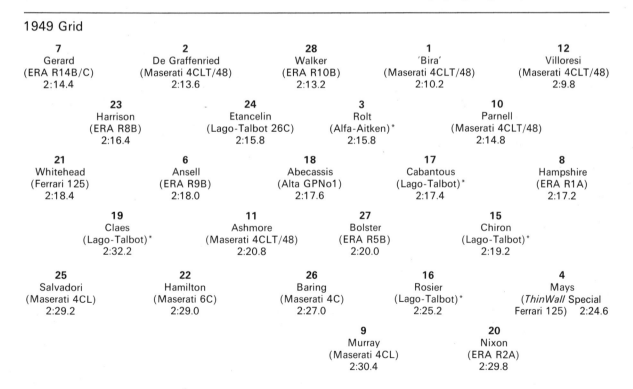

7 Gerard (ERA R14B/C) 2:14.4	**2** De Graffenried (Maserati 4CLT/48) 2:13.6	**28** Walker (ERA R10B) 2:13.2	**1** 'Bira' (Maserati 4CLT/48) 2:10.2	**12** Villoresi (Maserati 4CLT/48) 2:9.8
23 Harrison (ERA R8B) 2:16.4	**24** Etancelin (Lago-Talbot 26C) 2:15.8	**3** Rolt (Alfa-Aitken)* 2:15.8	**10** Parnell (Maserati 4CLT/48) 2:14.8	
21 Whitehead (Ferrari 125) 2:18.4	**6** Ansell (ERA R9B) 2:18.0	**18** Abecassis (Alta GPNo1) 2:17.6	**17** Cabantous (Lago-Talbot)* 2:17.4	**8** Hampshire (ERA R1A) 2:17.2
19 Claes (Lago-Talbot)* 2:32.2	**11** Ashmore (Maserati 4CLT/48) 2:20.8	**27** Bolster (ERA R5B) 2:20.0	**15** Chiron (Lago-Talbot)* 2:19.2	
25 Salvadori (Maserati 4CL) 2:29.2	**22** Hamilton (Maserati 6C) 2:29.0	**26** Baring (Maserati 4C) 2:27.0	**16** Rosier (Lago-Talbot)* 2:25.2	**4** Mays (*ThinWall* Special Ferrari 125) 2:24.6
		9 Murray (Maserati 4CL) 2:30.4	**20** Nixon (ERA R2A) 2:29.8	

*Denotes un-supercharged engines

Non-starters/non-arrivals: 5 R.E. Ansell/Bainbridge (Maserati 4CL) – 14 Mathieson/Johnson (ERA E-Type) – 29 Schell/Duntov (Lago-Talbot) – 30 Richardson (RRA)

spread obsolescence. 'Bira' made a superb start, rushing into the broad sweep of Woodcote Corner two lengths clear of Villoresi who had De Graffenried and Parnell with him, and the indomitable Gerard looming high above in the old English upright ERA.

Villoresi quickly got the measure of 'Bira' and his bright-red Maserati led its blue-and-yellow sister on lap three, the pair of them drawing away from the pack. On lap sixteen 'Bira' regained his lead, but only for two laps before Villoresi's works-prepared car showed its power advantage and stormed through again. 'Gigi' Villoresi swept round smoothly until lap twenty-four when 'Bira' was back in the lead, and the Ambrosiana car began to fall away, stopped in the pits for fuel and a discussion ending lap 27 and restarted fourth.

Parnell in the second Ambrosiana car had been third when Villoresi stopped, and so gained second place, just yards ahead of De Graffenried's white-crossed car. Abecassis was flying around fifth and remarkably fast in the traditionally testy Alta, with Ashmore sixth.

By the thirty-lap mark 'Bira' had lapped all but the second, third and fourth place men, and was averaging just over 80 mph on a circuit made unpopularly slow by that too-tight Club Chicane. Abecassis pressed-on undismayed when the Alta shed a length of exhaust pipe which bounded along the track in front of the pits, and simultaneously Villoresi sped into his pit for a quick stop, only to retire when his engine's oil pressure vanished.

Poor 'Bira' was suffering a recurrence of his 1948

brake fade, and Parnell closed slowly as down in the field Chiron went out once more with transmission breakage, Baring retired with a water leak, and Harrison's ERA broke its engine. At 40-laps 'Bira' was still leading, at 80.12 mph, and 41.4 seconds clear of Parnell who was in turn 20.4 seconds clear of De Graffenried. Walker was fourth but his ERA soon went out with braking problems, and Gerard was next in line followed by Etancelin.

Abecassis lost much time as the Alta's carburettor float chamber came loose, and just before fifty laps 'Bira's' braking caught him out at Club and he thumped into the straw bales, unfortunately collecting a hidden marker barrel which deranged his Maserati's front suspension. His race was run, so Parnell inherited first place with the Swiss Baron 23.6 seconds behind at half-distance, Gerard third and Billy Cotton delighting the crowd with some hard driving in Hampshire's ERA fourth. The Rosier and Etancelin Talbots in fifth and sixth place seemed set to complete the distance without a fuel stop, and were beginning to look threatening.

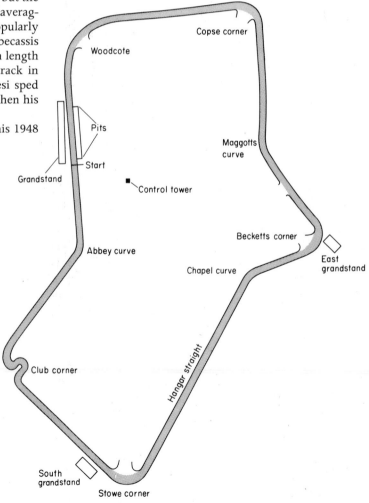

The notorious Club Chicane and its straw bale barriers, with Villoresi leading the 1949 Grand Prix from Etancelin, Walker, Harrison, Abecassis, Rolt, a Maserati and Ansell. Someone is already in trouble with the bales . . .

Parnell's glory lasted just six laps until his back-axle oil plug popped out, and while the leak was hastily staunched De Graffenried rasped by into the lead. Parnell made three more stops, retiring after sixty-nine laps when the back-axle broke. Meanwhile near-tragedy struck at Stowe as Bolster's ERA rolled wildly over the straw bales and severely injured its half-ejected driver. He lay by the trackside for 25 minutes before the ambulance arrived, sparking a terrific controversy about the use of straw-bales and the efficiency of Silverstone's medical services.

By sixty laps (180 miles) De Graffenried led at 78.11 mph, and was over three minutes ahead of Gerard with Parnell third but soon to retire. Behind Cotton and the Talbots lay Ashmore, who had lost 2 minutes trying to revive his car out on the circuit, while Abecassis had fought his way back into seventh place in a gritty drive with the Alta which amazed many observers by its longevity and speed.

Salvadori spun and stalled out on the circuit, push-started the Maserati and leapt aboard unaided, while Rosier plodded past the fourth-place ERA. With ninety miles to go Gerard began driving with new-found determination to whittle down the Swiss' lead, while Mays had been driving determinedly all afternoon but could do nothing with the *ThinWall* Ferrari's desperate handling. Its combination of swing axles and a very short wheelbase rendered it an unmanageable beast, and in disgust Mays came into his pit to hand over to BRM Chief Mechanic Ken Richardson. Unfortunately Richardson's experience was very limited, and on lap eighty-two it proved insufficient as the *ThinWall* took charge out of Abbey Curve and spun wildly through the spectator ropes, felling five onlookers who luckily escaped with minor injuries.

The other Ferrari had got away from Folland after he took over from Peter Whitehead, and he had a wild spin out of Maggotts after striking one of the all-too-common oil patches. Hamilton, whose wife was expecting a happy event, had some lurid slides on the oil, and afterwards declared that if she was not already a mother, he at least was a father!

At eighty-five laps De Graffenried slithered in for his second refuelling stop, allowing Gerard to close within a minute. But the Leicester garage owner's one and only stop was to come, on lap fifty-four. He got away after just 45 seconds, but then the ERA began to fluff and falter, and he settled back to tour

37

home second. De Graffenried tore home happily to win, 65 seconds clear of the green ERA which was a lap clear of Rosier – the only man who succeeded in running the whole race non-stop.

As a motor race, the 1949 event was an improvement, but six people in hospital at the end of the day was a stark reminder that motor racing was dangerous.

Results

1 Baron E. De Graffenried (1.49 Maserati – driver) 3 hrs 52 mins 50.2 secs, 77.31 mph; **2** F.R. Gerard (1.48 ERA – driver) 3 hrs 53 mins 55.4 secs, 76.95 mph; **3** L. Rosier (4.48 Lago-Talbot – driver) 99 laps; **4** D. Hampshire/W.E. Cotton (1.48 ERA – D. Hampshire) 99 laps; **5** P. Etancelin (4.48 Lago-Talbot – driver) 97 laps; **6** F. Ashmore (1.49 Maserati – Scuderia Ambrosiana) 97 laps; **7** G. Abecassis (1.49 Alta – driver) 96 laps; **8** P.N. Whitehead/D. Folland (1.49 Ferrari – 'Scuderia Ferrari') 95 laps; **9** G.E. Ansell (1.48 ERA – driver) 94 laps; **10** J. Claes (4.48 Lago-Talbot – Ecurie Belge) 92 laps; **11** D. Hamilton/P. Fotheringham-Parker (1.49 Maserati – D. Hamilton) 92 laps.

FASTEST LAP 'B. Bira' (1.49 Maserati – Prince Birabongse) lap 40, 2 mins 11 secs, 82.44 mph.

RETIREMENTS A.P.R. Rolt (3.44 Alfa Romeo – driver) 15 laps, back-axle; G. Nixon (1.48 ERA – driver) 25 laps, engine; L. Villoresi (1.49 Maserati – Scuderia Ambrosiana) 36 laps, engine; A.A. Baring (1.49 Maserati 4C – driver) 38 laps, water leak; Y. Giraud-Cabantous (4.48 Lago-Talbot – G. Grignard) 39 laps, oil loss, seized piston; L. Chiron (4.48 Lago-Talbot – Ecurie France) 41 laps, broken UJ; 'Bira' (1.49 Maserati – Prince Birabongse) 47 laps, accident; P.D.C. Walker (1.48 ERA – P.N. Whitehead) 50 laps, brakes; J.V. Bolster (1.48 ERA – P.N. Bell) 52 laps, accident; D. Murray (1.49 Maserati – driver) 64 laps, engine; R.F. Salvadori (1.49 Maserati – driver) 65 laps, burned valve; R. Parnell (1.49 Maserati – Scuderia Ambrosiana) 69 laps, transmission; K. Richardson/R. Mays (1.49 *ThinWall* Special Ferrari – G.A. Vandervell) 81 laps, accident.

Swiss winner – 1949; Baron de Graffenried brings home Enrico Plate's Maserati to a jubilant reception from the team patron on the left, their mechanics, and the Alta crew in the background.

1950 Silverstone

May 13, Silverstone, 70 laps of 2.889-mile circuit
approximately 202.23 miles

Today, the 1950 British Grand Prix is recalled as the inaugural round of the newly-devised World Drivers' Championship, but at the time it achieved far more significance from the FIA's award to the RAC of the courtesy title 'The 11th *Grand Prix d'Europe* (incorporating the 2nd British Grand Prix)', and the presence of King George VI, Queen Elizabeth and other members of the Royal Family.

The RAC's race programme enthused; '. . . this is the first time that the Reigning Sovereign has attended a Motor Race in Great Britain and it is to be hoped that this race will find favour with Their Majesties and with all who have gathered here today or who may be listening to this event "on the air".'

'Royal Silverstone' established the Grand Prix as a national sporting institution, as important in its own field as the Derby was to horse-racing, or an England-Australia test match at Lord's was to cricket. The programme authors went on to produce a rather quaint 'explanation' of the FIA's prestige *Grand Prix d'Europe* title. They reasoned: 'If a Grand Prix is to ordinary races as a test match is to club cricket, then the Grand Prix d'Europe has no cricketing parallel,

but may perhaps be likened to the Olympic Games . . .'!

Well, perhaps logic never was their strong point, but the organizers had at last attracted Alfa Corse to their Grand Prix. The team had lost only one race since their post-war revival, in 1946, and were now returning to racing after a season's lay-off in 1949. Under the direction of racing manager Guidotti their soon-to-be-famous 'Three Fs' team was to make its debut at Silverstone. Fangio, Farina and Fagioli were to drive their latest Tipo 158 cars, while as a gesture to their English hosts the Alfa Romeo management provided a fourth 158 for Reg Parnell, the most experienced of all British racing drivers at that time. Guidotti was acting as reserve driver, in place of the listed Piero Taruffi.

The outcome of the race was assured as soon as the big Alfa trucks, emblazoned with '*Alfa Romeo, Gomme Pirelli*' lettering bumped into the Silverstone paddock, but there were seventeen other runners. Maseratis were fielded by Scuderia Ambrosiana for the Davids, Murray and Hampshire, Enrico Platé was listed as the entrant of 'Bira's' car, while Joe Fry, Chiron, Baron de Graffenried and Bonetto were to

1950 Grid

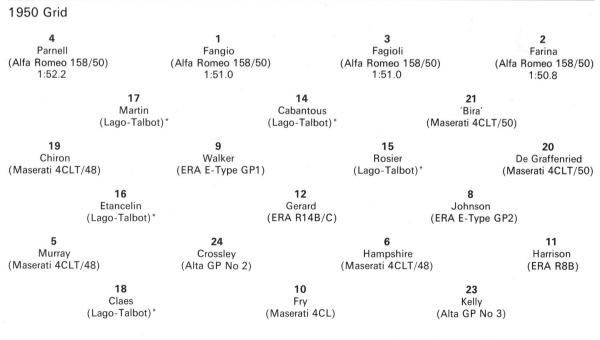

4 Parnell (Alfa Romeo 158/50) 1:52.2	**1** Fangio (Alfa Romeo 158/50) 1:51.0	**3** Fagioli (Alfa Romeo 158/50) 1:51.0	**2** Farina (Alfa Romeo 158/50) 1:50.8

17 Martin (Lago-Talbot)*	**14** Cabantous (Lago-Talbot)*	**21** 'Bira' (Maserati 4CLT/50)

19 Chiron (Maserati 4CLT/48)	**9** Walker (ERA E-Type GP1)	**15** Rosier (Lago-Talbot)*	**20** De Graffenried (Maserati 4CLT/50)

16 Etancelin (Lago-Talbot)*	**12** Gerard (ERA R14B/C)	**8** Johnson (ERA E-Type GP2)

5 Murray (Maserati 4CLT/48)	**24** Crossley (Alta GP No 2)	**6** Hampshire (Maserati 4CLT/48)	**11** Harrison (ERA R8B)

18 Claes (Lago-Talbot)*	**10** Fry (Maserati 4CL)	**23** Kelly (Alta GP No 3)

*Denotes unsupercharged engines

Non-starter: 22 Bonetto (Maserati 4CLT)

The luckless E-Type ERA warming-up under Silverstone sun, for the 1950 Grand Prix d'Europe.

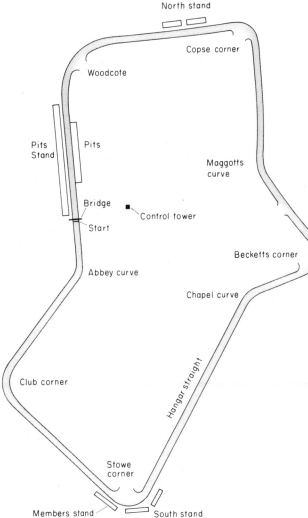

drive their own cars, all but the latter arriving to do so. Automobiles Talbot entered four of their big unblown 4½-litre 'sixes' for Giraud-Cabantous, Rosier, Etancelin, and Martin, while Claes had his own sister car in yellow Ecurie Belge colours. T.A.S.O. Mathieson entered Johnson's E-Type ERA ('It embodied all the worst features of the pre-war German cars'), while earlier and more reliable models were fielded for Walker, Harrison and Gerard. The two private post-war Altas of Irishman Joe Kelly and Geoffrey Crossley completed the entry.

Thursday practice saw the big wine-red Alfas wailing round the revised circuit, minus the previous year's chicane at Club and with most other corners eased and made faster. Farina did a 1:50.8 lap, to average 93.85 mph, or 0.5 mph faster than the lap record for the previous year's BRDC course, which took a wider path at Stowe. Fangio's car was recognizable by its yellow cowl, while Farina's was blue, Fagioli's white and Parnell's – of course – green. Farina equalled his good time on the Friday, and while his team-mates improved, none could challenge his pole position for the race.

Saturday was bright and clear, and by 6 am Silverstone's car parks were beginning to fill. After the 500 cc heats and final had given overall victory to Wing-Commander Aikens' Iota-Triumph from the youthful pair Moss and Collins, Raymond Mays gave a three-lap demonstration in the sensational pale-green V16 BRM. It was announced that the car would make its racing debut in the BRDC *Daily Express* meeting in August, and then the Royal Party toured the circuit and Earl Howe introduced them to the Grand Prix drivers.

While the Grenadier Guards band played, Howe took his place between the King and Queen and explained the procedure to them as the grid formed up with the four sparkling Alfa Romeos obviously omnipotent on the front row. Then the flag fell, and Farina catapulted away to lead into Woodcote from Fagioli, Fangio and Parnell. Walker's E-Type pulled off the grid straight into its pit, while Johnson's staggered off-course at Woodcote on lap two with its supercharger in pieces. Rolt quickly rejoined with Walker's car, but gearbox trouble soon put it out.

Nothing could interrupt the Italian display of speed and power at the head of the field, with Farina still leading at the five-lap mark by 0.6 seconds from Fangio, Fagioli and Parnell. 'Bira' and De Graffenried led the chase, while Fagioli moved to the fore by ten laps, Fangio at fifteen laps and Farina again at the twenty-lap mark.

The Swiss aristocrat's Maserati clattered to a stop when a con-rod broke before Abbey Curve, allowing Cabantous to inherit sixth place. Chiron drove on despite his Maserati throwing oil, until it swamped the car's clutch and the gearbox broke, and Kelly lost time with clutch problems.

At thirty laps Farina was 2.8 seconds clear of Fagioli, who was swopping his place every few miles with Fangio, while Parnell ran dutifully fourth throughout, his Alfa's radiator grille having been stove in by one of the numerous Silverstone hares. At forty laps Fangio was within 0.4 seconds of Farina whose average was a cool 90.8 mph.

'Bira' abruptly disappeared from fifth place when fuel starvation stopped the Maserati on Hangar Straight, Rosier sliding into sixth place behind the steady Cabantous. The three regular Alfa drivers all made slick 25-second fuel stops, Parnell's taking 5 seconds longer, Fry handed over to Shawe-Taylor at his stop and Crossley lost time when his pit's pressure-hose system failed, then abandoned out at Copse Corner. Murray's engine failed soon after his stop, and at the fifty-lap mark Fangio led Farina by 1.2 seconds and he had forced the race average up to 91.01 mph. Farina repassed to take the lead, and at the sixty-lap mark Fangio was running 0.6 seconds behind him. Then his Alfa slid on oil at Stowe, thumping a bale in a wild flurry of dust and straw. An oil-line was damaged in this incident, and as he felt his straight-eight engine beginning to tighten the burly Argentinian was forced to retire.

With five laps to go, Farina led Fagioli by nearly 42 seconds, but he eased right back and allowed 'The Abruzzi Robber' to close within 3 seconds as they wailed out of Abbey towards the finish line. Parnell was a popular third in this race which had a foregone conclusion, while the ever-reliable Gerard rumbled under the flag in sixth place, first home driver to finish in a British car and so winning the Fred G. Craner Memorial Trophy.

It had by no means been a great race, but 'Royal Silverstone' was a landmark in the history of the British Grand Prix, for it made airfield racing respectable, and much, much better was soon to come.

Results

1 G. Farina (1.48 Alfa Romeo – Alfa Romeo SpA) 2 hrs 13 mins 23.6 secs, 90.95 mph; 2 L. Fagioli (1.48 Alfa Romeo – Alfa Romeo SpA) 2 hrs 13 mins 26.2 secs, 90.92 mph; 3 R. Parnell (1.48 Maserati – Alfa Romeo SpA) 2 hrs 14 mins 15.6 secs, 90.37 mph; 4 Y. Giraud-Cabantous (4.48 Lago-Talbot – Automobiles Talbot) 68 laps; 5 L. Rosier (4.48 Lago-Talbot – Automobiles Talbot) 68 laps; 6 F.R. Gerard (1.48 ERA – driver) 67 laps; 7 T.C. Harrison (1.48 ERA – driver) 67 laps; 8 P. Etancelin (4.48 Lago-Talbot – Automobiles Talbot) 65 laps; 9 D.A. Hampshire (1.49 Maserati – Scuderia Ambrosiana) 67 laps; 10 J.G. Fry (1.49 Maserati – driver) 64 laps; 11 J. Claes (4.48 Lago-Talbot – Ecurie Belge) 64 laps.

RETIREMENTS L.G. Johnson (1.48 ERA – T.A.S.O. Mathieson) 2 laps, supercharger; P.D.C. Walker/A.P.R. Rolt (1.48 ERA – driver) 9 laps, gearbox; E. Martin (4.48 Lago-Talbot – Automobiles Talbot) 12 laps, engine; Baron E. De Graffenried (1.49 Maserati – driver) 36 laps, con-rod; L. Chiron (1.49 Maserati – driver) 24 laps, oil leaks, clutch; 'B. Bira' (1.49 Maserati – Enrico Platé) 49 laps, fuel starvation; D. Murray (1.49 Maserati – Scuderia Ambrosiana) 44 laps, engine; J.M. Fangio (1.48 Alfa Romeo – Alfa Romeo SpA) 62 laps, oil leaks, con-rod.

RUNNING AT FINISH BUT TOO FAR BEHIND TO BE CLASSIFIED J. Kelly (1.48 Alta – driver) 57 laps; G. Crossley (1.48 Alta – driver) 43 laps.

'Oh no you don't!', Dr Giuseppe Farina wields mind over matter in his slithering – but winning – Alfa Romeo.

1951 Silverstone

July 14, Silverstone, 90 laps of 2.889-mile circuit
approximately 260 miles

Following their triumphant 1950 season, in which Farina clinched the first properly organized Driver's World Championship from Fangio, Alfa Corse knew that their basically thirteen-year-old *Alfettas* were nearing the end of the road. Their straight-eight engines had been developed to fever pitch, yielding 385 bhp at a wild 8,500 rpm and gulping fuel at 1.5 mpg as much to cool the engine internals as to produce actual power. Over at Maranello, Ferrari had found increasingly competitive potential from their much more economical unsupercharged 4.5-litre V12s and it was against this background that the 1951 British Grand Prix was set.

Farina had won the Belgian Grand Prix for Alfa, but he was trailed home by the Ferraris of Ascari and Villoresi. Fangio and Fagioli shared the winning Alfa at Reims, again leading home two Ferraris, and now the two deadly Italian rivals came to Silverstone.

There were four Tipo 159 Alfa Romeos, with De Dion rear suspensions to control wheel movements more adequately than had the swing-axles of 1950. Farina's, Fangio's and Consalvo Sanesi's were 159Bs with extra oval section long-range tanks slung alongside the engine, while Bonetto had the original 'Monza 159A' of 1950 with a small extra tank slung in the cockpit, and the need for two fuel stops.

Ferrari entered three Tipo 375 unblown V12s, 24-plug versions for Ascari and the ageing Villoresi and an older 12-plug model for the Argentinian Froilan Gonzalez. Peter Whitehead was to handle Vandervell's latest 4.5-litre *ThinWall Special*, and Lago-Talbots were fielded by Rosier, Hamilton, Chiron and Claes while Etancelin's could not be repaired in time after a breakage at Reims.

Bob Gerard and Brian Shawe-Taylor ran their ERAs, David Murray and John James their creaky Maserati 4CLTs, and Fotheringham-Parker was trying again in his even older 4CL. Irishman Joe Kelly had his fragile two-stage blown Alta, and BRM arrived too late to practice with hastily-prepared centrifugally-supercharged V16s for Peter Walker and Reg Parnell. All three entries from Amedée Gordini's team (for Trintignant, Manzon and Simon) were scratched after troubles at Reims.

During practice the works Ferraris all thundered around the circuit under 1 minute 46 seconds, and the burly Gonzalez demanded attention as he lapped at a shattering 1 minute 43.4 seconds, 100.65 mph to

smash Farina's 97.19 mph record set in May. Fangio and Farina fought back, driving their cars with light fuel loads and using every centimetre of road to record 44.4 and 45.0, while Ascari and Villoresi were quicker than Sanesi and Bonetto on 45.4 and 45.8 respectively.

Clearly the stage was set for an almighty battle, the like of which British crowds had not seen since 1938. Before the race Peter Walker and Peter Whitehead did a lap of honour in their Le Mans-winning C-Type Jaguar with Moss, who had made fastest lap there, perched on its tail. The day was overcast but warm, and on the warming-up lap the weary BRM mechanics' hearts sank as Parnell's car sounded flat. A change of plugs re-orchestrated those 16-cylinders and they whooped joyously as Parnell re-started. Earl Howe assured both BRM drivers 'We're all with you, whatever happens . . .'.

From the flag the front row blasted away in a crash of sound not matched since 1938 at Donington. Gonzalez and Fangio hurtled away side-by-side, but Farina found more traction and plunged between them while the other Italian cars were all within touching distance, weaving around that first crazy lap.

Bonetto screamed across the timing line first, from Gonzalez, Farina, Ascari, Fangio, Villoresi, Sanesi and Whitehead who was falling behind and was already dubious about the *ThinWall*'s brakes. Next time round and Gonzalez was in the lead from Bonetto, with Ascari third. Parnell's yowling BRM had slashed through the field onto Whitehead's tail. Parker's Maserati had its bonnet flapping and made two early stops, and after five laps Gonzalez was 5.8 seconds in the lead.

He had taken his Ferrari almost literally by the scruff of the neck and was hurling it around Silverstone with total abandon. Fangio and Farina were cornering their heavy, fuel-bloated Alfas in long balanced slides, closing up for the lead, and at ten laps Fangio caught and passed his compatriot. He drew away until Gonzalez held the gap at 5–6 seconds and the Argentinian pair began to drop the rest of the field.

Fangio's fifth lap had been at a record 97.55 mph, and his thirteenth was to average 98.84 mph. Gonzalez was chased by Farina, Ascari and Bonetto who had a fist-waving Villoresi trying to find a way

1951 Grid

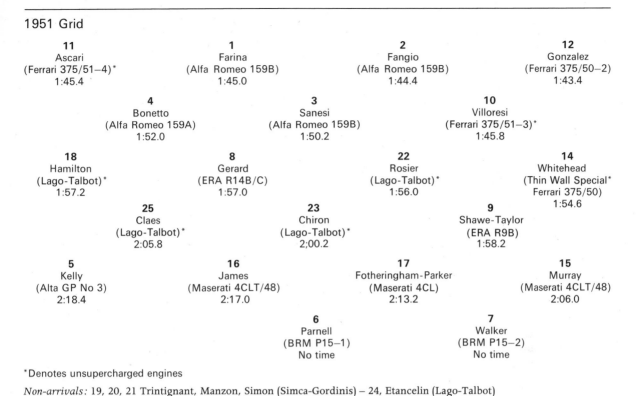

11 Ascari (Ferrari 375/51–4)* 1:45.4	**1** Farina (Alfa Romeo 159B) 1:45.0	**2** Fangio (Alfa Romeo 159B) 1:44.4	**12** Gonzalez (Ferrari 375/50–2) 1:43.4
	4 Bonetto (Alfa Romeo 159A) 1:52.0	**3** Sanesi (Alfa Romeo 159B) 1:50.2	**10** Villoresi (Ferrari 375/51–3)* 1:45.8
18 Hamilton (Lago-Talbot)* 1:57.2	**8** Gerard (ERA R14B/C) 1:57.0	**22** Rosier (Lago-Talbot)* 1:56.0	**14** Whitehead (Thin Wall Special* Ferrari 375/50) 1:54.6
	25 Claes (Lago-Talbot)* 2:05.8	**23** Chiron (Lago-Talbot)* 2;00.2	**9** Shawe-Taylor (ERA R9B) 1:58.2
5 Kelly (Alta GP No 3) 2:18.4	**16** James (Maserati 4CLT/48) 2:17.0	**17** Fotheringham-Parker (Maserati 4CL) 2:13.2	**15** Murray (Maserati 4CLT/48) 2:06.0
		6 Parnell (BRM P15–1) No time	**7** Walker (BRM P15–2) No time

*Denotes unsupercharged engines

Non-arrivals: 19, 20, 21 Trintignant, Manzon, Simon (Simca-Gordinis) – 24, Etancelin (Lago-Talbot)

past, because Sanesi was trying to find a way past *him*. Parnell was screaming round in the handsome BRM, keeping to a strict 10,500 rpm rev limit and troubled by front wheel patter under braking. Whitehead had settled for safety in the *Thinwall*, and he was ninth, some way ahead of Walker's second BRM and then Shawe-Taylor on his own in the ERA.

On lap 14 Sanesi barrelled into Stowe Corner in a terrific slide, held it and surprised Villoresi into

'He had taken his Ferrari by the scruff of the neck and was hurling it round Silverstone with total abandon' – Gonzalez thunders past the farm.

letting him by, while Gonzalez had closed right up onto Fangio's tail, 0.4 seconds behind at an average of over 95 mph.

In the pits Parker lost 2 minutes with ignition trouble, Claes had all twelve plugs changed in his dual-ignition Talbot, Kelly had similar problems and Parker stopped again. Hamilton spun at Copse, and at twenty-five laps Fangio had drawn 5.6 seconds away from 'Pepe' Gonzalez and had forced the race average up to 95.92 mph as his immense fuel load burned off.

Gonzalez couldn't get Beckett's right, and on one lap he had hit a marker tub, bounded over it, and weaved through the straw bales to press on regardless and angry and put in a 99.04 mph lap which left tuffets and stones all round the circuit!

Chiron lost 20 seconds having the Talbot's dampers adjusted, and Bonetto's small-tanked Alfa made the first refuelling stop on lap twenty-nine, rejoining after 35 seconds. Simultaneously James retired his Maserati with a split radiator.

At thirty laps the race average still soared, Fangio flashing by at 96.09 mph just 1.6 seconds clear of Gonzalez. Whitehead lost time having his brakes adjusted, Hamilton came in for oil, showed a cut arm which could not be treated, and downed two swift beers! Sanesi bellowed in on lap forty-one for fuel and fresh rear wheels, but one jammed on its splines and

the stop cost 2 minutes 52 seconds before he could rejoin. Parnell's BRM howled by to take his sixth place, despite a 30-second fuel stop which had Parnell hopping out of the car and complaining that cockpit heat was becoming unbearable.

Farina shot into his pit on lap forty-six for a 55-second fuel and rear tyre stop. Walker's BRM halted for just 25 seconds but two later stops as his cockpit became too hot for comfort prevented his following Parnell past Sanesi.

Then it was the leader's turn, and on lap 49 Fangio bustled into his pit, his car was refuelled and its rear wheels changed in 49 seconds and he hurled it back into the race, 1 minute 13 seconds behind Gonzalez's thundering Ferrari. Ascari was third, ahead of Farina.

Shawe-Taylor was running well among the backmarkers, in eighth place ahead of a resigned Whitehead, with Rosier, Gerard and Hamilton in an oil-soaked Talbot following on. Kelly was miles behind in his troublesome Alta. Murray's Maserati made a slow stop as it was refuelled from churns, its driver's overalls were soaked in oil and the car was reluctant to restart. Chiron had made a 5½-minute stop to investigate brake trouble and retired after forty-one laps, and then the works Ferraris began to come in . . .

Villoresi was first. Ten gallons rushed in from two churns, and he was away again after 32 seconds. Ascari came in for fuel and rear wheels, and was away in 33 seconds, after quickly downing a glass of water. Then Gonzalez was flagged-in, but he ignored the signal at first and then hustled in on lap sixty-one, stalling his engine. He stumbled from his cockpit, was pushed back in as fuel gurgled down the filler neck, a mechanic applied the electric starter, the big V12 boomed into life and he was away again in 23 seconds! While Gonzalez was thinking about stopping, Ascari had come in quietly with the sister car, and retired with transmission trouble, looking thoughtfully at Gonzalez's machine during its brief stop . . .

At seventy laps 'The Pampas Bull' had averaged 96.33 mph and led Fangio by 1 minute 19.2 seconds. Fangio was trying immensely hard in his maroon car, which juddered wildly into and through the corners under the enormous stresses he was imposing. Farina was third, but a lap behind, and Villoresi could not come to grips with the grim-faced *Dottore*. Bonetto was fifth, another lap down, and Sanesi sixth two laps behind until Parnell caught and slashed past him to partisan cheers and waves.

Suddenly that noxious sinus-snagging smell of a burning clutch wafted across the circuit, and it was Farina coasting down to Club where he hastily abandoned the Alfa as its engine bay seemed to be on fire. Hamilton spun while trying to double Kelly at Stowe, just as Gonzalez rushed up to lap them both. Parker went out when his Maserati broke an oil pipe, and then Gonzalez began to ease his pace, allowing Fangio to gain as much as a second a lap but by that time it was all too little, too late.

So the burly Gonzalez thundered home to win the British Grand Prix having taken on the Alfas and outfought them almost single-handed. Fangio came home second, tired but happy for his compatriot, 50 seconds behind, and Villoresi, Bonetto, Parnell and Sanesi followed on. Special cheers were deserved by the BRM pair for despite failing brakes their engines were as crisp as when they had started, Parnell had skinned his hand on the bucking steering wheel and both he and Walker had burned their left legs against hot cockpit panelling.

It had been a terrific, historic motor race, the best yet in post-war Britain.

'An' thenna she go lika dat!' – Dr Farina explains his troubles to a dubious audience.

Fifth for Britain, with heat exhaustion and burned feet – Reg Parnell fought an heroic battle with this supercharged V16 BRM, as team-mate Peter Walker suffered similarly in bringing his sister car home seventh.

Results

1 J.F. Gonzalez (4.49 Ferrari – Scuderia Ferrari) 2 hrs 42 mins 18.2 secs, 96.11 mph; **2** J.M. Fangio (1.48 Alfa Romeo – Alfa Romeo SpA) 2 hrs 43 mins 09.2 secs, 95.61 mph; **3** L. Villoresi (4.49 Ferrari – Scuderia Ferrari) 88 laps; **4** F. Bonetto (1.48 Alfa Romeo – Alfa Romeo SpA) 87 laps; **5** R. Parnell (1.48 BRM – BRM Ltd) 85 laps; **6** C. Sanesi (1.48 Alfa Romeo – Alfa Romeo SpA) 84 laps; **7** P.D.C. Walker (1.48 BRM – BRM Ltd) 84 laps; **8** B.N. Shawe-Taylor (1.48 ERA – driver) 84 laps; **9** P.N. Whitehead (4.49 *Thin Wall* Special Ferrari – G.A. Vandervell) 83 laps; **10** L. Rosier (4.48 Lago-Talbot – driver) 83 laps; **11** F.R. Gerard (1.48 ERA – driver) 82 laps; **12** J.D. Hamilton (4.48 Lago-Talbot – driver) 81 laps; **13** J. Claes (4.48 Lago-Talbot – driver), 80 laps.

FASTEST LAP G. Farina (1.48 Alfa Romeo – Alfa Romeo SpA) lap 38, 1 min 44.0 secs, 99.99 mph.

RETIREMENTS Farina lap 75, clutch; A. Ascari (4.49 Ferrari – Scuderia Ferrari) 56 laps, gearbox; D. Murray (1.49 Maserati – driver) 45 laps, broken valve spring; J. James (1.49 Maserati – driver) 23 laps, split radiator; P. Fotheringham-Parker (1.49 Maserati – driver) 46 laps, broken oil-pipe; L. Chiron (4.48 Lago-Talbot – Ecurie Rosier) 41 laps, brakes.

1952 Silverstone

July 19, Silverstone, 85 laps of 2.926-mile circuit
approximately 248.7 miles

The RAC delegated organization of their 1952 Grand Prix to the BRDC, lessees of the Silverstone site, and they performed an admirable job to arrange a veritable feast of speed with financial assistance and publicity from *The Daily Express*. The circuit had been revised, with new pits, race control, stands and start area moved to the straight between Woodcote and Copse Corners, abandoning the original site after Abbey Curve.

The BRDC achieved a very high-class entry, which

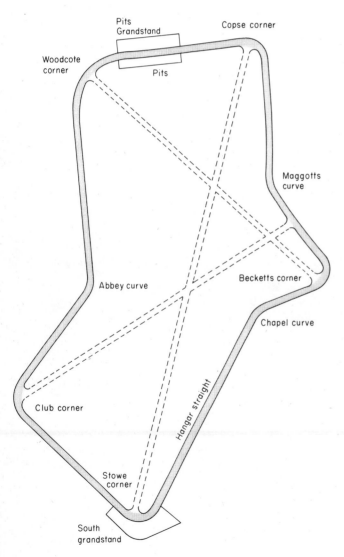

included no less than eight Ferraris. There were three works-entered 4-cylinder Tipo 500s for Ascari, Farina and Piero Taruffi, and three similar private entries for the Swiss Rudi Fischer, the Frenchman Rosier and for Englishman Roy Salvadori in Bobby Baird's latest acquisition. Two older unblown 2-litre V12 cars were to be driven by Peter Hirt for Ecurie Espadon team-patron Fischer, and by Peter Whitehead. Rosier's car non-started, but seven Ferraris in the race was a record.

Amedée Gordini brought three 6-cylinder cars as works entries for his hard-charging star driver Maurice Trintignant, Robert Manzon and 'B. Bira', while an older 1430 cc 4-cylinder car was running *sans* its 1951 supercharger for Johnny Claes, entered by Ecurie Belge.

Enrico Platé entered his two cut-and-shut 4CLT-based Maserati-Plates for De Graffenried and Harry Schell, son of the Ecurie Bleu proprietor who had brought the Delahayes to Donington pre-war. New Maserati A6 GCMs were entered by the South American Escuderia Bandeirantes for the Brazilian Bianco and his Uruguayan fellow-tourist Heitel Cantoni.

Facing this strong foreign entry was the best British field yet assembled, headed by Connaught Engineering's four new A-Type cars for their sponsor Kenneth McAlpine, and Dennis Poore, Eric Thompson and Ken Downing. Five new Cooper-Bristols were fielded for Mike Hawthorn, Alan Brown, Eric Brandon, Murray and Parnell. John Heath and George Abecassis entered three of their new single-seater HWMs with Alta engines for Hamilton, Peter Collins and Lance Macklin, while the Australian Tony Gaze ran his ex-works 1951 model. Singleton entries included Stirling Moss in the advanced new G-Type ERA with a Bristol 6-cylinder engine similar to the Coopers, while Graham Whitehead ran the new Alta which he campaigned in partnership with his half-brother, Peter. Tony Crook had a stripped two-seater Frazer Nash with Bristol engine, but Ken Wharton non-started his sister single-seater model. Bill Aston (a veteran of fifty-two) entered his fractious air-cooled flat-four engined Aston-Butterworth.

The BRDC stage-managed their Grand Prix to perfection, arranging a European-style parade of the cars and drivers, while the Rover gas turbine car and the successful Alpine Rally Sunbeams made demonstration laps. A thirty-five-lap Formule Libre race

1952 Grid

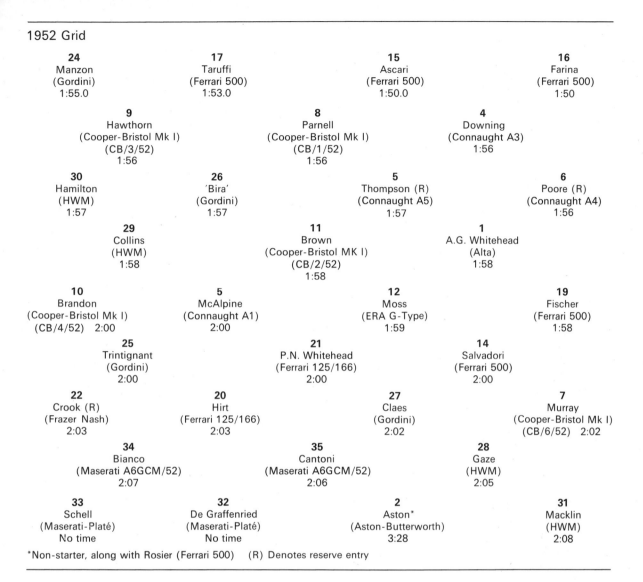

24 Manzon (Gordini) 1:55.0	**17** Taruffi (Ferrari 500) 1:53.0	**15** Ascari (Ferrari 500) 1:50.0	**16** Farina (Ferrari 500) 1:50
	9 Hawthorn (Cooper-Bristol Mk I) (CB/3/52) 1:56	**8** Parnell (Cooper-Bristol Mk I) (CB/1/52) 1:56	**4** Downing (Connaught A3) 1:56
30 Hamilton (HWM) 1:57	**26** 'Bira' (Gordini) 1:57	**5** Thompson (R) (Connaught A5) 1:57	**6** Poore (R) (Connaught A4) 1:56
	29 Collins (HWM) 1:58	**11** Brown (Cooper-Bristol MK I) (CB/2/52) 1:58	**1** A.G. Whitehead (Alta) 1:58
10 Brandon (Cooper-Bristol Mk I) (CB/4/52) 2:00	**5** McAlpine (Connaught A1) 2:00	**12** Moss (ERA G-Type) 1:59	**19** Fischer (Ferrari 500) 1:58
	25 Trintignant (Gordini) 2:00	**21** P.N. Whitehead (Ferrari 125/166) 2:00	**14** Salvadori (Ferrari 500) 2:00
22 Crook (R) (Frazer Nash) 2:03	**20** Hirt (Ferrari 125/166) 2:03	**27** Claes (Gordini) 2:02	**7** Murray (Cooper-Bristol Mk I) (CB/6/52) 2:02
	34 Bianco (Maserati A6GCM/52) 2:07	**35** Cantoni (Maserati A6GCM/52) 2:06	**28** Gaze (HWM) 2:05
33 Schell (Maserati-Platé) No time	**32** De Graffenried (Maserati-Platé) No time	**2** Aston* (Aston-Butterworth) 3:28	**31** Macklin (HWM) 2:08

*Non-starter, along with Rosier (Ferrari 500)   (R) Denotes reserve entry

preceded the Grand Prix, won by Taruffi in the *ThinWall Special* who shared fastest lap at 1:49.0, 96.67 mph with Gonzalez's V16 BRM (before its retirement).

Nine green cars on the first four rows of the grid was an encouraging sight for British eyes, but it made no odds to Ascari, who shot well away from Farina as the flag fell. Poore was hard on their heels in the Connaught, with Downing, Parnell, Thompson, Hawthorn and Taruffi (who had muffed his start) blaring by ahead of 'Bira', Moss, Salvadori, Hamilton and Collins.

Brown stopped with brake problems, Manzon lost 3 minutes with clutch trouble and then retired, while Taruffi got into his stride and moved into fifth place at five laps, fourth at ten and then passed Poore for third place as the Englishman spun on oil on lap

The aces – Alberto Ascari, his friend and mentor Luigi Villoresi, and the rugged 'Nino' Farina – all three were British Grand Prix winners.

Ascari's Ferrari '500' led all the way.

14. As the Ferraris became comfortably established, the Connaughts just did not have the pace to close with them, the Cooper-Bristols were having troubles, and the HWMs were nowhere.

On lap twenty-seven Farina dodged into the pits, losing 3 minutes and four places while plugs were changed in an attempt to cure misfiring, but it was to no avail and he began lagging badly, being passed by Thompson. Hirt went out with brake failure, Murray's Ecurie Ecosse Cooper-Bristol died at Woodcote, and Hamilton and Gaze were in trouble with their HWMs. Moss' curious-looking ERA was underpowered and he spun it in his efforts to compensate, before having to retire as the cylinder head was lifting. 'Bira' abandoned the Gordini beyond Club with transmission troubles, and both Brown and Brandon were in difficulties with the water-pump belts on their Bristol engines.

To general amazement, the Connaughts began making fuel stops, Thompson halting for 1 minute with the rev-counter u/s and taking on fuel, oil and water. Poore was next, losing 55 seconds and giving Hawthorn his third place, the tall blond Farnham boy's Cooper-Bristol running superbly in direct contrast to its sister cars.

At fifty laps Ascari led at an average of 91.01 mph, with Taruffi second and Hawthorn only 55 seconds behind in third place and averaging 88.24 mph. Schell had stopped his Platé during the first two Connaught stops, taking on fuel and oil, and on laps 50 and 51 the Downing and McAlpine A-Types swept in, losing 49 and 45 seconds respectively. One lap later it was Macklin's turn in the HWM, and three laps later an unhappy De Graffenried had both his understeering Platé's front wheels changed.

Hamilton was out with engine failure, and Gaze surrendered to ruptured gaskets in his wide-bodied HWM.

So the Ferraris barked on their consistent way, non-stop, and the somnolent crowd saw Brown stop for oil, Graham Whitehead for fuel, and Collins lose 9 minutes while misfiring was traced to a faulty magneto.

Ascari led Taruffi all the way home in a faultless Ferrari demonstration of speed, reliability, and the long-range essential in a modern Grand Prix car. Hawthorn was a fine third, enhancing his burgeoning reputation and doing full justice to his father's impeccable preparation of the Bob Chase-owned car. The Poore and Thompson Connaughts were in the points in a heartening British display, while a distinctly ruffled Farina nursed his flat Ferrari home into sixth place.

Results

1 A. Ascari (1.98 Ferrari – Scuderia Ferrari) 2 hrs 44 mins 11 secs, 90.92 mph; 2 P. Taruffi (1.98 Ferrari – Scuderia Ferrari) 84 laps; 3 J.M. Hawthorn (1.97 Cooper-Bristol – L.D. Hawthorn) 83 laps; 4 D. Poore (1.96 Connaught – driver) 83 laps; 5 E. Thompson (1.96 Connaught – driver) 82 laps; 6 G. Farina (1.98 Ferrari – Scuderia Ferrari) 82 laps; 7 R. Parnell (1.97 Cooper-Bristol – A.H.M. Bryde) 82 laps; 8 R.F. Salvadori (1.98 Ferrari – G. Caprara) 82 laps; 9 K.H. Downing (1.96 Connaught – driver) 82 laps; 10 P.N. Whitehead (1.99 Ferrari – driver) 81 laps; 11 'B. Bira' (1.99 Gordini – Equipe Gordini) 81 laps; 12 A.G. Whitehead (1.96 Alta – driver) 80 laps; 13 L. Macklin (1.96 HWM – HWM Ltd) 80 laps; 14 R. Fischer (1.98 Ferrari – Ecurie Espadon) 80 laps; 15 J. Claes (1.5 Gordini – Ecurie Belge) 79 laps; 16 K. McAlpine (1.96 Connaught – driver) 79 laps; 17 H. Schell (1.99 Maserati-Plate – Enrico Plate) 78 laps; 18 G. Bianco (1.99 Maserati – Escuderia Bandeirantes) 77 laps; 19 Baron E. De Graffenried (1.99 Maserati-Plate – driver) 76 laps; 20 E. Brandon (1.97 Cooper-Bristol – Ecurie Richmond) 76 laps; 21 T.A.D. Crook (1.97 Frazer-Nash – driver) 75 laps; 22 A. Brown (1.97 Cooper-Bristol – Ecurie Richmond) 69 laps.

FASTEST LAP   Ascari 1 min 52 secs, 94.08 mph.

RETIREMENTS   D. Murray (1.97 Cooper-Bristol – Ecurie Ecosse), engine; S. Moss (1.97 ERA – ERA Ltd), engine; P. Hirt (1.99 Ferrari – Ecurie Espadon), brakes; R. Manzon (1.99 Gordini – Equipe Gordini), transmission; M. Trintignant (1.99 Gordini – Equipe Gordini), transmission; F.A.O. Gaze (1.96 HWM – driver), blown gaskets; P. Collins (1.96 HWM – HWM Ltd), ignition; J.D. Hamilton (1.96 HWM – HWM Ltd), engine; H. Cantoni (1.99 Maserati – Escuderia Bandeirantes).

1953 Silverstone

July 18, Silverstone, 90 laps of 2.926-mile circuit
approximately 263.3 miles

Competition was much more fierce in 1953 as the new 6-cylinder Maseratis became more reliable and began to match the Ferraris. Fangio had recovered from his Monza crash early in 1952 and was fully capable of taking on the Ferrari strength of Ascari, Farina, Villoresi and Hawthorn with his by now much smoother-driving team-mate Gonzalez. But Ascari had won the first three races of the year, with a Maserati third each time, and then at Reims it was left to Mike Hawthorn to out-fumble both Fangio and Gonzalez in the closing laps – a solitary Ferrari against the two Maseratis. Thus the teams came to Silverstone set for a battle perhaps as hard-fought as Gonzalez's classic of 1951, but it did not work out that way.

Both Italian works teams were unchanged from Reims, with the usual Ferrari quartet of Tipo 500s ranged against the Maserati A6GCMs of Fangio, Gonzalez, Bonetto and a youthful Argentinian newcomer named Onofre Marimon, son of one of Fangio's old *Carretera* road-racing rivals. A fifth Ferrari 500 came from Ecurie Rosier for the iron-haired forty-eight-year-old Frenchman, and 'Tulo' De Graffenried had a private white-bonneted Maserati A6GCM. Completing the foreign entry was Equipe Gordini, with three of their 'racing on a shoe-string' 6-cylinder cars for Trintignant, Schell and the ex-motor-cycle Champion of France, Jean Behra.

HWM fielded four tatty-looking single-seaters for Macklin, Collins, Hamilton and Jack Fairman, and Connaught ran three Hilborn-Travers fuel-injected A-Types for McAlpine, Salvadori and the evergreen

Tony Rolt expresses his feelings to Ken Wharton, during practice with Rob Walker's A-Type Connaught.

'Bira'. Ian Stewart was to run Ecurie Ecosse's normally carburated Connaught, and Rolt was in R.R.C. Walker's similarly dark-blue sister car.

Jimmy Stewart, a Scot from Dumbarton with a teenage brother named Jackie, was to drive Ecurie Ecosse's Cooper-Bristol Mk 1. Three 1953 Cooper-Bristol Mk IIs were entered by the manufacturer for Ken Wharton, by Bob Gerard, and by Bob Chase (Mike Hawthorn's mentor) for Alan Brown. Three more front-engined Cooper Mk IIs were entered, all Alta-powered, but Moss' blew up disastrously at Reims which left just Whitehead and Crook to race their's at Silverstone. Chiron had entered his OSCA, but he withdrew from many mid-season races, including this Grand Prix.

Practice saw the Ferrari/Maserati battle well and truly joined, as Ascari was quickest at 1:48.0, followed by Gonzalez and Hawthorn with '49-dead' and Fangio with a lap at 1:50.0, equalled by Farina. Villoresi and Marimon were both on 1:51.0 to complete a brilliant Italian team line-up in the first two rows of the starting grid.

The cars assembled after Earl Howe had unveiled the 'Bira'-designed Pat Fairfield Memorial which had been moved to Silverstone after fourteen years languishing amid the brambles at Donington Park. The whole field began to creep as Kenneth Evans raised the Union Jack, then streamed away to Copse in a deafening blare of noise. Fangio led into Copse, and Ascari led out as the graceful Maserati skidded wide. Villoresi and Gonzalez led the rest, and a furious De Graffenried chased away last after stalling on the grid.

On lap 2 Gonzalez shouldered past Fangio to chase the leading Ferrari, and Hawthorn was ahead of Marimon in fourth place until he came pelting into Woodcote's broad sweep far too fast, bounded off course through a low fence and spun luridly along the grass verge below the packed grandstands. He kept his head, caught the car on its last revolution and with a harassed glance over his shoulder grabbed first gear and belted back into the fray, his face bleaching as his fright reaction developed!

A lap later Ugolini waved him in to check the car, and a slight fuel leak was corrected. Meanwhile Ascari was making fast driving look easy as he drove away with typical grace, and set a new Formula 2 race record of 1:51.0 – 94.93 mph – on his second lap.

1953 Grid

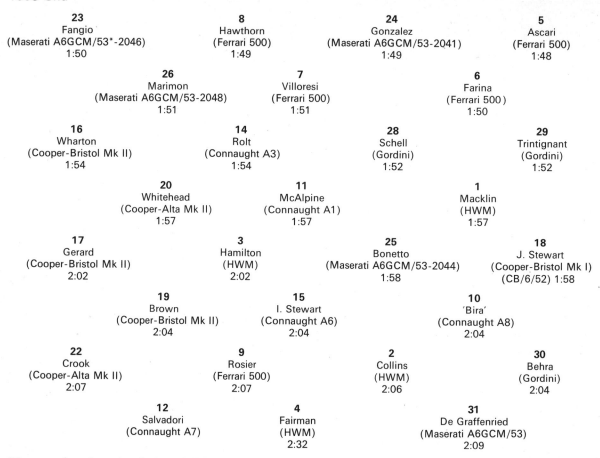

23 Fangio (Maserati A6GCM/53*-2046) 1:50	**8** Hawthorn (Ferrari 500) 1:49	**24** Gonzalez (Maserati A6GCM/53-2041) 1:49	**5** Ascari (Ferrari 500) 1:48
	26 Marimon (Maserati A6GCM/53-2048) 1:51	**7** Villoresi (Ferrari 500) 1:51	**6** Farina (Ferrari 500) 1:50
16 Wharton (Cooper-Bristol Mk II) 1:54	**14** Rolt (Connaught A3) 1:54	**28** Schell (Gordini) 1:52	**29** Trintignant (Gordini) 1:52
	20 Whitehead (Cooper-Alta Mk II) 1:57	**11** McAlpine (Connaught A1) 1:57	**1** Macklin (HWM) 1:57
17 Gerard (Cooper-Bristol Mk II) 2:02	**3** Hamilton (HWM) 2:02	**25** Bonetto (Maserati A6GCM/53-2044) 1:58	**18** J. Stewart (Cooper-Bristol Mk I) (CB/6/52) 1:58
	19 Brown (Cooper-Bristol Mk II) 2:04	**15** I. Stewart (Connaught A6) 2:04	**10** 'Bira' (Connaught A8) 2:04
22 Crook (Cooper-Alta Mk II) 2:07	**9** Rosier (Ferrari 500) 2:07	**2** Collins (HWM) 2:06	**30** Behra (Gordini) 2:04
	12 Salvadori (Connaught A7)	**4** Fairman (HWM) 2:32	**31** De Graffenried (Maserati A6GCM/53) 2:09

*These cars have been described as A6SSGs but works records indicate that A6GCMs were the F2 cars for both 1952 and '53. I have indicated the later body-style by '/53'.

Non-arrivals: 21 Moss (Cooper-Alta) – 20 Whitehead (Cooper-Alta) – 27 Chiron (OSCA)
Listed reserve drivers: 17 D.A. Clarke – 18 N. Sanderson

Gonzalez equalled it next time round to prove the Maserati as good a car, and on lap 4 Ascari flashed round in 1:50.0 – 95.79 mph. These were the opening feints in a 263-mile race, and Ascari's speed in his fuel-laden car was the product of sheer virtuosity.

Already problems had struck the home runners. Crook had fuel system failure, McAlpine split a hose, and both were out on the first lap. Wharton was in and out to investigate disappearing oil pressure, and then Schell's Gordini made three stops in the first six laps and retired with magneto failure. As he made his final stop Trintignant rejoined with his broken exhaust system lashed up, and on lap 8 Peter Whitehead came in for brake adjustment.

Race officials studied Gonzalez's car intently as it appeared to be spraying oil, and Lugo was asked to bring him in. He ignored the stewards so they black-flagged his driver, who also turned a blind eye for three laps before swirling into the pits in genuine fury. By this time the leak had run dry, and after a stormy scene he tucked his head down on his chins and thrashed back onto the track. Certainly the circuit was oily, and the race average fell for a while as Ascari ran 15 seconds clear of Fangio and 30 seconds ahead of Villoresi, while Farina and Marimon were close together a minute or more adrift.

Stewart retired the Connaught on lap 25 after four stops to investigate a bad misfire, Trintignant and Hamilton had both gone out, and De Graffenried was in constant trouble with misfiring. Wharton needed oil and Whitehead had further brake adjustment in his Cooper-Alta. Bonetto's works Maserati had been delayed with a choked carburettor jet, Gerard gave up when his Cooper's front spring chattered loose, and Behra dropped out when his Gordini's fuel pump

50

Froilan Gonzalez warms-up his Maserati along Silverstone's main runway amongst typical racing car transport of the day. The C-Type Jaguar was Bill Holt's entry in the supporting sports car race, and the single-seater is Horace Richards' Formule Libre HAR.

Pushin' and Shovin': this rear of the grid quartet at the start of the 1953 Grand Prix includes a startled Duncan Hamilton (HWM), teeth-gritting Tony Crook (Cooper-Alta), and a resigned Louis Rosier (Ferrari), while Roy Salvadori dodges his Connaught past them all. The bus formed the timekeepers' box in those days.

failed. 'Bira' stopped for water and a plug-change, and on lap 35 Macklin's HWM retired with its clutch housing split, and De Graffenried abandoned as his car's clutch pedal broke off.

Neither Ferrari nor Maserati showed measurable superiority over the other, but between them they blew British opposition into the weeds more effectively than they had in 1952. Just before half-distance a rare place-change among the leaders saw Marimon displace Farina for fifth place in his blue-and-yellow Maserati, and at the forty-fifth lap Ascari led consistently from Fangio, Villoresi, Gonzalez, Marimon and Farina, with Rolt's Walker-blue Connaught chasing them round in seventh place.

Salvadori lost eighth place on lap 51 when a rear radius rod cracked on his Connaught, and soon afterwards Fairman's HWM was abandoned with clutch failure. Brown had lost 13 minutes having a broken steering wheel replaced, and then on lap 56 Gonzalez hustled into the pits to refuel and take on two gallons of oil.

Collins crashed his HWM at Chapel Curve, and at sixty laps Ascari was a full 41 seconds clear of Fangio. Then trouble struck the Italian cars, for six laps later Villoresi's Ferrari shattered its back-axle, and Marimon's Maserati died at Copse Corner and was abandoned.

Wharton's pit-crew loaded 10 gallons of fuel in a brisk 20 seconds and Rolt lost a minute refuelling on lap 67. All this time Hawthorn had been climbing through the field although mutedly after his enormous spin and subsequent stop which dropped him back to last place. He was thirteenth at 20 laps, twelfth at 30, and ninth at 40 laps. Salvadori's retirement gave him a place, and on lap 66 he got past Rolt for fifth just as Villoresi and Marimon went out.

As the race ran into its closing stages the sky darkened, and a savage hail shower slattered across the circuit, followed by heavy rain which had the low-lying sections flooding rapidly. Just as the shower began Rolt veered off course on his seventy-

first time through Becketts. A half-shaft had snapped, and Jimmy Stewart found himself sixth behind Hawthorn. The tartan-shirted Scot was really flying along, but a deep puddle caught him out at Copse Corner and he thudded into the bank to end a promising drive. Even the experienced 'Bira' spun twice, and then the sun broke through, the rain stopped, and Ascari led the way home to win his second consecutive British Grand Prix, by exactly 1 minute from Fangio. Bonetto replaced Stewart in sixth place, 'Bira' brought the first British car home seventh and Wharton was the first British driver to finish, in eighth place with the sadly delayed works Cooper. Ferrari had beaten Maserati once more, but only narrowly, and Ascari had lapped third-place Farina twice in the sister car. He was all that stood between Fangio, Maserati and a Grande Epreuve victory, and although that combination did win at Monza to close the season, the Championship was again Ascari's for Ferrari.

Results

1 A. Ascari (1.98 Ferrari – Scuderia Ferrari) 2 hrs 50 mins, 92.97 mph; **2** J.M. Fangio (1.98 Maserati – Officine Alfferi Maserati) 2 hrs 51 mins; **3** G. Farina (1.98 Ferrari – Scuderia Ferrari) 88 laps; **4** J.F. Gonzalez (1.98 Maserati – Officine Alfieri Maserati) 88 laps; **5** J.M. Hawthorn (1.98 Ferrari – Scuderia Ferrari) 87 laps; **6** F. Bonetto (1.98 Maserati – Officine Alfieri Maserati) 82 laps; **7** 'B. Bira' (1.96 Connaught – Connaught Engineering), 82 laps; **8** K. Wharton (1.97 Cooper-Bristol – Cooper Car Co Ltd) 80 laps; **9** P. N. Whitehead (1.96 Cooper-Alta – Atlantic Stable) 78 laps.

FASTEST LAP Gonzalez and Ascari, 1 min 50 secs, 95.79 mph.

RETIREMENTS K. McAlpine (1.96 Connaught – Connaught Engineering), start-line: T.A.D. Crook (1.96 Cooper-Alta – driver), start-line, fuel-feed; F.R. Gerard (1.97 Cooper-Bristol – driver) 8 laps; J.D. Hamilton (1.96 HWM – John Heath) 14 laps, clutch; M. Trintignant (1.99 Gordini – Automobiles Gordini), back-axle, 15 laps; I. Stewart (1.96 Connaught – Ecurie Ecosse) 26 laps, ignition; J. Behra (1.99 Gordini – Automobiles Gordini) 30 laps, fuel feed; L. Macklin (1.96 HWM – John Heath), 31 laps, clutch housing; R.F. Salvadori (1.96 Connaught – Connaught Engineering) 50 laps, cracked radius arm; J. Fairman (1.96 HWM – John Heath) 54 laps, clutch; P.J. Collins (1.96 HWM – John Heath) 56 laps, accident; A. Brown (1.97 Cooper-Bristol – R.J. Chase) 61 laps, belt; O. Marimon (1.98 Maserati – Officine Alfieri Maserati) 67 laps, engine; L. Villoresi (1.98 Ferrari – Scuderia Ferrari) 67 laps, back-axle; A.P.R. Rolt (1.96 Connaught – R.R.C. Walker) 71 laps, half-shaft; J.R. Stewart (1.97 Cooper-Bristol – Ecurie Ecosse) 79 laps, accident.

Second year running: Ascari in the 1953 Ferrari Tipo 500.

1954 Silverstone

July 17, Silverstone, 90 laps of 2.926-mile circuit
approximately 263.3 miles

The motor racing World was still staggering from the impact of Mercedes-Benz's return to Grand Prix racing when the teams arrived at Silverstone. The Daimler-Benz racing team was flushed with their French triumph and were set to improve their unlucky British showings of 1937–8. Herrmann's Reims engine had blown up too thoroughly to allow a third car for Silverstone, so just two *stromlinienwagen* W196s were available, for Fangio and Karl Kling. They were little changed from Reims trim, apart from three-pointed star embellishers in the radiator air intakes.

Scuderia Ferrari entered three cars, all Tipo 625 4-cylinder models based on the Formula 2 500s. Drivers were Gonzalez, Hawthorn and Trintignant. Parnell and Rosier had their private 625s. Officine Alfieri Maserati had delivered seven of their new 250F models, running three as works entries for Ascari and Villoresi (both on loan from Lancia whose new cars were unready), and for Marimon. Private 250Fs were entered by Gilby Engineering for Salvadori, by 'Bira', by 'Pa' Moss for his son Stirling and by Alfred Owen's BRM organization for Ken Wharton. Schell and Roberto Mieres had interim Maseratis with 1954 250F engines in old Formula 2 A6GCM chassis, while Gordini fielded three 2½-litre 6-cylinder cars for Behra, the Belgian André Pilette and for Clemar Bucci from the Argentine.

G.A. Vandervell ran his embryo 2.3-litre *Vanwall Special* Grand Prix car with curious surface cooler on the nose for Collins, and five Connaughts were all privately entered A-Types with 2-litre engines. Leslie Marr and Leslie Thorne (in the Ecosse car) had standard chassis cars, while the Walker car was for John Riseley-Prichard. Bill Whitehouse's car and Sir Jeremy Boles' for Don Beauman were long-chassis variants. All were on normal Amal carburettors.

Horace Gould, Gerard and Brandon ran Cooper-Bristol Mk IIs, and the wealthy Peter Whitehead boasted a new 2470 cc Alta engine in his Cooper special.

Practice was dull and wet, but on the Friday morning Fangio sang his crisp straight-eight Mercedes around the circuit in 1:45.0, to average 100.35 mph, bettering by 0.19 seconds Farina's best-ever lap in the Formule Libre *ThinWall Special* Ferrari with its two extra litres and four more cylinders! It was not an easy drive, however, and the ex-World Champion

The popular Gonzalez plots his countryman's downfall for the second time in four years: Silverstone, 1954.

brought his car in with its broad nose dented and torn where he had struck marker barrels. Gonzalez and Hawthorn were timed at 1:46.0 and Moss proved his value in a Continental car with a 1:47.0 which put him on the outside of the front row. Behra, Salvadori and Trintigant all equalled Kling's 1:48.0 but the times are far too pat to be true.

Saturday dawned wet and blustery, but the showers dissipated before the supporting events got under way, and by the time the Grand Prix grid formed up the circuit had dried although rain was threatening to return. Maserati were in a dreadful state as their works-prepared cars had arrived late and all four had to start from the back of the grid alongside Rosier's Ferrari which had also missed practice. Villoresi's car suddenly gushed oil, and the team were allowed to install him in the spare before flag-fall.

Gonzalez made a superb start, catapulting away from Moss, Hawthorn and Fangio into Copse Corner. Marimon and Ascari both took flyers from the back rows, and as the field howled back into sight from Abbey Curve, past the old start area into Woodcote Corner, Gonzalez led from Hawthorn, Fangio, Moss and Behra. Marimon had passed nineteen cars to run

1954 Grid

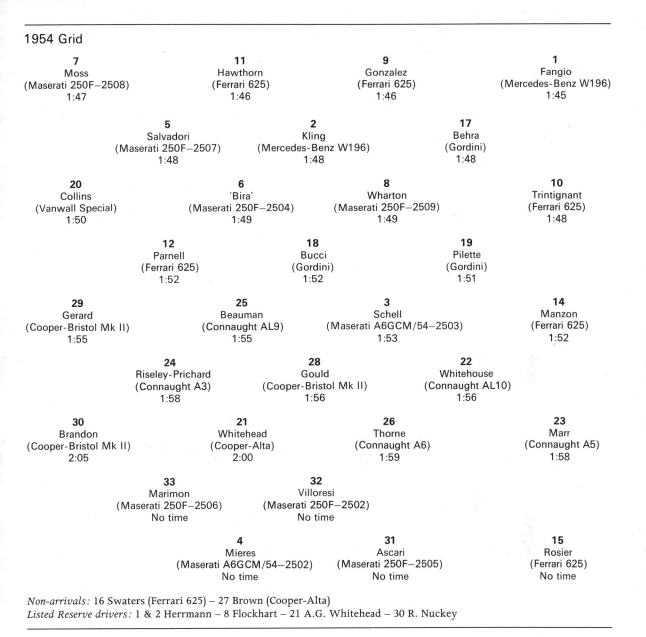

7
Moss
(Maserati 250F–2508)
1:47

11
Hawthorn
(Ferrari 625)
1:46

9
Gonzalez
(Ferrari 625)
1:46

1
Fangio
(Mercedes-Benz W196)
1:45

5
Salvadori
(Maserati 250F–2507)
1:48

2
Kling
(Mercedes-Benz W196)
1:48

17
Behra
(Gordini)
1:48

20
Collins
(Vanwall Special)
1:50

6
'Bira'
(Maserati 250F–2504)
1:49

8
Wharton
(Maserati 250F–2509)
1:49

10
Trintignant
(Ferrari 625)
1:48

12
Parnell
(Ferrari 625)
1:52

18
Bucci
(Gordini)
1:52

19
Pilette
(Gordini)
1:51

29
Gerard
(Cooper-Bristol Mk II)
1:55

25
Beauman
(Connaught AL9)
1:55

3
Schell
(Maserati A6GCM/54–2503)
1:53

14
Manzon
(Ferrari 625)
1:52

24
Riseley-Prichard
(Connaught A3)
1:58

28
Gould
(Cooper-Bristol Mk II)
1:56

22
Whitehouse
(Connaught AL10)
1:56

30
Brandon
(Cooper-Bristol Mk II)
2:05

21
Whitehead
(Cooper-Alta)
2:00

26
Thorne
(Connaught A6)
1:59

23
Marr
(Connaught A5)
1:58

33
Marimon
(Maserati 250F–2506)
No time

32
Villoresi
(Maserati 250F–2502)
No time

4
Mieres
(Maserati A6GCM/54–2502)
No time

31
Ascari
(Maserati 250F–2505)
No time

15
Rosier
(Ferrari 625)
No time

Non-arrivals: 16 Swaters (Ferrari 625) – 27 Brown (Cooper-Alta)
Listed Reserve drivers: 1 & 2 Herrmann – 8 Flockhart – 21 A.G. Whitehead – 30 R. Nuckey

sixth, while Ascari was thirteenth, behind Kling, Trintignant, Wharton, Schell and Collins. Whitehead went straight to his pit with a broken oil union.

Marimon spun at Abbey on lap 3, but two laps later Fangio was second behind Gonzalez and Hawthorn's Ferrari had a significant dent in its tail. At ten laps Gonzalez was 3 seconds clear of Fangio, at 15 laps he had only a second in hand. Moss and

View from the pit gallery, 1954, with the Ferraris of Hawthorn (looking on thoughtfully in jerkin and helmet), Trintignant and Manzon about to be joined by Gonzalez. The Salvadori Maserati (5) is just visible behind.

Hawthorn were scrapping for third place, and then it began to rain.

Meanwhile Ascari had been up to seventh place before lap 9 when his Maserati's steering stiffened and he had to stop. He drove hard to regain lost ground, only to shatter an inlet valve and suffer a brief engine fire after twenty-two laps as he pulled off past the pits.

Both Mercedes were in trouble on the wet circuit with their new and under-developed Continental racing tyres and Collins picked off Kling for eighth place just before the new Vanwall's head joint failed. Nuckey, Rosier and Whitehead were already out of the race, and as the shower abated, the circuit began to dry 'on the line'.

Villoresi had been signalled in after twenty-six laps to give his car to Ascari. Bucci lost control of his Gordini on a newly-surfaced patch at Copse and thumped the bank, Parnell's new Ferrari broke its engine and was abandoned at Club, and on lap 31 Salvadori lost eighth place in a stop to re-secure a trailing tank strap.

Moss and Hawthorn were passing and re-passing to the bi-partisan crowd's great glee, while Beauman, Riseley-Prichard and Gerard were having a comfortable battle for the '2-litre class'. Ascari was driving hard to regain ground in Villoresi's Maserati when it snapped a con-rod on lap 41, and put the great Italian out of his last British Grand Prix.

At half-distance Gonzalez had averaged 94.08 mph and was driving with all the studied calm of Ascari in 1952–3. He was 3 seconds clear of Fangio, whose unmanageable Mercedes bore unmistakable signs of contact with more marker barrels. Moss was third by 25 seconds, Hawthorn fourth 10 seconds behind, and Behra and Marimon fifth and sixth.

It began to rain heavily, and Fangio's Mercedes had dents on both sides of the nose, third gear had gone, he was holding in fourth and howling up to 9,600 rpm in a desperate effort to keep touch with his fellow-countryman and former team-mate. But he could not even hold off Moss and Hawthorn, who trod carefully past the sliding Mercedes to great cheers from the crowd. While the Italian cars plumed on calmly and controllably through the rain, Fangio was in deep trouble with his silver car yawing and bobbing through the corners. Behra's spirited drive in the Gordini ended on lap 55 when the rear-suspension broke, and 'Bira' (who had 'flu) handed-over his car to Ron Flockhart on lap 42. Unfortunately the Scot slid off at Copse on his third lap, squelched into the earth bank and was thrown out as the car rolled. Wet and rueful, he walked back to the pits, unhurt.

So Gonzalez sailed on and on, and Moss and Hawthorn looked settled for second and third places until suddenly the Moss luck struck again and his Maserati snapped a drive-shaft, sloughing to a stop just ten laps from home.

Ferrari were thus awarded a 1–2 finish, Marimon was third after a thoroughly good performance in what was sadly his last Grand Prix race, and Fangio nursed the Mercedes home fourth to complete an Argentinian points-scoring trio. Gerard's unobtrusive ride in the Cooper-Bristol brought the first British car home in tenth place, but for most of the damp crowd the light had gone out with Moss' wretched luck . . . perhaps 1955 would be his year?

Results

1 J.F. Gonzalez (2.49 Ferrari – Scuderia Ferrari) 2 hrs 56 mins 14.0 secs, 89.69 mph; 2 J.M. Hawthorn (2.49 Ferrari – Scuderia Ferrari) 2 hrs 57 mins 24.0 secs; 3 O. Marimon (2.49 Maserati – Officine Alfieri Maserati) 89 laps; 4 J.M. Fangio (2.49 Mercedes-Benz – Daimler-Benz AG) 89 laps; 5 M. Trintignant (2.49 Ferrari – Scuderia Ferrari) 87 laps; 6 R. Mieres (2.49 Maserati – driver) 87 laps; 7 K. Kling (2.49 Mercedes-Benz – Daimler-Benz AG) 87 laps; 8 K. Wharton (2.49 Maserati – A.G.B. Owen) 86 laps; 9 A. Pilette (2.49 Gordini – Automobiles Gordini) 86 laps; 10 F.R. Gerard (1.97 Cooper-Bristol – driver) 85 laps; 11 D. Beauman (1.96 Connaught – Sir Jeremy Boles Bt) 84 laps; 12 H. Schell (2.49 Maserati – driver) 83 laps; 13 L. Marr (1.96 Connaught – driver) 82 laps; 14 L. Thorne (1.96 Connaught – Ecurie Ecosse) 78 laps; 15 H. Gould (1.97 Cooper-Bristol) 44 laps.

FASTEST LAP Gonzalez, Hawthorn, Moss, Ascari, Marimon, Behra and Fangio 1 min 50.0 secs, 95.79 mph.

RETIREMENTS R. Nuckey (1.97 Cooper-Bristol – driver) 2 laps, engine; L. Rosier (2.49 Ferrari – driver) 3 laps, engine; P.N. Whitehead (2.46 Cooper-Alta – driver) 3 laps, engine; R. Manzon (2.49 Ferrari – driver) 16 laps, engine; P.J. Collins (2.23 Vanwall Special – G.A. Vandervell) 17 laps, blown gasket; C. Bucci (2.49 Gordini – Automobiles Gordini) 18 laps, accident; A. Ascari (2.49 Maserati – Officine Alfieri Maserati) 21 laps, valve; R. Parnell (2.49 Ferrari – driver) 25 laps, engine; J. Riseley-Prichard (1.96 Connaught – R.R.C. Walker) 40 laps, steering; L. Villoresi/ A. Ascari (2.49 Maserati-Officine Alfieri Maserati) 40 laps, con-rod; 'B. Bira'/R. Flockhart (2.49 Maserati – driver) 44 laps, accident; R.F. Salvadori (2.49 Maserati – Gilby Engineering Co Ltd) 53 laps, gearbox; J. Behra (2.49 Gordini – Automobiles Gordini) 55 laps, rear suspension; Whitehouse (1.96 Connaught – driver) 64 laps, engine; S.C. Moss (2.49 Maserati – A.E. Moss) 80 laps, back-axle.

1955 Aintree

July 16, Aintree, 90 laps of 3-mile circuit
approximately 270 miles

The RAC's delegation of their Grande Epreuve to the BRDC had not been altogether popular with the country's older major club, the BARC. In 1955 the governing body consequently handed responsibility for the British World Championship race to John Morgan of the BARC, and the race moved north-west to Liverpool and the new motor racing circuit laid out around Mrs Mirabel Topham's Grand National turf course at Aintree.

The 1955 season was unfortunately dominated by one event, the Mercedes crash at Le Mans which killed eighty-one spectators and injured many more. In its wake the French, Swiss, German and Spanish Grands Prix were all cancelled, and the face of the season changed. In the early races Fangio's now slipper-bodied Mercedes-Benz W196s had won in the Argentine, Belgium and Holland, while Trintignant had come home a delighted victor for Ferrari at Monaco where only one of the Mercedes, driven by Moss, had been classified as a finisher.

Moss' prowess with his private Maserati in 1954 had won him factory support from the Modena company, and then a place in the Mercedes team alongside Fangio, Kling and their guest drivers. He had run home dutifully second in Belgium and Holland, and with the prospect of a British driver winning the British Grand Prix, pre-race publicity attracted a huge crowd to the Liverpool stadium. In those heady times of exuberantly ridiculous crowd figures, an attendance of 150,000 was quoted.

Daimler-Benz AG sent five W196s, for Fangio, Kling, Moss and the Italian Taruffi. Fangio and Moss had short-chassis models, Kling and Taruffi the medium-length cars, all with outboard front brakes. The practice hack was an early 1955 medium-length model, with its massive front drum brakes mounted inboard.

Maserati came to Aintree with previous experience of the circuit, and were as confident as they could be against the might of Mercedes. They had three neat, un-louvred bodies on their 1955 big-port-engined 250Fs for Behra, Mieres and Luigi Musso, and a much-louvred 1954 model for André Simon. Ferrari ran three of their now woefully inadequate 625s, for Hawthorn, Trintignant and Eugenio Castellotti. The young Italian had been seconded from the now defunct Lancia team, whose finances had dried up almost coincidentally with the death of their star driver, Ascari, in a Ferrari testing crash at Monza.

Gordini had three of his ageing, hastily-prepared cars for Manzon, Hernano da Silva Ramos and a newcomer from sports car racing named Mike Sparken. Vanwall entered two of their Cooper-chassised cars, for Wharton and Schell; McAlpine had the prototype B-series Connaught with stream-lined bodywork, Fairman the works' similar experimental car, Marr the first production streamliner and Rolt Rob Walker's new open-wheeled B-Type. Four private Maseratis included the much-modified 250Fs of the Owen Organization and Stirling Moss Ltd – driven by Collins and Macklin respectively – Salvadori in the Gilby car and Gould with his ex-'Bira' model. Completing the field was a hastily concocted 'Formula 1 special'; a Manx-tailed Cooper central-seat sports car with a '2.2'-litre Bristol engine shoe-horned into its central bay. The driver was a tough Australian newcomer named Jack Brabham, and it was the first mid-engined car to run in a British Grand Prix race, since Auto Union had won at Donington.

Mercedes' four drivers and chief engineer Uhlenhaut ground round and round in practice, the hack car covering twice race distance with nothing serious going wrong. Moss was quickest, at 2:00.4, Fangio next at 2:00.6, and then Behra got amongst them with his Maserati, at 2:01.4 quicker than both Kling (2.0) and Taruffi (3.0).

Race day was brilliantly sunny and hot, but smoke and a stomach-wrenching smell from a nearby chemical works did little for the stadium's rural charm. Fangio walloped into the lead as the flag began its fall, with Moss inches behind and Behra slow to find traction. As the smoke cleared and the pack bawled away into Waterways Corner, Schell and Marr were left stalled on the grid . . . the Vanwall driver wasting his good grid place, and furious!

The field could be seen streaming into the infield loop, and already four silver cars dominated: Fangio, Moss, Kling and Taruffi, but Behra was among them in third place as they flicked through Melling Crossing and boomed through Tatts to complete the lap.

Fangio and Moss were away on their own, Simon's Maserati had a dented tail and his gearchange was faulty so he stopped, while Hawthorn's Ferrari had also been bunted in the tail. On lap 3 Fangio side-

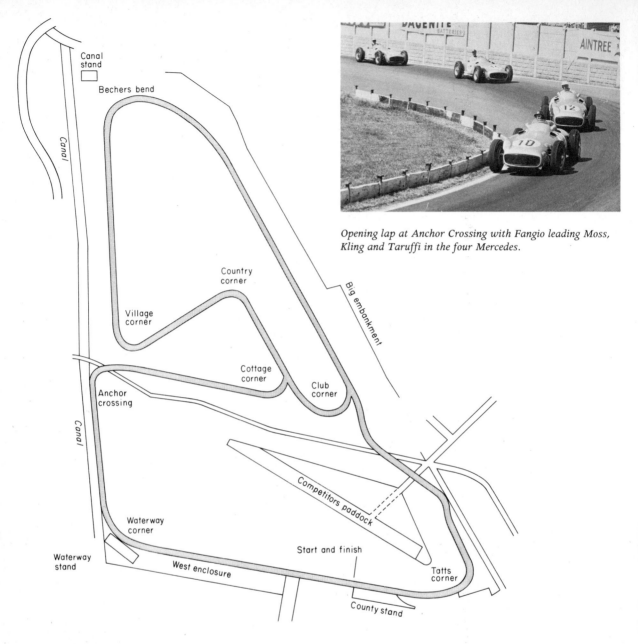

Opening lap at Anchor Crossing with Fangio leading Moss, Kling and Taruffi in the four Mercedes.

stepped to let Moss lead his own Grand Prix, and Behra was just keeping touch behind them and dropping the rest of the field. Mieres was going well and had joyfully displaced Taruffi for fifth, while Musso was snapping at the silver-haired Italian's heels.

Brabham's hastily completed Cooper was heartbreakingly slow, and was lapped on lap 5, while Schell was charging through from the back as only he could, was up to eleventh and gaining on Trintignant. Behra's car abruptly poured smoke and stopped at Waterways, and at ten laps Moss was 1.5 seconds clear of Fangio, with Kling third by 30 seconds and Mieres, Taruffi and Musso close behind. Hawthorn was being pressed by Collins and Trintignant was being caught by Schell. Castellotti flurried into his pit and complained that his car would not *go*.

Musso briefly displaced Taruffi, and the crowd took Schell to their hearts as he carved past Trintignant and set off after the Collins/Hawthorn duel. Hawthorn was lolling in his cockpit, badly affected by the heat, and first Collins then Schell blasted by.

Manzon abandoned his Gordini, and Rolt had a fright as his Connaught's throttle linkage lost its spring and the power stayed on into Melling. He switched off and coasted into the Walker pit. On lap

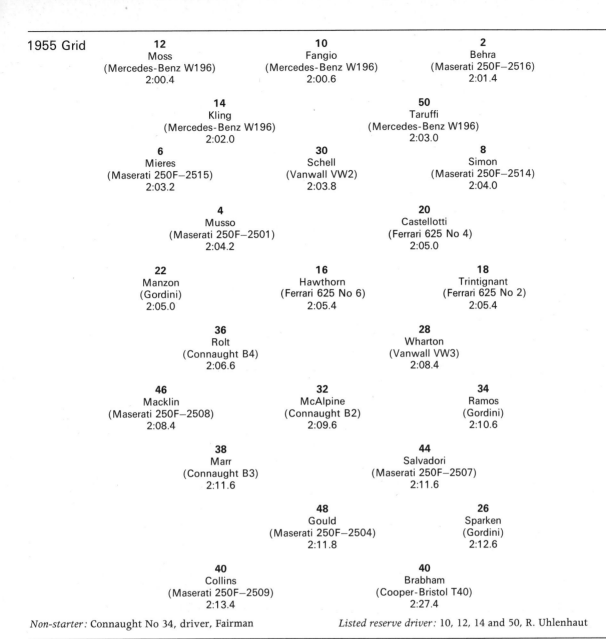

1955 Grid

12 Moss (Mercedes-Benz W196) 2:00.4	**10** Fangio (Mercedes-Benz W196) 2:00.6	**2** Behra (Maserati 250F–2516) 2:01.4

14 Kling (Mercedes-Benz W196) 2:02.0	**50** Taruffi (Mercedes-Benz W196) 2:03.0

6 Mieres (Maserati 250F–2515) 2:03.2	**30** Schell (Vanwall VW2) 2:03.8	**8** Simon (Maserati 250F–2514) 2:04.0

4 Musso (Maserati 250F–2501) 2:04.2	**20** Castellotti (Ferrari 625 No 4) 2:05.0

22 Manzon (Gordini) 2:05.0	**16** Hawthorn (Ferrari 625 No 6) 2:05.4	**18** Trintignant (Ferrari 625 No 2) 2:05.4

36 Rolt (Connaught B4) 2:06.6	**28** Wharton (Vanwall VW3) 2:08.4

46 Macklin (Maserati 250F–2508) 2:08.4	**32** McAlpine (Connaught B2) 2:09.6	**34** Ramos (Gordini) 2:10.6

38 Marr (Connaught B3) 2:11.6	**44** Salvadori (Maserati 250F–2507) 2:11.6

48 Gould (Maserati 250F–2504) 2:11.8	**26** Sparken (Gordini) 2:12.6

40 Collins (Maserati 250F–2509) 2:13.4	**40** Brabham (Cooper-Bristol T40) 2:27.4

Non-starter: Connaught No 34, driver, Fairman   *Listed reserve driver:* 10, 12, 14 and 50, R. Uhlenhaut

17 Fangio surged ahead of Moss, Simon rejoined the race and Gould and Wharton stopped for attention. On lap 20 Fangio and Moss, slicing through traffic with surgical skill, were 40 seconds clear from Kling and Mieres, with Taruffi, Collins, Schell and Hawthorn flickering by in close company. Then Schell's throttle pedal broke off under his pressure, Marr spun, stalled and wrenched a brake pipe, and Castellotti gave up sans transmission.

Moss wanted to lead again, tried at Tatts Corner, but Fangio stayed put impassively and 'the Boy' snapped dutifully back onto line behind him. Next time into Tatts McAlpine's woolly-sounding Con-

naught got in the way, and he almost stopped in an effort to leave them free passage.

Salvadori went out with clutch failure, as did Collins, Rolt's throttle was repaired and Peter Walker took over to rejoin. On lap 32 Wharton's Vanwall burst an oil line and gushed lubricant back into the pits. On lap 37 Musso displaced Taruffi, McAlpine gave up and Moss was 4 seconds ahead of Fangio.

Brabham abandoned his Cooper with engine failure on lap 41, and Moss got the better of passing some back-markers who held up Fangio for 5 seconds more. At half-distance Neubauer put out the 'RG' signs ('Regolare' for Fangio's benefit), but Taruffi was urged

necine duel which ended in the Frenchman's Ferrari breaking a plug which wrecked its cylinder head. Schell found to his joy that Wharton's Vanwall handled better than his original car, and he unlapped himself once from Castellotti and powered away after the silver cars.

Neubauer was showing the 'PI' signs ('Piano', easy), Moss' lead over Fangio was around 4 seconds and they had lapped everyone save Kling. Sparken's sole surviving Gordini was wheezing round slower and slower, and with seventy-five laps gone only ten cars survived and the Aintree course looked empty.

On lap 88 Moss seemed to pull out all the stops just for the fun of it, and he hurtled round 3.8 seconds quicker than his preceding lap to set a record of 2:00.4, 89.70 mph. On the last lap he slowed right down at Melling for Fangio to join up, and the pair crackled across the line with Moss becoming the first Englishman to win his home Grand Prix, by 0.2-second from his mentor. Kling and Taruffi followed through to complete the only 1–2–3–4 finish in Daimler-Benz racing history, and the poor record of 1954 had been corrected indelibly.

So one of the home drivers had won the race, but when would we build the cars to carry them?

Results

1 S.C. Moss (2.49 Mercedes – Daimler-Benz AG) 3 hrs 7 mins 21.2 secs, 86.47 mph; **2** J.M. Fangio (2.49 Mercedes) 3 hrs 7 mins 21.4 secs; **3** K. Kling (2.49 Mercedes-Benz) 3 hrs 8 mins 33.0 secs; **4** P. Taruffi (2.49 Mercedes-Benz) 89 laps; **5** L. Musso (2.49 Maserati – Officine Alfieri Maserati) 89 laps; **6** J.M. Hawthorn/E. Castellotti (2.49 Ferrari – Scuderia Ferrari) 89 laps; **7** M. Sparken (2.47 Gordini – Equipe Gordini) 81 laps; **8** L. Macklin (2.49 Maserati – Stirling Moss Ltd) 79 laps; **9** H. Schell/K. Wharton (2.49 Vanwall – G.A. Vandervell) 72 laps.

FASTEST LAP   Moss 2 mins 00.4 secs, 89.7 mph.

RETIREMENTS   R. Manzon (2.47 Gordini – Equipe Gordini) 5 laps, transmission; J. Behra (2.49 Maserati – Officine Alfieri Maserati) 10 laps, oil-pipe; A. Simon (2.49 Maserati – Officine Alfieri Maserati) 10 laps, gearbox; E. Castellotti (2.49 Ferrari – Scuderia Ferrari) 17 laps, transmission; L. Marr (2.47 Connaught – driver) 18 laps, brakes; A.P.R. Rolt/P.D.C. Walker (2.47 Connaught – R.R.C. Walker) 19 laps, throttle; H. Schell (2.49 Vanwall – G.A. Vandervell) 21 laps, throttle; H. Gould (2.49 Maserati – driver) 22 laps, brakes; R.F. Salvadori (2.49 Maserati – Gilby Engineering Co Ltd) 24 laps, oil-pressure; H. da Silva Ramos (2.47 Gordini – Equipe Gordini) 27 laps, engine; P.J. Collins (2.49 Maserati – A.G.B. Owen) 29 laps, clutch; K. McAlpine (2.47 Connaught – Connaught Engineering) 31 laps, oil-pressure; J.A. Brabham ('2.2'* Cooper-Bristol – Cooper Cars Ltd) 31 laps, valve; R. Mieres (2.49 Maserati – Officine Alfieri Maserati) 48 laps, piston; M. Trintignant (2.49 Ferrari – Scuderia Ferrari) 60 laps, cylinder head.

*In reality a normal 1.97 engine, but GP regs included a 2-litre minimum limit!

Moss's face showing signs of a hard afternoon's work as he raises the Daily Telegraph *Trophy after his historic Aintree victory.*

on to retake Musso's Maserati fifth place behind Mieres. Then the Brazilian's 250F burned a piston on lap 48, Musso found himself fourth and Taruffi was fifth, driving harder as his compatriot's car began puffing smoke.

Macklin spun Moss' Maserati on the Vanwall oil at Melling, walked to the pits for assistance and was push-started again. Hawthorn felt sick and handed over to Castellotti while Schell had brow-beaten his team into fixing Wharton's car and he rejoined in it.

Taruffi barged past Musso on lap 55, and Mercedes' silver fleet were running 1–2–3–4 at last. Behind them Castellotti and Trintignant indulged in an inter-

1956 Silverstone

July 14, Silverstone, 101 laps of 2.926-mile circuit
approximately 295.5 miles

The Grand Prix returned to its spiritual home at Silverstone for the 1956 event, and with soaring lap speeds under the developing $2\frac{1}{2}$-litre formula the BRDC set race distance at one-hundred-and-one laps to ensure the three-hour duration necessary to qualify for Championship status.

Mercedes had retired from racing at the close of the 1955 season, Fangio had gone to Ferrari and Moss to his old friends at Maserati. First blood in the Argentine had gone to Fangio and Musso for the Prancing Horse, Moss replied with a good win at Monaco, and then Peter Collins came good to win both the Belgian and French Grands Prix for Ferrari.

The Maranello team were using modified versions of the side-tanked Lancia D50 V8 cars which Gianni Lancia had presented to Ferrari late the previous year, after his own racing programme had collapsed. Four were entered at Silverstone, for Fangio, Collins, Castellotti and the Spanish Marques Alfonse de Portago. Maserati responded with three full works cars for Moss, Behra and Cesare Perdisa, and were looking after the Spaniard Francesco Godia-Sales' privately-owned car. Piotti's private 250F was entered for Villoresi, now years past his stylish peak, and there were six more of the handsome 6-cylinder Maseratis: Scuderia Guastalla's for Umberto Maglioli; Gilby Engineering's for Salvadori, and their own cars for Rosier, Bruce Halford, Brabham and Gould.

Vandervell's Vanwalls had long since lost their *Special* tag, and over the winter they had been completely redesigned with a new light-weight chassis by Colin Chapman of Lotus sports car fame, and a new aerodynamic teardrop body shell by Frank Costin. Moss gave the new version a superb debut in the International Trophy race on this circuit in May when he led from start to finish. Then he had returned to his Maserati contract, leaving Schell and Trintignant as Vanwall's regular pilots. Schell was big-hearted and always aggressive if not exactly in the front-line, and at Reims he had given the works Ferraris a big fright by catching them up after a pit stop and running amongst them for many laps. For this home race Vandervell brought the much-loved Gonzalez back from semi-retirement in the Argentine.

The Owen Organization had produced an all-new, very small 4-cylinder $2\frac{1}{2}$-litre BRM late in '55, and three of these P25s were entered for Hawthorn, Flockhart and Tony Brooks who – as an amateur – had won the previous year's Syracuse Grand Prix for Connaught against a strong Maserati works team.

Connaught, increasingly short of money, fielded three B-Type *Syracuse* cars for Fairman, Ulsterman Desmond Titterington, and the one-handed Archie Scott-Brown. Gordini had two straight-eight cars for Ramos and Manzon, and the field was completed by the evergreen Bob Gerard in a genuinely 2.2-litre Cooper-Bristol and by Paul Emery's Alta-engined Emeryson.

Race morning was shrouded by clammy mist and low cloud, but the track stayed dry. As Hawthorn popped his BRM's clutch at flag-fall, the little car perked-up its nose and bulleted away to lead into Copse with team-mate Brooks hot on its heels from the third row! In comparison Gonzalez's Vanwall sheared a drive-shaft in the middle of the pack and sighed to a sad halt before the pits, but partisan cheers thundered out at the end of that lap as first Hawthorn then Brooks blared by in their BRMs, having left the pack for dead.

Fangio, Schell, Castellotti, Salvadori and Collins roared by in hot pursuit, but the BRMs comfortably extended their lead. Flockhart was less fortunate in the third Bourne car, its engine failing on lap 3, while Brabham abandoned the ex-Owen Maserati ('the worst buy I ever made') two laps later.

Fangio broke clear of the bobbing, weaving mob chasing the leaders and he reeled-in Brooks, taking his second place on lap 6 but unable to close the 5-seconds gap to Hawthorn. Vanwall's challenge evaporated as Schell trundled into the pits with a broken rear damper, while Trintignant was feeling his way round in his relatively strange car in eleventh place.

Moss established himself fourth, ahead of a terrific battle for fifth between Collins and Salvadori who was always at home at Silverstone, and who got the better of the works Ferrari. Some way behind came Scott-Brown, De Portago and Castellotti engaged in a rare tussle, then on lap 8 Fangio hurtled into Becketts in a big understeer, the Ferrari's tail suddenly flicked out into wild oversteer and he spun, rejoining behind Collins.

As Moss settled down he picked off Brooks on lap 11, while behind him Collins side-stepped to let the grim-faced Fangio through. Scott-Brown was now leading two furious works Ferrari drivers, and

1956 Grid

2
Collins
(Lancia-Ferrari D50)
1:43

23
Hawthorn
(BRM P25—251)
1:43

1
Fangio
(Lancia-Ferrari D50)
1:42

7
Moss
(Maserati 250F—2522)
1:41

28
Salvadori
(Maserati 250F—2507)
1:44

18
Gonzalez
(Vanwall VW1)
1:44

16
Schell
(Vanwall VW2)
1:44

20
Titterington
(Connaught B2)
1:46

19
Scott-Brown
(Connaught B7)
1:45

24
Brooks
(BRM P25—252)
1:45

3
Castellotti
(Lancia-Ferrari D50)
1:44

31
Gould
(Maserati 250F—2514)
1:48

8
Behra
(Maserati 250F—2521)
1:47

4
De Portago
(Lancia-Ferrari D50)
1:47

15
Manzon
(Gordini '8')
1:49

25
Flockhart*
(BRM P25—253)
1:49

17
Trintignant
(Vanwall VW4)
1:49

9
Perdisa
(Maserati 250F—2501)
1:49

21
Fairman
(Connaught B5)
1:51

29
Halford
(Maserati 250F—2504)
1:51

11
Villoresi
(Maserati 250F—2519)
1:50

10
Godia
(Maserati 250F—2524)
1:55

12
Maglioli
(Maserati 250F—2515)
1:54

32
Emery
(Emeryson-Alta)
1:54

26
Gerard
(Cooper-Bristol T23)
1:53

30
Brabham
(Maserati 250F—2509)
2:01

27
Rosier
(Maserati 250F—2506)
1:59

14
Ramos
(Gordini '8')
1:56

*Listed reserve driver: 25 who replaced Wharton.

Non-arrivals: 5 Gendebien (Ferrari) — 6 Volonterio (Maserati) — 22 M. Oliver (Connaught)

The only time he managed it – Juan Manuel Fangio blares the Lancia-Ferrari under the chequered flag to win the British Grand Prix.

Titterington was closing on them in the second Connaught. Four British drivers were leading the race, a BRM was first and the Connaughts were giving works Ferraris a big fright. But on lap 15 Moss took Hawthorn into Copse, Fangio excised Brooks from fourth place and went after Salvadori in third, and on lap 16 Scott-Brown's immense effort ended at Becketts when a rear hub collapsed.

Once Moss was in the lead he drew smoothly away from Hawthorn, the remarkable Salvadori, Fangio, Brooks and Collins. Schell had rejoined with his Vanwall repaired, but Trintignant's sister car was in with fuel-feed problems. Emery abandoned, Titterington's Connaught needed a plug-change, and as Hawthorn was slowing Salvadori lanced by at Copse to give Maserati first and second.

Hawthorn was glancing anxiously into his cockpit, for liquid grease was spraying onto his hip from a split drive-shaft gaiter. When this had happened at Goodwood the transmission had seized and Hawthorn's BRM had flipped, so ending lap 23 he trundled prudently into the pits and withdrew from his last drive for the Bourne team.

Fangio's Lancia-Ferrari was slithering and yawing

The 1956 start, with the Hawthorn and Brooks BRMs already to the fore.

about as oil and a few spots of drizzle coated the circuit. On lap 28 Moss lapped Behra much to the Frenchman's disgust, and Castellotti could not shake off the less experienced De Portago. Castellotti stopped to investigate poor performance, Maglioli, Halford and Rosier had abandoned their Maseratis, and on lap 40 Brooks surged in to complain of a sticking throttle. After attention he rejoined, but at the fast Abbey Curve it stuck again, the BRM rushed off onto the grass verge, spun back across the track and somersaulted. Luckily Brooks was thrown clear, to escape with a broken jaw, for the car exploded into flames and burned by the trackside for some time. BRM had taped a pencil to its broken throttle linkage by way of repair!

On Salvadori's Maserati a tank-strap came loose on lap 48, just as it had in this race two years previously, and he was forced to stop. He rejoined fourth, but Fangio was second, 40 seconds behind Moss until the Maserati peeled into its pit for a 20-second oil stop. The 250F was never so healthy after its restart, and Fangio closed within 5 seconds which gap Moss managed to maintain only by enormous effort.

At half-distance only Moss, Fangio, Collins and Salvadori were on the same lap, and while Moss was driving hard, Fangio was driving on and over his car's limit, losing and regaining control from second to second. Then Collins saw his water temperature rise, oil pressure sink and abandoned on lap 64. Behra's off-tune Maserati was easy to handle on the slime and as he reeled in De Portago, the Spaniard was called in and Collins took over, finding this car more controllable than his original.

Salvadori was put out by fuel starvation after a superb performance, and Moss and Fangio were alone on the same lap until the sixty-ninth tour when the leading Maserati dived into its pit to investigate power-loss. Ignition leads were changed, and Moss rejoined second, but a relieved Fangio now found he could leave the ailing Maserati with comparatively little effort.

Titterington's delayed Connaught shattered its engine, and Moss was forced to stop for more oil. Castellotti had spun and buckled a front wheel and suspension, so he came in and gave the car to De Portago, who drove on carefully. Fangio doubled Collins on lap 90, and three laps later was set to lap Moss when the Maserati's gearbox broke up. It was all over, Fangio sat back to tour round to his first and only British Grand Prix win, while a string of lame ducks and reliable plodders followed him in. De Portago was black-flagged as his damaged car looked lethal, and after much discussion he was allowed to wait just before the finish line, and trundle across as Fangio took the flag.

British cars now had the speed, but that was useless without reliability. To finish first you must first finish . . . as Vanwall intended to do in 1957.

Results

1 J.M. Fangio (2.48 Lancia-Ferrari – Scuderia Ferrari) 2 hrs 59 mins 47.0 secs, 98.65 mph; 2 Marques A. de Portago/ P.J. Collins (2.48 Lancia-Ferrari – Scuderia Ferrari) 100 laps; 3 J. Behra (2.49 Maserati – Officine Alfieri Maserati) 99 laps; 4 J. Fairman (2.47 Connaught – Connaught Engineering) 98 laps; 5 H. Gould (2.49 Maserati – driver) 97 laps; 6 L. Villoresi (2.49 Maserati – driver) 96 laps; 7 C. Perdisa (2.49 Maserati – Officine Alfieri Maserati) 95 laps; 8 F. Godia-Sales (2.49 Maserati – Officine Alfieri Maserati) 94 laps; 9 R. Manzon (2.49 Gordini – Amedee Gordini) 94 laps; 10 E. Castellotti/Marques A. de Portago (2.48 Lancia-Ferrari – Scuderia Ferrari) 92 laps; 11 F.R. Gerard (2.24 Cooper-Bristol – driver) 88 laps.

FASTEST LAP S.C. Moss (2.49 Maserati – Officine Alfieri Maserati) 1 min 43.2 secs, 102.104 mph.

RETIREMENTS J.F. Gonzalez (2.49 Vanwall – G.A. Vandervell) 0 laps, drive-shaft; R. Flockhart (2.49 BRM – A.G.B. Owen) 2 laps, engine; J.A. Brabham (2.49 Maserati – driver) 4 laps, blown engine; P. Emery (2.48 Emeryson-Alta – driver) 13 laps, ignition; A. Scott-Brown (2.47 Connaught – Connaught Engineering) 17 laps, stub axle; U. Maglioli (2.49 Maserati – Scuderia Guastalla) 22 laps, gearbox; B. Halford (2.49 Maserati – driver) 24 laps, piston; J.M. Hawthorn (2.49 BRM – A.G.B. Owen) 24 laps, universal joint; L. Rosier (2.49 Maserati – driver) 24 laps, magneto; C.A.S. Brooks (2.49 BRM – A.G.B. Owen) 41 laps, accident; R.F. Salvadori (2.49 Maserati – Gilby Engineering Co Ltd) 59 laps, fuel system; P.J. Collins (2.48 Lancia-Ferrari – Scuderia Ferrari) 64 laps, oil-pressure; H. da Silva Ramos (2.49 Gordini – Equipe Gordini) 72 laps, back-axle; M. Trintignant (2.49 Vanwall – G.A. Vandervell) 75 laps, fuel line; D. Titterington (2.47 Connaught – Connaught Engineering) 75 laps, cam-rod; H. Schell (2.49 Vanwall – G.A. Vandervell) 87 laps, fuel line; S.C. Moss 95 laps, back-axle.

Chief Mechanic Parenti, Champagne bottle in hand, Andreina – Fangio's constant travelling companion – the rest of the Ferrari team and hangers-on march up the pit row to greet their winner, 1956.

1957 Aintree

July 20, Aintree, 90 laps of 3-mile circuit
approximately 270 miles

In this season British fortunes began to fulfil the promise of the preceding year. Fangio was with Maserati, his first love, and he won the Argentine, Monaco and French Grands Prix and was clearly set for a fifth World Championship title to add to his narrow fourth victory of 1956. But at Monaco Brooks' Vanwall had finished second to the forty-six-year-old *maestro*, and Vandervell's small, efficient team were showing solid promise. It was the BARC's turn to organize the Grand Prix at Aintree, and the CSI granted them the courtesy title of *Grand Prix d'Europe* once more.

Vanwall fielded three cars, for Moss, Brooks and their new find, Stuart Lewis-Evans, who had led the Reims race comfortably the previous Sunday, in only his second Vanwall drive. Brooks overturned an Aston Martin in the Le Mans 24-Hours race three weeks before the Grand Prix, and arrived at Aintree still stiff and sore. Maserati had four late-model 250Fs, three lightweights for Fangio, Behra and the indefatigable Schell, while their latest Argentinian tourist, Carlos Menditeguy, was to use their much-developed test car, 2501. Scuderia Ferrari had removed the side tank fairings among intensive developments to their latest Lancia V8 cars and they fielded four of them for Hawthorn, Collins, Musso and Trintignant.

BRM had difficulty with injured drivers, and fielded two of their fragile P25s for Les Leston and Fairman. Private Maserati 250Fs were to be handled by Ivor Bueb and the Swede Joakim Bonnier, while Gould practised but did not start in his late model.

Then there were three mid-engined Coopers; two of the latest Formula 2 chassis for Brabham (Rob Walker's car) and Salvadori (the works'), carrying 1.9-litre Coventry-Climax 4-cylinder engines driving through modified Citroen transaxles, and Bob Gerard's 2.2-litre Bristol-engined special.

A regretted absentee was Connaught, for their modest finances had tottered earlier in the year as the Belgian and Dutch races were cancelled, and when the BARC said they were not going to pay starting money for the British race it was the final straw. Rodney Clarke and Kenneth McAlpine had decided to close down the company rather than risk bankruptcy, and the brave story of Connaught had come to an end.

Practice was dominated by Vanwall, Moss trying all three cars and taking pole position in Brooks' but only just bettering the remarkable Lewis-Evans' time in the same machine. Brooks improved late in practice as his stiff limbs loosened up and he regained the rhythm of fast driving. Moss and Brooks sandwiched Behra's red Maserati with their green Van-

Final top-up, Moss checks the cockpit as Vanwall mechanics gush fuel into the leading car, and then push him back into the race. Moss' face tells it all . . .

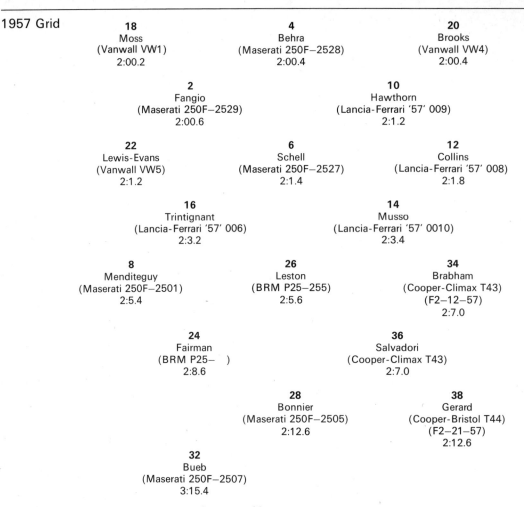

1957 Grid

18
Moss
(Vanwall VW1)
2:00.2

4
Behra
(Maserati 250F—2528)
2:00.4

20
Brooks
(Vanwall VW4)
2:00.4

2
Fangio
(Maserati 250F—2529)
2:00.6

10
Hawthorn
(Lancia-Ferrari '57' 009)
2:1.2

22
Lewis-Evans
(Vanwall VW5)
2:1.2

6
Schell
(Maserati 250F—2527)
2:1.4

12
Collins
(Lancia-Ferrari '57' 008)
2:1.8

16
Trintignant
(Lancia-Ferrari '57' 006)
2:3.2

14
Musso
(Lancia-Ferrari '57' 0010)
2:3.4

8
Menditeguy
(Maserati 250F—2501)
2:5.4

26
Leston
(BRM P25—255)
2:5.6

34
Brabham
(Cooper-Climax T43)
(F2—12—57)
2:7.0

24
Fairman
(BRM P25—   )
2:8.6

36
Salvadori
(Cooper-Climax T43)
2:7.0

28
Bonnier
(Maserati 250F—2505)
2:12.6

38
Gerard
(Cooper-Bristol T44)
(F2—21—57)
2:12.6

32
Bueb
(Maserati 250F—2507)
3:15.4

Non-starter: Maserati No 30, 250F—2514, driver, Gould

---

walls on the front row, and Fangio was relegated to a most unusual second-row start.

Raceday morning began with rain, but a strong wind quickly chased it away, and when the Grand Prix grid assembled the track was virtually dry. Behra set his rear tyres alight in a fearsome start, but was first into Waterways only for Moss to slide the Vanwall's long drooping snout ahead halfway round that first lap. Behra shot by the pits second, with Hawthorn, Brooks, Collins, Schell, Musso, Fangio and and the rest flickering by in his wake.

Moss settled down to break his opposition, and the strangely quiet Vanwall boomed away into an increasing lead. Brooks decided a duel with Hawthorn was unwise so sat back to be towed round fourth although Collins was closing, and his intention was to keep his car running and healthy in case one of his fitter teammates should require it.

Fangio was falling back, first Musso then Lewis-

Evans charging by him, and back in the field Leston's BRM was baulking the little Cooper-Climaxes, for once they got by they scuttled away from the front-engined car. Bueb was the first pit-caller, on lap 8, for plugs.

At ten laps Moss was scratching hard and his lead over Behra had grown to 7.5 seconds, while the Frenchman was doing his best to stave off Hawthorn. Brooks was harrassed by Musso, but then the Italian spun and was passed by both Lewis-Evans and Fangio. Moss rushed on, proving conclusively that his Vanwall was the fastest of contemporary Grand Prix cars, while the new interim Coopers had tagged on to the tail-end of the Italian works car group and were worrying at Trintignant's Ferrari.

On lap 21 Moss appeared at Tatts and accelerated under the huge grandstands with a stammer spoiling that civilized exhaust note, and Behra had chopped 1.5 seconds off what had been a 9-second lead. Next

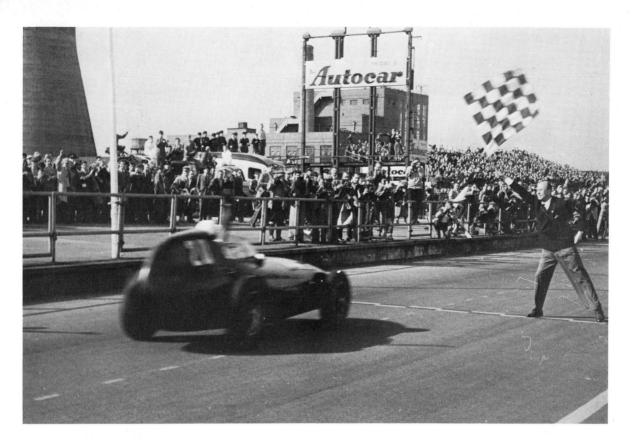

lap, and the tall green car veered into the pits, the bonnet was off, magneto earth wire plucked off, bonnet back on and Moss surged away. But still the car fluffed. In again, and team manager David Yorke signalled Brooks to surrender his car. In it came on lap 26, Moss leapt aboard and bulleted back into the race down in ninth place.

Behra was driving hard in the leading Maserati, being informed of Moss's revival by his pit, and the tension became electric as the large crowd *willed* the Vanwall forward. Schell's Maserati steamed into the pits with overheating to give Moss eighth place, and the white-helmeted Englishman set about the lap record in his chase through the field. He caught Menditeguy, and passed him. He caught Fangio, on lap 35, and passed him. Behra was driving a polished race to lead from Hawthorn, with Collins third and being caught by Lewis-Evans in the other Vanwall. Moss displaced Musso to run fifth at forty laps, and there were only Collins, Lewis-Evans and Hawthorn between him and Behra's leading car.

Menditeguy shuddered into the pits with his 250F's prop-shaft cracked and vibrating furiously, Schell's car had broken its water pump and Collins' Ferrari was falling back off-song. Salvadori picked off Trintignant for eighth place on lap 43, and Brabham was following him through. Moss was gaining

The moment we had waited so many years for: British driver, British car, winning the British Grand Prix.

Tony Brooks and Stirling Moss, the man who kept his car in contention despite unhealed Le Mans injuries, and the man who took it over to win the race, frame a proud pair of British racing peers – Earl Howe, and Lord Selsdon.

rapidly on Collins, with the crowd cheering him on all round the circuit. Schell finally gave up his battle with overheating, Salvadori was holding off a very miffed Trintignant who had Brabham's little car in his mirrors, then came the BRMs, Gerard in the unsuccessful Cooper-Bristol 'special' and Brooks in the Moss Vanwall which was weakening by the minute.

At half-distance, forty-five laps, Behra was maintaining a comfortable 9-second lead from Hawthorn, with Lewis-Evans 20 seconds behind. Collins had fallen 21 seconds behind the third-place Vanwall, but Moss was gobbling him up and two laps later the Vanwalls were 3–4 with Moss really flying!

Both BRMs broke their engines after a sorry showing, on lap 49 Fangio abandoned with deranged valvegear, and on lap 53 Collins gave up with a water leak. Behra was waved on and began to drive really hard, equalling the lap record, but Moss was breaking it and gaining.

Ferrari pulled in Trintignant to give his car to Collins, but after three laps Collins returned it with thanks, and the Frenchman rejoined. By lap 65 the two Vanwalls were right with Hawthorn, the gap between Behra and Moss was 36 seconds, and the Vanwall star set a new lap record at 1:59.2 in his efforts to come to grips. Musso, fifth, was lapped by Behra, and on lap 69 the Frenchman was 22 seconds clear of Hawthorn who had Lewis-Evans and Moss all over him.

Moss was lining up to take both his countrymen when disaster struck Behra. The leading Maserati's clutch-flywheel assembly shattered abruptly, and as the Hawthorn/Moss/Lewis-Evans trio blasted past the coasting car, the Ferrari punctured its left-rear tyre on debris. As Hawthorn slowed, the Vanwalls slammed by and completing lap 69 Moss appeared in the lead through Melling Crossing from his teammate, with Behra coasting towards his pit to retire and Hawthorn cork-screwing along with a flat tyre!

Everybody in the packed grandstands leaped to their feet, cheering wildly, and with Musso nearly a lap down and Hawthorn delayed, the Vanwalls eased off and began to cruise comfortably round. It was a wonderful picture, but on lap 73 it was shattered as Moss appeared on his own, for Lewis-Evans had lost contact and coasted to a halt at Cottage Corner with the Vanwall's throttle linkage detached. He began to work on the car, and puttered into the pits for a permanent repair as Moss completed his eightieth lap. Brooks had retired the third Vanwall by this time, and then Lewis-Evans was ushered back into the race in a handicapped seventh place.

Moss led by miles from Musso, who had Hawthorn a minute behind him, followed by Salvadori and Trintignant. Brabham lost sixth place when his clutch exploded, which elevated Gerard and Bueb in the sick Gilby Maserati. Moss stopped for fuel on lap 79, giving the spectators opposite the pits a bad fright until his intentions became clear, but rejoining still 40 seconds clear of Musso.

Salvadori came in for fuel on lap 82, reporting 'ticking noises' from the rear of the little works Cooper, and two laps later his spirited drive ended in gearbox failure. He limped round towards the finish line, and waited for Moss to take the flag.

Everyone in that Aintree crowd had their fingers crossed for the green car, and as Moss accelerated out of Tatts Corner and took that chequered flag the crowd erupted in delight, flooded onto the course and acclaimed an historic British victory in their home race against the strongest opposition which the red cars could offer.

Long after that day's racing had finished, Aintree was packed with revellers, savouring that great victory, for 20 July 1957 saw one of those great sporting occasions on which nobody wanted the sun to set. It was a beginning – and today the end is not yet in sight.

Results

1 S.C. Moss/C.A.S. Brooks (2.49 Vanwall – G.A. Vandervell) 3 hrs 6 mins 37.8 secs, 86.8 mph; 2 L. Musso (2.49 Lancia-Ferrari – Scuderia Ferrari) 3 hrs 7 mins 3.4 secs; 3 J.M. Hawthorn (2.49 Lancia-Ferrari – Scuderia Ferrari) 3 hrs 7 mins 20.6 secs; 4 M. Trintignant (2.49 Lancia-Ferrari – Scuderia Ferrari) 88 laps; 5 R.F. Salvadori (1.96 Cooper-Climax – Cooper Car Co Ltd) 85 laps; 6 F.R. Gerard (2.24 Cooper-Bristol – Bob Gerard Cars Ltd) 82 laps; 7 S. Lewis-Evans (2.49 Vanwall – G.A. Vandervell) 82 laps; 8 I. Bueb (2.49 Maserati – Gilby Engineering Co Ltd) 71 laps.

FASTEST LAP   Moss, 1 min 59.2 secs, 90.6 mph.

RETIREMENTS   J. Bonnier (2.49 Maserati – driver) 18 laps, gearbox; C. Menditeguy (2.49 Maserati – Officine Alfieri Maserati) 35 laps, transmission; H. Schell (2.49 Maserati – Officine Alfieri Maserati) 39 laps, water pump; L. Leston (2.49 BRM – Owen Racing Organization) 45 laps, engine; J. Fairman (2.49 BRM – Owen Racing Organisation) 48 laps, engine; C.A.S. Brooks (2.49 Vanwall – G.A. Vandervell) 51 laps, fuel pump; P.J. Collins (2.49 Lancia-Ferrari – Scuderia Ferrari) 53 laps, water line; J. Behra (2.49 Maserati – Officine Alfieri Maserati) 69 laps, clutch; J.A. Brabham (1.96 Cooper-Climax – R.R.C. Walker) 75 laps, clutch.

1958 Silverstone

July 19, Silverstone, 75 laps of 2.926-mile circuit
approximately 219.5 miles

The new season saw fundamental changes to the character of Formula 1 Grand Prix racing which gave the emergent British 'special builders' the chance they needed to get onto terms with the now established constructors, such as Vanwall and Ferrari. Financial difficulties had seen the demise of Maserati as a serious works team at the end of 1957, and the CSI had bowed to oil company pressures by banning alcohol-based fuels and stipulating 130-octane 'AvGas' petrol in its place. Race distances were also relaxed, organizers being allowed to cut back from 500 kms to 300 kms distance if they wished, and from three hours' to two hours' duration.

This downgrading of Grand Prix-style racing allowed smaller cars to be constructed, with less fuel tankage. Vanwall and BRM worked hard during the winter months to convert their engines to run on petrol, which lacked the internal cooling properties of their former fuel brews, but Ferrari had been using more and more straight petrol in their fuels during 1957 and for the new season they had the new Dino 246 V6 engine developed specifically to run on 'normal' aviation spirit. The more modest demands of the shorter GP distance encouraged Formula 2 manufacturers like Lotus to follow Cooper's lead into Formula 1, designing and building their own rolling chassis around proprietary engines from Coventry-Climax.

Moss won the Argentine GP for Rob Walker in his little 1.9-litre F2-based Cooper-Climax, and Trintignant won Monaco in the same car. Moss won the Dutch GP, and Brooks the Belgian, for Vanwall, while Hawthorn won Ferrari's first GP of the year at Reims, where his team-mate Musso crashed fatally.

So to Silverstone, where Ferrari fielded three 246s for Hawthorn, Collins and the promising German Wolfgang von Trips. The usual Vanwall trio of Moss, Brooks and Lewis-Evans represented probably the greatest in-depth strength of any team. Cooper ran three cars, a 2.2-litre version for Salvadori, their senior driver, and 1960 cc models for Brabham and Ian Burgess. Trintignant was in Walker's sister car, and one 2.2 and two 1960 cc engines powered the Lotuses, a cigar-like 1957 Mark 12 for Cliff Allison, and two Vanwall-like Mark 16s for Graham Hill and Alan Stacey; the latter being a promising driver making his Grand Prix debut despite the handicap of having an artificial leg. BRM entered three revised

P25s for Schell, Behra and the American Masten Gregory, but the latter hurt himself during practice for a supporting event when he crashed Ecurie Ecosse's Lister-Jaguar sports car.

The field was completed by three 250F Maseratis; Bonnier in Scarlatti's lightweight '57 car, Gerino Gerini the ex-Piotti car, and Carroll Shelby the Centro-Sud team car which he had raced at Reims. Bernie Ecclestone ran his ex-works Connaughts for Bueb (the 'toothpaste-tube' wedge-shaped car) and Fairman in a normal *Syracuse*.

None of the Ferraris was as quick in practice as the efforts of their drivers and their furious exhaust notes would suggest, and Moss did 1:39.4 for Vanwall which was the fastest-ever Silverstone lap at that time. Brooks was next quickest on the Thursday, but on Friday Schell hurtled his BRM round in 1:39.8, Salvadori did 1:40.0 to beat all the Ferraris, and Allison in his spidery little 2.2 Lotus split Hawthorn and Collins on row two with a 1:40.4 to equal the Ferrari team leader's time.

Hawthorn hesitated at the start, Moss was first away but Collins took a flyer from row two and catapulted past the Vanwall to steal an immediate lead. In those opening laps Moss was forced into huge opposite-lock slides to match the Ferrari's surprising pace, and he had Hawthorn on his heels and the worrying sight of oil escaping from the Vanwall's engine bay. Schell was fourth in the BRM, watching his oil temperature and pressure gauges in mounting alarm, and he quickly slipped behind Lewis-Evans.

Brooks ran sixth ahead of a rough-and-tumble for seventh place involving Salvadori, Trips, Hill, Brabham and Behra. The Cooper pair combined efforts to cut out the rest, and as they ran clear Hill abandoned his Lotus as its oil pressure sagged. Its hot gearbox had previously burned his backside!

The Ferraris handled happily on full tanks, and Moss could do nothing about Collins' lead. Behra hit one of the numerous Silverstone hares and had a tyre punctured by a bone from the poor thing's body, Allison was unable to reproduce his practice speed and abandoned sans oil pressure, Stacey's sister Lotus was out with overheating, and Trintignant whizzed into the Walker pit on three cylinders, the fourth chimed in as he stopped, so he promptly whizzed back out again!

On lap 26 Moss' Vanwall abruptly belched blue

1958 Grid

2
Hawthorn
(Ferrari Dino 246)
1:40.4

10
Salvadori
(Cooper-Climax T45)
1:40.0

20
Schell
(BRM P25—257)
1:39.8

7
Moss
(Vanwall VW10)
1:39.4

9
Lewis-Evans
(Vanwall VW6)
1:41.4

1
Collins
(Ferrari Dino 246)
1:40.6

17
Allison
(Lotus-Climax 12)
1:40.4

3
Von Trips
(Ferrari Dino 246)
1:42.0

11
Brabham
(Cooper-Climax T45)
1:42.0

8
Brooks
(Vanwall VW5)
1:41.6

19
Behra
(BRM P25—256)
1:41.4

16
Hill
(Lotus-Climax 16)
1:43.0

22
Bonnier
(Maserati 250F—2529)
1:43.0

4
Trintignant
(Cooper-Climax T45)
1:42.6

6
Gerini
(Maserati 250F—2519)
1:53.0

15
Bueb
(Connaught B3)
1:51.4

12
Burgess
(Cooper-Climax T45)
1:45.4

5
Shelby
(Maserati 250F—2522)
1:44.2

18
Stacey
(Lotus-Climax 16)
1:58.8

14
Fairman
(Connaught B7)
1:58.8

Non-starter: 21 Gregory (BRM)

smoke and retired direct to the paddock round the end of the pits, so Ferrari were firmly first and second. Almost simultaneously Salvadori scuttled past Lewis-Evans, who loomed above him in the lofty Vanwall's cockpit, and Brabham was leading Trips and Brooks, who was quite out of touch.

Hawthorn stopped briefly for oil on lap 44, without losing his place to Salvadori, Collins lapped Brooks who was too depressed to respond, and then doubled Schell who was still nursing his car. He had found its oil pressure stabilizing as he eased off, but now he took exception to Collins' progress and hung-on grimly, being towed along by the leader towards the Brabham/Trips battle. The German was troubled by oil leaks and brakes pulling to the right, and on lap 59 his V6's bearings began to rattle, and sent him coasting into retirement in the pits.

Collins grew uncomfortable at Schell's continued presence, ran wide on a corner and waved the BRM through, whereupon the Franco-American blared by and forgot his oil problems as he went after Brabham.

Salvadori was being cooked in the Cooper's cockpit but was holding off a manful assault from Lewis-Evans, but nobody could match the Ferraris that day, and Collins sang home happily to become the second Englishman to win a British Grand Prix, his Ferrari putting a nail in the faltering myth of 'British supremacy', with Hawthorn second and delighted at his great friend's success. Salvadori's baby Cooper led Lewis-Evans to the line by just 0.2 seconds for third place, and the writing was clearly on the wall for all front-engined adherents who cared to read it. Schell happily survived for the fifth place he deserved, beating Brabham to the line by 8.4 seconds.

It was the last race of that season's 'happy time', for two weeks later Collins died on the Nurburgring. Hawthorn went on to beat Moss by one point to become the first British World Champion Driver, but Lewis-Evans suffered fatal burns in the last round, at Casablanca. Within three months Hawthorn too was gone, killed in a road accident on the Guildford Bypass, and the Moroccan calamity had persuaded Tony Vandervell to retire his Vanwall team, although the World Constructors' Championship was theirs. Somehow it had a bitter taste.

Results

1 P.J. Collins (2.41 Ferrari – Scuderia Ferrari) 2 hrs 9 mins 4.2 secs, 102.05 mph; 2 J.M. Hawthorn (2.41 Ferrari – Scuderia Ferrari) 2 hrs 9 mins 28.4 secs; 3 R.F. Salvadori (2.2 Cooper-Climax – Cooper Car Co) 2 hrs 9 mins 54.8 secs; 4 S. Lewis-Evans (2.49 Vanwall – G.A. Vandervell) 2 hrs 9 mins 55.0 secs; 5 H. Schell (2.49 BRM – A.G.B. Owen) 2 hrs 10 mins 19.0 secs; 6 J.A. Brabham (1.96 Cooper-Climax – Cooper Car Co) 2 hrs 10 mins 27.4 secs; 7 C.A.S. Brooks (2.49 Vanwall – G.A. Vandervell) 74 laps; 8 M. Trintignant (2.01 Cooper-Climax – R.R.C. Walker) 73 laps; 9 C. Shelby (2.49 Maserati – Scuderia Centro-Sud) 72 laps.

FASTEST LAP   Hawthorn 1 min 40.8 secs, 104.5 mph.

RETIREMENTS   J. Fairman (2.47 Connaught – B.C. Ecclestone) 8 laps, ignition; N.G. Hill (1.96 Lotus-Climax – Team Lotus) 18 laps, oil pressure; J. Behra (2.49 BRM – A.G.B. Owen) 20 laps, suspension; A. Stacey (1.96 Lotus-Climax – Team Lotus) 20 laps, oil pressure; I. Bueb (2.47 Connaught – B.C. Ecclestone) 20 laps, gearbox; C. Allison (2.2 Lotus-Climax – Team Lotus) 22 laps, engine; S.C. Moss (2.49 Vanwall – G.A. Vandervell) 26 laps, engine; I. Burgess (1.96 Cooper-Climax – Cooper Car Co) 41 laps, clutch; G. Gerini (2.49 Maserati – Scuderia Centro-Sud) 44 laps, gearbox; J. Bonnier (2.49 Maserati – driver) 50 laps, transmission; Count W. von Trips (2.41 Ferrari – Scuderia Ferrari) 60 laps, engine.

Copse Corner on the first lap of the 1958 Grand Prix, with Moss' tall Vanwall leading Collins' Ferrari, Schell's BRM and the car which was going to displace them all within a year – the Cooper-Climax, driven here by Salvadori.

The Happy Time for Peter Collins as he hustles his Ferrari past Silverstone's sun-soaked corn-fields towards his British Grand Prix victory. Two weeks later he was killed, at Nurburgring . . .

1959 Aintree

July 18, Aintree, 75 laps of 3-mile circuit
approximately 225 miles

By 1959 the so-called 'rear-engined revolution' had taken hold of Grand Prix racing. Coventry-Climax produced full 2½-litre versions of their dohc FPF 4-cylinder engines, and in the light and highly manoeuvrable Coopers with their crude suspension but minimal frontal area, they proved sufficient to dominate the season. Jack Brabham was Cooper's ace driver. He began the World Championship season by winning at Monaco but Bonnier's BRM beat him in Holland to give that unhappy marque their first-ever Grande Epreuve victory. Brooks and Phil Hill, driving front-engined Ferrari 246s, beat the Australian's Cooper at Reims, and while Moss had shown immense pace with a Cooper-Climax entered by Rob Walker early in the season he handled a British Racing Partnership-entered BRM P25 in the French event.

So to Aintree, where the BARC guaranteed starts to sixteen runners while the remaining eight places on the grid would be awarded to the next-fastest qualifiers in practice. Ferrari were strike-bound at Maranello and could not come, so for the first time in years there were no Italian factory cars in the British Grand Prix.

John and Charles Cooper entered three works cars, for Brabham, Gregory and their fast-rising New Zealand star, Bruce McLaren. Trintignant was in Walker's car once more, and Maserati-engined Coopers were entered for Burgess and Hans Herrmann by 'Mimo' Dei's private Scuderia Centro-Sud, and for Fairman by Tommy Atkins.

There were four BRM P25s, for Bonnier, Schell and Flockhart in works dark metallic green, and for Moss in BRP's pale green livery. The David Brown Organization entered two of their new front-engined 6-cylinder DBR4/250s for Salvadori and Shelby, and Lotus had three Mark 16s for Hill, Stacey and Innes Ireland. Vanwall came out of limbo with a lightweight version of their classical front-engined design for Brooks; released for his home event by Ferrari. Halford was to drive Fisher's ancient Connaught; Fritz d'Orey had a Centro-Sud Maserati 250F; and Brian Naylor his JBW-Maserati special.

The first practice was wet. Moss was quickest with the two Astons close behind, but on the dry Friday Brabham achieved a 1:58.0 to set a new practice record. Salvadori flung the powerful Aston Martin round to astonish everyone by equalling this time, and

Schell's BRM completed the front row 1.2 seconds slower. Brooks was in continual trouble and was buried unhappily near the back of the grid . . . this wasn't Vanwall's type of motor race.

It rained again on race morning, but a strong wind blew away the clouds (and the smell from the chemical works), and conditions were bright and dry as the grid formed up. Ireland was replaced by Stacey immediately before the start as he felt unwell, and Brabham led away into Waterways, with Schell and Bonnier in the BRMs, Gregory and Trintignant in the Coopers, then Moss, McLaren, Hill and Salvadori streaming along behind.

Fairman spun in the pack on lap 2, while Shelby rushed into the Aston pit shouting that he was being sprayed with fuel. It was just the overflow from his brimming tanks, and as he rushed away again, Salvadori scurried in with the same complaint. So both Astons lost their good grid positions, and the battle was on between Cooper-Climax and BRM.

Brabham dirt-tracked his way round, opposite-locking the Cooper with controlled exuberance. Schell, Bonnier, Gregory, Moss, Trintignant and McLaren were all over the track trying to outfumble each other, with Hill treading warily in their wash. Flockhart, Stacey and Naylor were next, then Salvadori gaining ground, and Brooks unhappy in the Vanwall. Chris Bristow was leading the F2 battle run concurrent with the Grand Prix for the first time, and David Piper had started two laps late after re-timing his engine.

On lap 8 Piper had the second-place battle burst around him at Tatts and this melée allowed Moss and Schell to break away with Gregory on his own, then Bonnier, Trintignant and McLaren racing as one. Shelby had one dud magneto, was on six plugs instead of all twelve and his engine lost edge, but Salvadori was storming round and catching Flockhart for tenth place.

By ten laps Brabham was fully 13 seconds clear of his pursuers, having had a clear road all the way; Trintignant had displaced Bonnier, and Gregory had been forced to ease off in deference to his car's water temperature.

Hill spun wildly across Mrs Topham's lawn at Tatts on lap 11, and Salvadori caught and passed the Lotus. The moustache bristled, Hill scrambled by the Aston once more and stuck out his elbows. Salvadori

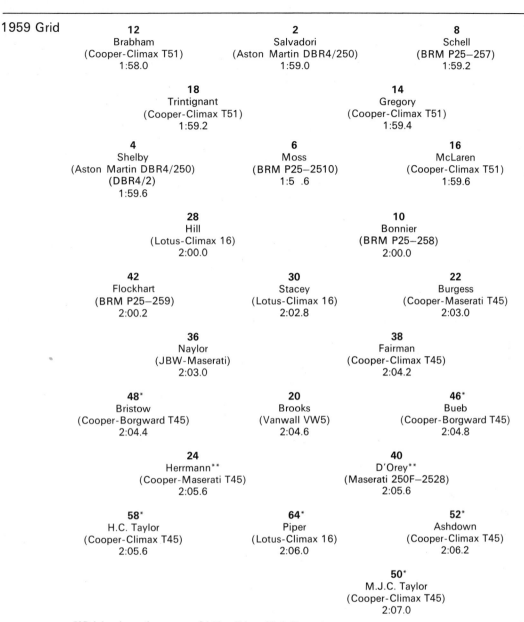

1959 Grid

12 Brabham (Cooper-Climax T51) 1:58.0	**2** Salvadori (Aston Martin DBR4/250) 1:59.0	**8** Schell (BRM P25–257) 1:59.2

18 Trintignant (Cooper-Climax T51) 1:59.2	**14** Gregory (Cooper-Climax T51) 1:59.4

4 Shelby (Aston Martin DBR4/250) (DBR4/2) 1:59.6	**6** Moss (BRM P25–2510) 1:5 .6	**16** McLaren (Cooper-Climax T51) 1:59.6

28 Hill (Lotus-Climax 16) 2:00.0	**10** Bonnier (BRM P25–258) 2:00.0

42 Flockhart (BRM P25–259) 2:00.2	**30** Stacey (Lotus-Climax 16) 2:02.8	**22** Burgess (Cooper-Maserati T45) 2:03.0

36 Naylor (JBW-Maserati) 2:03.0	**38** Fairman (Cooper-Climax T45) 2:04.2

48* Bristow (Cooper-Borgward T45) 2:04.4	**20** Brooks (Vanwall VW5) 2:04.6	**46*** Bueb (Cooper-Borgward T45) 2:04.8

24 Herrmann** (Cooper-Maserati T45) 2:05.6	**40** D'Orey** (Maserati 250F–2528) 2:05.6

58* H.C. Taylor (Cooper-Climax T45) 2:05.6	**64*** Piper (Lotus-Climax 16) 2:06.0	**52*** Ashdown (Cooper-Climax T45) 2:06.2

50*
M.J.C. Taylor
(Cooper-Climax T45)
2:07.0

**Driving in preference to, 24 Von Trips, 40 J. Bayards
*1500 cc Formula 2 cars

Non-starters: No 26 Fairman (Cooper-Climax T45), No 32, Stacey (Lotus-Climax 16) took over Ireland's car, No 34, Halford (Connaught), No 44*, T.P. Taylor (Beart-Cooper), No 54*, Greene (Cooper-Climax); No 56*, W.F. Moss (Cooper-Climax); No 60*, Parkes (Fry-Climax); No 62*, D. Taylor (Lotus-Climax)

bumped and barged the Lotus, and even *shouted* at Hill before scratching past again five laps later.

Brooks abandoned with misfiring and unpredictable braking. Trintignant passed Schell for third place on lap 15, their battle allowing McLaren to catch up and eventually push the BRM back one more place. Meanwhile Brabham was exactly 1 second per lap ahead of Moss at 17 laps, and then the 1957 victor

began whittling away at the Australian's advantage. He began lapping consistently below 2 minutes, and on lap 24 the BRM blared round in a record time of 1:58.6 and closed the gap to 15 seconds.

McLaren surprised both Trintignant and Schell by diving inside them into one of the slower corners and stealing off with 'their' third place. On lap 25 the blue Cooper passed the BRM, and Schell promptly

spun at Tatts, losing time but not his fifth place.

Behind him Bonnier abandoned sixth place as the BRM's throttle broke, Gregory was baulking Salvadori in a torrid duel, and up front Moss was sniping away at the lap record, smashing it at 1:58.2 on lap 28 and then again at 1:58.0 on lap 29. John Cooper kept Brabham informed and he maintained a 12–14 second cushion. By lap 35 he looked safe but just to be sure he did occasional flat-out laps and on lap 42 he equalled Moss' new lap record. But he could see his left-front tyre wearing heavily, and settled back as he knew a tyre stop with his bolt-on wheels would be disastrous.

Moss had to make a tyre change, and he hurtled after the Cooper, building on Brabham's easing pace to close to 10 seconds behind. On lap 49 he shot into the pits for a 31-second stop to change the left-rear wheel. He was away again before McLaren came by, but improving his practice time by two whole seconds had given Dunlop a beating.

Trintignant had lost second gear and fell away from Schell. Salvadori spun at Anchor Crossing, Brabham lapped him, Gregory was in the clear and Moss was furiously opposite-locking his BRM but with little chance of catching the leader. Schell lapped Shelby and stung him into hanging on to the BRM's tail, Hill was slowing and Flockhart spun into the ditch at Village as his oil pressure gauge pipe burst and flooded his pedals with oil. Gregory stopped for water, although his eased pace had stabilized the Cooper's temperature, and Salvadori and Shelby passed him.

Brabham obviously had the legs of the Moss BRM, but the pale-green car was flashing around Aintree with its driver showing all his virtuosity in an apparently irretrievable situation. He was cutting the gap by half a second a lap, lowering the record to 1:57.8. Cooper signalled Brabham to go easy on his tyres but kept him informed of his decreasing lead. Schell came in to change his left-rear wheel, and Bristow ran low on fuel past the pits, then stammered right round the course to refuel and rejoin without losing his F2 lead.

Nine laps to go, the Brabham-Moss gap 32 seconds, and Moss dived back into the pits for a few gallons of fuel. He had felt the car cough as fuel surged in the tighter corners, he was away again in 25 seconds but McLaren was rushing up onto his tail from Tatts. The Cooper shot by as Moss had the BRM accelerating on full song, and he retook second place within the lap. But the young New Zealander would not be shaken off. On lap 68 Moss did 1:57.6 to break away, and on lap 69 1:57.0. On the last lap McLaren threw everything into a last desperate effort, and as Brabham traipsed confidently beneath the chequered flag all eyes turned to Tatts for the second-place battle. McLaren equalled Moss' new record, drew alongside towards the line and just failed to steal the place by 0.2 second!

Results

1 J.A. Brabham (2.49 Cooper-Climax – Cooper Car Co Ltd) 2 hrs 30 mins 11.6 secs, 89.88 mph; **2** S.C. Moss (2.49 BRM – Owen Racing Organization with The British Racing Partnership) 2 hrs 30 mins 33.8 secs; **3** B.L. McLaren (2.49 Cooper-Climax – Cooper Car Co Ltd) 2 hrs 30 mins 34.0 secs; **4** H. Schell (2.49 BRM – Owen Racing Organization) 74 laps; **5** M. Trintignant (2.49 Cooper-Climax – R.R.C. Walker) 74 laps; **6** R.F. Salvadori (2.49 Aston Martin – David Brown) 74 laps; **7** M. Gregory (2.49 Cooper-Climax – Cooper Car Co) 73 laps; **8** A. Stacey (2.49 Lotus-Climax – Team Lotus) 71 laps; **9** N.G. Hill (2.49 Lotus-Climax – Team Lotus) 70 laps; **10** C. Bristow (1.5 Cooper-Borgward F2 – British Racing Partnership) 2 hrs 31 mins 32.6 secs, 70 laps at 83.14 mph; **11** H.C. Taylor (1.5 Cooper-Climax – R.H.H. Parnell) 69 laps; **12** P. Ashdown (1.5 Cooper-Climax – Alan Brown) 69 laps; **13** I. Bueb (1.5 Cooper-Borgward – British Racing Partnership) 69 laps.

FASTEST LAP Moss, and McLaren, 1 min 57.0 secs, 92.31 mph.

RETIREMENTS C.A.S. Brooks (2.49 Vanwall – G.A. Vandervell) 12 laps, ignition; M.J.C. Taylor (1.5 Cooper-Climax F2 – Alan Brown) 15 laps, transmission; J.B. Naylor (2.49 JBW-Maserati – driver) 17 laps, transmission; D.R. Piper (1.5 Lotus-Climax F2 – Dorchester Service Station) 19 laps, gasket; H. Herrmann (2.49 Cooper-Maserati – Scuderia Centro-Sud) 20 laps, clutch; I. Burgess (2.49 Cooper-Maserati – Scuderia Centro-Sud) 31 laps, transmission; J. Fairman (2.49 Cooper-Climax – C.T. Atkins) 36 laps, gearbox; J. Bonnier (2.49 BRM – Owen Racing Organization) 37 laps, brakes; R. Flockhart (2.49 BRM – Owen Racing Organization) 54 laps, accident; F. d'Orey (2.49 Maserati – Scuderia Centro-Sud) 57 laps, accident; C. Shelby (2.4 Aston-Martin – David Brown) 68 laps, ignition.

First lap at Aintree, 1959 with Brabham leading Schell, Salvadori, Bonnier, Gregory (14), Moss (6), Trintignant (18), McLaren (16), Hill (28) and the rest along the canalside into Anchor Crossing. Leaving it the Australian is already running clear, Moss goes wide in the pale-green BRP BRM and McLaren has his Cooper sideways ahead of Hill's front-engined Lotus.

1960 Silverstone

July 16, Silverstone, 77 laps of 2.926-mile circuit
approximately 225.3 miles

The last season of $2\frac{1}{2}$-litre racing had begun with McLaren winning the Argentine Grand Prix; Moss won at Monaco in Walker's new mid-engined Lotus-Climax 18, Brabham in Holland and again in Belgium where Moss had a severe accident during practice, and Bristow and Stacey died in the race. Brabham won again at Reims, and Cooper came to Silverstone set for their number one driver's fourth consecutive victory of the season. That was a feat not achieved since Ascari's run of success in 1952.

Brabham and McLaren were in the works' new lowline Cooper-Climaxes, while the third works car was hired for the occasion by Lance Reventlow whose front-engined Scarab team over from California had run out of spares at Reims. BRM fielded three new mid-engined P48s for Bonnier, Graham Hill and Dan Gurney; Lotus three Mark 18s for Ireland, Jim Clark and multiple motor-cycle World Champion John Surtees, who was in his first four-wheeled racing season. This was his second *Grande Epreueve* appearance. Scuderia Ferrari fielded just two of their obsolescent Dino 246 front-engined cars, for Trips and Phil Hill.

The private Yeoman Credit Cooper team welcomed Brooks into the fold after his one final fling in the lightweight Vanwall at Reims, and he took Halford's place with team-mates Olivier Gendebien and Henry Taylor. Scuderia Centro-Sud ran two red Coopers with Maserati engines for Gregory and Burgess, and Aston Martin had two new, short-chassis lightweight front-engined DBR5/250s for Salvadori and Trintignant. Keith Greene had the Gilby Cooper-Maserati, Fairman Atkins' Cooper-Climax, Lucien Bianchi was in Fred Tuck's similar car and David Piper had Bob Bodle's front-engined Lotus-Climax 16.

Practice put Brabham on pole, a whole second quicker than Graham Hill, with McLaren and Bonnier mirroring the Cooper/BRM duo on the outside of the front row. Trips was the quicker Ferrari driver, but only by dint of some desperately hard motoring. Chuck Daigh proved 4 seconds per lap quicker than Reventlow, his Scarab boss, and he took over the rented works Cooper, while Gino Munaron's Ferrari-engined Cooper of the Scuderia Castellotti arrived too late for practice but was allowed to start from the back of the grid.

Moss, still recuperating after his Belgian upset, dropped the starting flag, and Hill promptly stalled his BRM on the front row. He had been clobbered heavily from behind on the grid at Reims, but he was luckier this time as the field rushed by on both sides. Fate had a more piquant trick awaiting him . . .

Brooks and Taylor were also stranded as the smoke cleared, while Brabham and McLaren dived clear into Copse to lead a tangled mob of cars jostling and changing position as they streamed round those opening laps. Bonnier and Ireland shouldered past McLaren, and he was followed by Surtees, Clark, Phil Hill, Gurney, Trips and Gregory. Salvadori was next up, with Graham Hill and Brooks in his group and charging hard after their delay.

Ireland took second place from Bonnier's BRM, but on lap 8 Brabham was storming away in the lead

The battle between Brabham's Cooper and Graham Hill's BRM raged long and hard once the Londoner had soared through the field after stalling at the start. He took the lead, only to spin off with six laps to run . . .

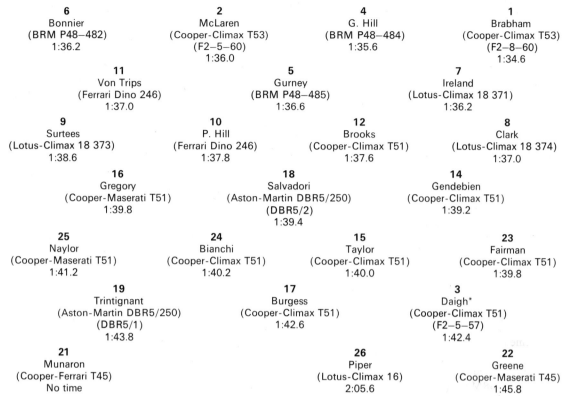

6 Bonnier (BRM P48–482) 1:36.2	**2** McLaren (Cooper-Climax T53) (F2–5–60) 1:36.0	**4** G. Hill (BRM P48–484) 1:35.6	**1** Brabham (Cooper-Climax T53) (F2–8–60) 1:34.6
	11 Von Trips (Ferrari Dino 246) 1:37.0	**5** Gurney (BRM P48–485) 1:36.6	**7** Ireland (Lotus-Climax 18 371) 1:36.2
9 Surtees (Lotus-Climax 18 373) 1:38.6	**10** P. Hill (Ferrari Dino 246) 1:37.8	**12** Brooks (Cooper-Climax T51) 1:37.6	**8** Clark (Lotus-Climax 18 374) 1:37.0
	16 Gregory (Cooper-Maserati T51) 1:39.8	**18** Salvadori (Aston-Martin DBR5/250) (DBR5/2) 1:39.4	**14** Gendebien (Cooper-Climax T51) 1:39.2
25 Naylor (Cooper-Maserati T51) 1:41.2	**24** Bianchi (Cooper-Climax T51) 1:40.2	**15** Taylor (Cooper-Climax T51) 1:40.0	**23** Fairman (Cooper-Climax T51) 1:39.8
	19 Trintignant (Aston-Martin DBR5/250) (DBR5/1) 1:43.8	**17** Burgess (Cooper-Climax T51) 1:42.6	**3** Daigh* (Cooper-Climax T51) (F2–5–57) 1:42.4
21 Munaron (Cooper-Ferrari T45) No time		**26** Piper (Lotus-Climax 16) 2:05.6	**22** Greene (Cooper-Maserati T45) 1:45.8

*Driving in preference to Reventlow

Non-starter: 20 Scarlatti (Cooper-Ferrari)

from the box-like Lotus, and Bonnier whizzed by the pits with Surtees, McLaren and Clark climbing all over him. Hill's BRM was right on the tail of the two luridly-driven Ferraris, and in one lap he passed them both and set off after Gurney, only to inherit his seventh place as the Californian slowed with gearchange trouble.

On lap 11 Surtees found a way past Bonnier, and much to the Swede's chagrin McLaren and Clark both outbraked him and followed Surtees through. The young Scot rapidly found a way past McLaren as well, which put Brabham first ahead of the works Lotus team.

Graham Hill had left the Ferraris for dead, and was closing on his Swedish team-mate in sixth place. Gregory was hurling his Cooper-Maserati after the Ferraris in gigantic broadsides, and keeping pace with them admirably. Brooks was eleventh, having climbed past Gendebien and Salvadori, and on lap 19 Graham Hill appeared on Bonnier's tail and passed him to chase after McLaren next time round.

The Londoner caught and passed the works Cooper in just two laps, and now Clark and fourth place were his targets. Brooks had caught Gregory, didn't like the look of his antics, and sat behind, waiting for a safe chance to pass.

On lap 28 the delayed BRM was right behind the twin Lotuses of Clark and Surtees, Ireland was just 4 seconds behind Brabham and both the Lotus and Cooper pits were signalling Hill's progress to their drivers. The crowd was enthralled by this fantastic drive, and on lap 30 Hill split Clark and Surtees, and next time round he had passed them both to notch one up against his old team. In thirty-one laps Hill had soared from twenty-first at the start to third, and at half-distance Brabham was getting the best of the traffic and drawing away from Ireland and Hill who were being shut off constantly by back-markers.

On lap 37 Hill slipped past Ireland into second place, and as the leaders broke clear of the traffic Brabham was 7 seconds ahead of the BRM. Although he was driving hard, Hill was neat and tidy, while Brabham now began to throw his Cooper about, hunching forward over the wheel. McLaren was in trouble and had been repassed by Bonnier for sixth place, while Brooks had disposed of the two Ferraris as Gregory zoomed into the pits to complain of a sticky throttle. Salvadori stopped to discuss peculiar handling and a power loss, and now that Graham Hill could see Brabham with no back-markers between them he simply demolished the Cooper's lead.

The gap was just 1.5 seconds on lap 51, inches on lap 52, and the two were wheel-to-wheel round much of lap 53. Brabham was slinging the Cooper's tail sideways through the corners, showering Hill with dust and grass trimmings, but on lap 55 the BRM found a niche as Brabham slid wide and Hill was through to the lead. Now the situation was reversed, for Brabham clung on like a leech and it was Hill's turn to watch his mirrors, fighting to maintain full concentration as his role changed from hunter to hunted. His brakes were wilting now, and he was having to pump them.

Ireland was falling back in third place, cocking his head to evaluate strange noises from his Lotus' suspension, and as he worried Surtees and Clark bustled by. On lap 58 Clark appeared in the pit lane, proceeding with caution after broken front suspension was quickly jury-rigged. Bonnier had his BRM suddenly squat down at the right-rear as its top spring mount broke away, and he corkscrewed into retirement trailing the tail of his car along the road.

On lap 70, Hill led Brabham by 1.5 seconds. It was just enough for BRM supporters to hope that the old jinx could finally be buried. Hill was finding it an immense strain, for he had been driving a virtually ten-tenths race since leaving the start-line, and now he knew only a few miles remained between him and victory in a Grande Epreuve. He was watching back-markers as he closed to lap them, watching Brabham bobbing about in his vibrating rear-view mirrors,

pumping his brakes into corners, and deciding his tactics for that last charge to the line.

Then he flashed past a backmarker into Copse, arrived too fast and the BRM snapped sideways. The mid-engine took charge, and Hill found himself planted backwards in the bank and away to his left was Brabham's Cooper, accelerating over the brow towards Maggott's Curve and his fourth consecutive Grand Prix victory. It was as sudden as that, and with six laps left Hill could only walk mournfully back to his pit. It was left to Surtees to come home a very good second, with Ireland worrying his way into third place. The last 2½-litre British Grand Prix had been a sensational motor race, but for Graham Hill it was to have been his best-ever chance of winning his home event.

Results

1 J.A. Brabham (2.49 Cooper-Climax – Cooper Car Co) 2 hrs 4 mins 24.6 secs, 108.69 mph; 2 J. Surtees (2.49 Lotus-Climax – Team Lotus) 2 hrs 5 mins 14.2 secs; 3 I. Ireland (2.49 Lotus-Climax – Team Lotus) 2 hrs 5 mins 54.2 secs; 4 B.L. McLaren (2.49 Cooper-Climax – Cooper Car Co) 76 laps; 5 C.A.S. Brooks (2.49 Cooper-Climax – Yeoman Credit Racing Team) 76 laps; 6 Count W. von Trips (2.49 Ferrari – Scuderia Ferrari) 75 laps; 7 P. Hill (2.49 Ferrari – Scuderia Ferrari) 75 laps; 8 H.C. Taylor (2.49 Cooper-Climax – Yeoman Credit Racing Team) 74 laps; 9 O. Gendebien (2.49 Cooper-Climax – Yeoman Credit Racing Team) 74 laps; 10 D.S. Gurney (2.49 BRM – Owen Racing Organization) 74 laps; 11 M. Trintignant (2.49 Aston Martin – David Brown) 72 laps; 12 D.R. Piper (2.49 Lotus-Climax – Robert Bodle Ltd) 72 laps; 13 J.B. Naylor (2.48 Cooper-Maserati – JBW Cars Ltd) 72 laps; 14 M. Gregory (2.48 Cooper-Maserati – Scuderia Centro-Sud) 71 laps; 15 G. Munaron (2.49 Cooper-Ferrari – Scuderia Eugenio Castellotti) 70 laps; 16 J. Clark (2.49 Lotus-Climax – Team Lotus) 70 laps.

FASTEST LAP N.G. Hill (2.49 BRM) 1 min 34.4 secs, 111.62 mph.

RETIREMENTS K. Greene (2.49 Cooper-Maserati – Gilby Engineering Co Ltd) 12 laps, overheating; R.F. Salvadori (2.49 Aston Martin – David Brown) 46 laps, steering; J. Fairman (2.49 Cooper-Climax – C.T. Atkins) 46 laps, fuel pump; C. Daigh (2.49 Cooper-Climax – Cooper Car Co) 58 laps, engine; I. Burgess (2.48 Cooper-Maserati – Scuderia Centro-Sud) 58 laps, valves; J. Bonnier (2.49 BRM – Owen Racing Organization) 61 laps, suspension; L. Bianchi (2.49 Cooper-Climax – Fred Tuck Cars Ltd) 63 laps, engine; N.G. Hill 72 laps, accident.

John Cooper with mechanics 'Noddy' Grohman, Mike Barney and 'Ginger' Devlin to his right, waves on Brabham after the fleeing BRM. The signal shows 'Placed second, 2 seconds behind, seven laps to go'.

1961 Aintree

July 15, Aintree, 75 laps of 3-mile circuit
approximately 225 miles

Liverpool produced truly awful weather conditions for the fourth Grand Prix to be staged at Aintree. It was the first to be run under the new 1½-litre Formula, and attracted a large and varied entry.

After their season as also-rans in 1960, Ferrari were dominating the new Formula with their mid-engined Dino 156 V6 cars. They had been humbled in the first race at Monaco, but only by Moss in Rob Walker's Lotus 18 and he had always been in a class on his own. Trips had led Phil Hill home in the Dutch Grand Prix, and in Belgium Hill had won from Trips, Richie Ginther and Gendebien, all in the new 'sharknose' Ferraris. At Reims, two weeks before the Aintree date, all the works Ferraris had struck trouble, but the day had been saved for Maranello by the older car entered by the FISA racing association, which 'new boy' Giancarlo Baghetti used to beat the Porsches on his Grand Prix debut.

While the British manufacturers could as yet only dream of their forthcoming V8 engines from Coventry-Climax and BRM, they were making do with Mk II Climax FPF in-line 'fours'. Brabham and McLaren used these engines in their works Coopers, as did Ireland and Clark in new slimline Lotus 21s, Moss in Rob Walker's 21-bodied Lotus 18 and even Graham Hill and Brooks in the interim P48 BRMs.

Yeoman Credit Coopers were to be driven by Surtees and Salvadori, UDT-Laystall (inheritors of the old BRP pale green colours) had twin Lotus 18s for Henry Taylor and Bianchi, and 'Lucky' Casner's Camoradi team fielded a Cooper for Gregory and a Lotus for Burgess. The promising Welshman, Jack Lewis, was running his new Cooper, and private Lotus 18s came from Tim Parnell (son of Reg who was running the Yeoman Credit team), Gerry Ashmore, Wolfgang Seidel and Louise Bryden-Brown for whom South African Tony Maggs was to drive. Tony Marsh had his much-modified 18, Keith Greene (son of Gilby Engineering proprietor Syd Greene) had the Gilby-Climax special, and Dei's Centro-Sud outfit were running two Cooper-Maseratis for Lorenzo Bandini and Massimo Natili.

Last, but certainly not least in terms of interest, was the experimental four-wheel drive Ferguson

P99, which Rob Walker's team was running ostensibly for Fairman, although Moss – as always – showed keen interest in such technical innovation.

Thursday practice was dry, Friday's very wet, and in the first sessions all three works Ferraris were

Phil Hill leads 'Taffy' von Trips, Richie Ginther, Stirling Moss, Jo Bonnier and Jimmy Clark on the opening lap at Aintree, 1961.

2
P. Hill
(Ferrari 156/02 V6)
1:58.8

6
Ginther
(Ferrari 156/04 V6)
1:58.8

8
Bonnier
(Porsche 718–2–03 4-cyl)
1:58.8

4
Von Trips
(Ferrari 156/05 V6)
1:58.8

28
Moss
(Lotus-Climax 18/21 '912' 4-cyl)
1:59.0

22
Brooks
(BRM-Climax P57–572 4-cyl)
1:59.0

16
Ireland
(Lotus-Climax 21 '933' 4-cyl)
1:59.2

18
Clark
(Lotus-Climax 21 '932' 4-cyl)
1:59.2

12
Brabham
(Cooper-Climax T55 4-cyl)
F1–10–62
1:59.4

34
Surtees
(Cooper-Climax T53 4-cyl)
1:59.6

20
G. Hill
(BRM-Climax P57–571 4-cyl)
2:00.0

10
Gurney
(Porsche 718–2–04 4-cyl)
2:00.2

36
Salvadori
(Cooper-Climax T53 4-cyl)
2:00.8

14
McLaren
(Cooper-Climax T55 4-cyl)
2:01.0

46
Lewis
(Cooper-Climax T53 4-cyl)
2:01.0

42
Gregory
(Cooper-Climax T53 4-cyl)
2:01.4

30
H. Taylor
(Lotus-Climax 18/21 '916' 4-cyl)
2:01.8

56
De Beaufort
(Porsche 718–2–01 4-cyl)
2:02.0

58
Baghetti
(Ferrari 156/03 V6)
2:02.0

26
Fairman
(Ferguson-Climax P99/01 4-cyl)
2:03.4

60
Bandini
(Cooper-Maserati T53 4-cyl)
2:03.6

52
Seidel
(Lotus Climax 18 '373' 4-cyl)
2:04.2

54
Greene
(Gilby-Climax 4-cyl)
2:06.0

50
Maggs
(Lotus-Climax 18 '903' 4-cyl)
2:06.4

44
Burgess
(Lotus-Climax 18 '905' 4-cyl)
2:06.6

40
Ashmore
(Lotus-Climax 18 '919' 4-cyl)
2:08.2

48
Marsh
(Lotus-Climax 18 '909' 4-cyl)
2:09.6

62
Natili
(Cooper-Maserati T51 4-cyl)
2:10.2

38
Parnell
(Lotus-Climax 18 '904' 4-cyl)
2:16.8

32
Bianchi
(Lotus-Climax 18/21 '917' 4-cyl)
2:18.8

timed at 1:58.8, and after a great effort Bonnier matched them with his effectively year-old F2-based Porsche. Moss was 0.2 second slower, and Brooks showed a popular return to his old form, on the same time as his former Vanwall team-mate.

On Saturday, the heavens opened, and Dunlop found huge demand for their new high-hysteresis rain tyres. The back rows of the grid crept as the flag was raised, and as it fell an unruly scrum of thirty cars foamed away towards the aptly-named Waterways Corner. The works Ferraris were already in command, Phil Hill first and the only man not driving in someone else's spray, then Trips, Ginther, Moss, Bonnier, Clark, Brooks, Graham Hill, Brabham, Ireland, Salvadori, Gurney and the rest floundering along in the murk as best they could.

Natili's engine died almost immediately, Surtees was rammed from behind and Ireland spun. He jarred his hand which he had hurt while playing around with his light aeroplane, and as he did not like racing in the rain anyway, and his hand hurt badly, he sat back to wade around last.

Ending lap 3 the Ferraris were still towing Moss and Bonnier, and next time round the Swede had been dropped and only the dark-blue Lotus stayed in touch with the red trio in the lead. On lap 6 Ginther lost his place to Moss as he ploughed heavily into a deep puddle, and through the fast and spooky swerve at Melling, Henry Taylor lost control and crashed heavily into some advertizing hoardings. It took some time to cut him from the wreckage, and he was taken to hospital with broken ribs.

Next time round, Phil Hill was in the spray from backmarkers and as he slowed Trips and Moss caught him into Tatts where they lined up to lap the Gilby. Trips emerged from the ensuing cloud of spray in the lead, leaving Hill to sort out Moss while Ginther was treading warily, literally in their wake.

Surtees spun wildly out of Tatts, later stopping to have a trailing tail-pipe removed, Graham Hill had

taken Bonnier and many engines were stammering as moisture affected their electrics. On lap 10 the sodden spectators cheered Moss as he plumed past Phil Hill for second place and on lap 14 he closed with Trips and challenged for the lead. He sat a second behind the Ferrari watching for the slightest mistake which might let him through, but the German drove faultlessly and refused to be shaken.

Fairman brought the Ferguson in misfiring, and an electrical wire was found to have shorted against a chassis tube, probably damaged when the four-wheel drive car ran over wreckage from Taylor's crash. Brabham displaced Graham Hill for fifth, Salvadori had seen off Clark and the flagging Bonnier for seventh, and Surtees was catching Baghetti after his early delays only to go out on lap 24 with no final drive.

On this same lap Trips plumed through Melling ahead of Moss, who slithered into sight broadside, fish-tailed, spun right round and continued his chase as if nothing had happened, but now 10 seconds behind. Four laps later Trips doubled Baghetti into Waterways, and as the young Italian attempted to keep in touch he lost control on a puddle and the FISA Ferrari clattered backwards through the horse railings. Bianchi spun across Mrs Topham's grass at Melling, and Phil Hill slithered towards a gatepost at very high speed on the approach to the same tricky 'S'. This frightened him considerably, and on lap 35

It was wet! Moss in the Walker Lotus 18/21.

Yes, Ferrari suspensions really did do that under braking. Trips on his winning way at Aintree.

he had eased-off and let Ginther through for third. Brabham began catching the Ferrari, and Graham Hill in sixth place was being assailed by Clark.

The rain was easing, drizzled to a stop, and the circuit began to dry. As it dried Clark took off, as did Brooks although two laps behind after a pit-stop, and meanwhile Ginther was blaring round closer to Moss and on lap 40 he took second place and Moss was in obvious trouble as Phil Hill too passed him. On lap 45 the blue Lotus flurried into its pit, a broken brake bridge pipe was found which had allowed all the fluid to dribble away, and with the track now dry shortage of brakes spelled retirement.

Graham Hill's BRM went out with valve spring trouble, and with Moss out Ginther slowed to let Phil Hill regain his rightful second place with Trips cruising along 20 seconds in the lead. Brabham was over a minute behind Ginther in fourth place, while the Ferguson had been carelessly push-started after a pit-stop which left the stewards no option but to disqualify it. Moss took it out to do some development laps, and Tavoni signalled the news to his Ferrari drivers in case they should misjudge its speed into corners. Then a political flutter began in the pits, and Moss was blackflagged out of the race for good.

Right at the end the track dried almost completely, and Clark closed up on Brabham only to be sidelined by an oil leak at sixty-three laps. Salvadori could not hold off Bonnier in the dry, losing his inherited fifth place. Gurney caught and passed McLaren for seventh, and way back in ninth place Brooks was having a final fling in his last British Grand Prix and set a new $1\frac{1}{2}$-litre lap record of 1:57.8, within 0.8 seconds of the best-ever $2\frac{1}{2}$-litre race lap.

Ferrari wailed home 1–2–3, and the International state of the sport was as always mirrored by the drivers – a German first, from two Americans, an Australian, a Swede and an Englishman.

Results

1 Count W. von Trips (1.47 Ferrari – SEFAC Ferrari) 2 hrs 40 mins 53.6 secs, 83.91 mph; 2 P. Hill (1.47 Ferrari – SEFAC Ferrari) 2 hrs 41 mins 39.6 secs; 3 P.R. Ginther (1.47 Ferrari – SEFAC Ferrari) 2 hrs 41 mins 40.4 secs; 4 J.A. Brabham (1.49 Cooper-Climax – Cooper Car Co), 2 hrs 42 mins 02.2 secs; 5 J. Bonnier (1.49 Porsche – Porsche System Engineering) 2 hrs 41 mins 09.8 secs; 6 R.F. Salvadori (1.49 Cooper-Climax – Yeoman Credit Racing Team) 2 hrs 42 mins 19.8 secs; 7 D.S. Gurney (1.49 Porsche – Porsche System Engineering) 74 laps; 8 B.L. McLaren (1.49 Cooper-Climax – Cooper Car Co) 73 laps; 9 C.A.S. Brooks (1.49 BRM-Climax – Owen Racing Organization) 73 laps; 10 I. Ireland (1.49 Lotus-Climax – Team Lotus) 72 laps; 11 M. Gregory (1.49 Cooper-Climax – Camoradi International) 71 laps; 12 L. Bandini (1.4 Cooper-Maserati – Scuderia Centro-Sud) 71 laps; 13 A. Maggs (1.49 Lotus-Climax – Mrs Louise Bryden-Brown) 69 laps; 14 I. Burgess (1.49 Lotus-Climax – Camoradi International) 69 laps; 15 K. Greene (1.49 Gilby-Climax) – Gilby Engineering Co Ltd) 69 laps; 16 Count C.G. de Beaufort (1.49 Porsche – Ecurie Maarsbergen) 69 laps; 17 W. Seidel (1.49 Lotus-Climax – Scuderia Colonia) 58 laps.

FASTEST LAP   C.A.S. Brooks 1 min 57.8 secs, 91.68 mph.

RETIREMENTS   M. Natili (1.4 Cooper-Maserati – Scuderia Centro-Sud) 0 laps, transmission; H.C. Taylor (1.49 Lotus-Climax – UDT Laystall Racing Team) 6 laps, accident; G. Ashmore (1.49 Lotus-Climax – driver) 8 laps, misfiring; J. Lewis (1.49 Cooper-Climax – H & L Motors) 8 laps, handling; T. Parnell (1.49 Lotus-Climax – R.H.H. Parnell) 13 laps, clutch; J. Surtees (1.49 Cooper-Climax – Yeoman Credit Racing Team) 24 laps, drop gears; A. Marsh (1.49 Lotus-Climax – driver) 26 laps, misfiring; G. Baghetti (1.47 Ferrari – Scuderia Sant'Ambroeus) 29 laps, accident; N.G. Hill (1.49 BRM-Climax – Owen Racing Organization) 44 laps, valve springs; S.C. Moss (1.49 Lotus-Climax – R.R.C. Walker Racing Team) 45 laps, brakes; L. Bianchi (1.49 Lotus-Climax – UDT Laystall Racing Team) 46 laps, gearbox; J. Fairman/S.C. Moss (1.49 Ferguson-Climax – R.R.C. Walker Racing Team) 57 laps, disqualified; J. Clark (1.49 Lotus-Climax – Team Lotus) 63 laps, broken oilpipe.

1962 Aintree

July 21, Aintree, 75 laps of 3-mile circuit
approximately 225 miles

Despite a storm of protest the RAC again delegated their Grand Prix to the BARC and Aintree for 1962, instead of continuing the long-established alternating policy with Silverstone. The new British V8 engines had drawn Ferrari's teeth this season, Graham Hill had won his first *Grande Epreuve* for BRM in the opening round at Zandvoort, and McLaren had won for Cooper at Monaco. Jimmy Clark scored his maiden success in the new monocoque-chassised Lotus 25 at Spa, while Gurney had won with Porsche's new air-cooled flat-eight in the French Grand Prix and in the minor race at Solitude on Porsche's own door-step.

Ferrari had been missing races due to continued industrial unrest at home, and they were represented at Aintree by Phil Hill in a lone 120-degree V6 car, in 1961 trim but for a gearbox mounted ahead of the final-drive assembly. Gurney and Bonnier handled the neat new air-cooled 8-cylinder Porsche 804s, Graham Hill and Ginther the new BRM P57 V8s, McLaren and Maggs works Cooper-Climax V8s, and Clark had his V8-engined Lotus 25 with team-mate Trevor Taylor in the spaceframe-chassised V8-powered 24.

Reg Parnell's Bowmaker-financed team fielded two Lola-Climax V8s for Surtees and the veteran Salvadori (in his last Formula 1 season), and private Lotus 24s with V8 engines were fielded by UDT-Laystall for Ireland and Gregory, by Jack Brabham whose own prototype F1 car was nearing completion and by the wealthy Wolfgang Seidel whose BRM-engined car was brand new. Rob Walker had to scratch his entry for Trintignant as the Lotus 24 had been written off at Rouen. The Swiss Scuderia Filipinetti withdrew their entry for the ex-motor-cyclist Jo Siffert when they were offered laughable appearance money. John Campbell-Jones' Emeryson had been wrecked at Solitude, and Greene's new Gilby-BRM V8 was not ready in time. This left the Climax 4-cylinder cars of Burgess and Lewis (Coopers), Jay Chamberlain and Tony Shelly (Lotus 18s) and Tony Settember's Emeryson to join De Beaufort's Porsche at the tail of the field.

Thursday practice was warm and sunny but a headwind on Railway Straight prevented record times. Clark's Aintree '200' record with the Lotus 24 in April stood at 1:54.0, but the timekeepers persisted in working to fifths-of-seconds, and there was some disgust at the dead-heats this produced. Gurney, Ginther and Ireland were all credited with 1:55.2,

then Clark got down to 1:54.0. Friday was a quicker day, and Surtees got down within 0.2 seconds of Clark's record, with Ireland and McLaren chasing him. Then the final session saw the skies cloud over, the wind drop, and Clark went out calmly for a fantastic 1:53.6 to ensure pole position. Down the field, Lewis was the only 4-cylinder runner below 2 minutes, in the Ecurie Galloise Cooper.

Saturday began with the inevitable Liverpudlian rain, but the sun was out before noon, the circuit dried and the grid assembled on a brilliant afternoon. Ireland broke a gearbox selector fork on the warm-up lap, and there was nothing his mechanics could do but remove the broken pieces, leaving him without second and third gears. As the flag was raised he could find no gears at all, and raised his hands helplessly to warn drivers behind of his predicament.

Somehow they all managed to weave and dodge around him as the flag fell, and Clark made a copybook start to take a long lead on the return from Tatts, with Surtees, Gurney, McLaren, Brabham, Graham Hill, Gregory, Salvadori, Phil Hill, Bonnier, Maggs, Ginther, and Taylor trailing him through.

Ireland's car was being worked on in the pits, and after four laps Clark was away on his own, with a bunch including Surtees, Gurney, McLaren, Brabham and Graham Hill drawing away from the mid-field runners. Surtees was flying around, and by lap 8 he had closed with his former Lotus team-mate, and both had lapped at 1:57.4. Clark pressed harder, took 0.4 seconds off his best time and drew away. Surtees fought back, equalling the blue-helmeted Scotsman's time, but he could not better it and was only just holding on to the Lotus.

Gurney had McLaren pressing him hard, Graham Hill had displaced Brabham's apple-green Lotus, and while Clark inexorably drew 4 seconds away from the second-place Lola, McLaren fought past Gurney's Porsche on lap 13. Taylor had a carburettor choke tube pop through the opening behind his head and land in his lap, Ireland had got going on Clark's eighth lap, and Shelly and Seidel had already abandoned.

Surtees settled for a consistent second place; Clark drew away into an increasingly dominant lead. Bonnier stopped at his pit on lap 26 to complain of gearchange troubles, and on the next lap his team-mate's clutch began to slip and Brabham whipped by

1962 Grid

20
Clark
(Lotus-Climax 25 R2)
1:53.6

24
Surtees
(Lola-Climax T4 BRGP-42)
1:54.2

32
Ireland
(Lotus-Climax 24 942)
1:54.4

16
McLaren
(Cooper-Climax T60)
(F1–17–61)
1:54.6

12
G. Hill
(BRM P57–5781)
1:54.6

8
Gurney
(Porsche 804–03)
1:54.8

10
Bonnier
(Porsche 804–02)
1:55.2

14
Ginther
(BRM P57–5784)
1:55.2

30
Brabham
(Lotus-Climax 24 947)
1:55.4

22
Taylor
(Lotus-Climax 24 949)
1:56.0

26
Salvadori
(Lola-Climax T4 BRGP43)
1:56.2

2
P. Hill
(Ferrari 156/07 V6)
1:56.2

18
Maggs
(Cooper-Climax T60)
(F1–18–61)
1:57.0

34
Gregory
(Lotus-Climax 24 944)
1:57.2

42
Lewis
(Cooper-Climax T53)*
1:59.4

36
Burgess
(Cooper-Climax Sp)
2:00.6

54
De Beaufort
(Porsche 718–2–01)*
2:01.4

48
Shelly
(Lotus-Climax 18/21)*
2:02.4

40
Settember
(Emeryson-Climax 1004)*
2:02.4

46
Chamberlain
(Lotus-Climax 18 905)*
2:03.4

44
Seidel
(Lotus-BRM 24 946)
2:11.6

*4-cylinder cars

Non-starters: 38 Campbell-Jones (Emeryson) – 50 Greene (Gilby-BRM) – 52 Siffert (Lotus-BRM)

into fifth place. Bonnier did one tentative lap before abandoning with final-drive failure and on lap 28 Salvadori's Lola began stammering with a flat battery which had to be replaced. Unfortunately a massive short somewhere flattened the replacement battery, so he too went out.

On lap 34 Clark doubled the disinterested Phil Hill in his obsolete Ferrari, and a lap later he added Ginther to his tally. At half-distance he was 14 seconds clear of Surtees with McLaren 30 seconds behind trailed by Graham Hill and Brabham. Gurney was lagging in sixth place with Gregory catching him, Taylor was back up to eleventh and Burgess was driving hard in the leading 4-cylinder.

Gurney succumbed to Maggs and Gregory, and on lap 44 Ginther had a stop out in the country as he persuaded his car's fuel pumps to function once more. Phil Hill retired with ignition failure, Clark doubled his team-mate and the yellow-helmeted Yorkshireman hung on to be towed through the field past Gurney. Burgess interrupted his good drive in a refuelling stop which let Lewis and Settember by, but there were few retirements and Ireland found no profit in limping his three-speed Lotus around at the tail of the field.

On lap 67 Clark doubled Brabham and lined up to pass Graham Hill, but with only eight laps to run he decided not to rub it in, eased off, and trailed the BRM to the line. Taylor, who had kept in touch, had more to gain, and he flew past both his team leader

Jimmy Clark's monocoque Lotus 25 leading Surtees' Lola, Gurney's flat-eight air cooled Porsche and Maggs' lapped Cooper during the sunny 1962 Grand Prix at Aintree.

Concentration – Clark in the Lotus 25.

and the BRM to finish one lap behind instead of two.

Jimmy Clark had won his second Grande Epreuve in supreme style on his own soil. He was only twenty-six, and he was writing the introduction to a legend.

Results

1 J. Clark (1.49 Lotus-Climax – Team Lotus) 2 hrs 26 mins 20.8 secs, 92.25 mph; **2** J. Surtees (1.49 Lola-Climax – Bowmaker Racing Team) 2 hrs 27 mins 10.0 secs; **3** B.L. McLaren (1.49 Cooper-Climax – Cooper Car Co) 2 hrs 28 mins 5.6 secs; **4** N.G. Hill (1.49 BRM – Owen Racing Organization) 2 hrs 28 mins 17.6 secs; **5** J.A. Brabham (1.49 Lotus-Climax – Brabham Racing Organization) 74 laps; **6** A. Maggs (1.49 Cooper-Climax – Cooper Car Co) 74 laps; **7** M. Gregory (1.49 Lotus-Climax – UDT Laystall Racing Team) 74 laps; **8** T.P. Taylor (1.49 Lotus-Climax – Team Lotus) 74 laps; **9** D.S. Gurney (1.49 Porsche – Porsche System Engineering) 73 laps; **10** J. Lewis (1.49 Cooper-Climax – Ecurie Galloise) 72 laps; **11** A. Settember (1.49 Emeryson-Climax – Emeryson Cars Ltd) 71 laps; **12** I. Burgess (1.49 Cooper-Climax – Anglo-American Equipe) 71 laps; **13** P.R. Ginther (1.49 BRM – Owen Racing Organization) 70 laps; **14** Count C.G. de Beaufort (1.49 Porsche – Ecurie Maarsbergen) 69 laps; **15** J. Chamberlain (1.49 Lotus-Climax – Ecurie Excelsior) 64 laps; **16** I. Ireland (1.49 Lotus-Climax – UDT-Laystall Racing Team) 61 laps.

FASTEST LAP   Clark, 1 min 55.0 secs, 93.91 mph.

RETIREMENTS   A. Shelly (1.49 Lotus-Climax – J. Dalton) 6 laps, overheating; W. Seidel (1.49 Lotus-BRM – Autosport Team Wolfgang Seidel) 11 laps, brakes; J. Bonnier (1.49 Porsche – Porsche System Engineering) 27 laps, gearbox; R.F. Salvadori (1.49 Lola-Climax – Bowmaker Racing Team) 35 laps, ignition; P. Hill (1.47 Ferrari – SEFAC Ferrari) 47 laps, ignition.

1963 Silverstone

July 20, Silverstone, 82 laps of 2.926-mile circuit
approximately 240 miles

After two years at the well-appointed but remote and decidedly malodorous Aintree circuit, the Grand Prix returned to its airfield home at Silverstone in 1963. Silverstone could be awful if it rained, beautiful if the sun shone, and for the BRDC's feast of speed this July weekend the sun beat down unabatingly.

Team Lotus arrived with Jimmy Clark having three consecutive Grande Epreuve victories to his credit, in Belgium, Holland and France. His 25 had a fuel-injected Climax V8 engine while Taylor's sister car used a carburettor version. Both rich-green monocoque cars were sporting broad yellow 'speed stripes' for the first time. Other Climax V8 users included Brabham's new works team of spaceframe cars for himself and Gurney, the works Coopers for McLaren and Maggs, Rob Walker's Cooper for Bonnier, Reg Parnell's Lola for his nineteen-year-old New Zealand discovery Chris Amon, and a similar privately-entered car for ex-motorcyclist Bob Anderson.

Works P57 BRM V8s were to run for reigning World Champion Graham Hill and Ginther, while Centro-Sud entered a works-prepared, red-painted sister car for Lorenzo Bandini. BRM V8 engines also appeared in two British Racing Partnership-entered cars – their own monocoque BRP for Ireland, and a spaceframe Lotus 24 for Jim Hall – in the Hugh Powell-financed Scirocco cars for Settember and Burgess; in Parnell's 24s for Gregory and motorcycle World Champion Mike Hailwood; in Swiss driver Jo Siffert's 24 and in Ian Raby's private Gilby special. Scuderia Ferrari brought two of their latest V6 cars but had just one driver, Surtees, to run them.

Practice saw Hill and Brabham down to 1:36.0 in the first session, but in the second on Thursday afternoon Clark went to work with a 1:34.4 which proved good enough for pole position, with Gurney, Hill and Brabham joining him on the four-strong front row.

Maggs' Cooper refused to fire on the grid, and as the flag fell only twenty-two cars got away, dodging wildly around the stranded bottle-green car. As the oil and rubber smoke cleared, mechanics pushed Maggs into the pits, while the works Brabhams of Jack himself and Gurney led that opening lap, with McLaren, Hill and Clark blurring by as one. Clark was not to be denied, he lanced into third place on lap 2, displaced Gurney on lap 3 and took Brabham for the lead on lap 4 to break clear of all pursuers.

Maggs entered the race three laps late, and Campbell-Jones was already in trouble and heading into the pits. Clark was rushing away on his own, leaving the Brabhams, McLaren, Hill and Surtees tussling for second place. Taylor led the midfield group, with Bonnier, Ireland, Ginther, Hall, Bandini and Amon all over each other. Anderson led the privateers, and Clark was hauling away to gain half a second a lap from his pursuers.

McLaren's engine broke at Chapel on lap 7, and Ireland was clear of the midfield group and charging after the depleted second-place dice. Taylor dived into his pit to report a defective fuel pump, and at ten laps Clark was fully 10 seconds clear of Brabham, Gurney, Hill and Surtees.

As Clark drove on in a faultless exhibition of effortless skill, Gurney moved ahead of Brabham to see if he could make any impression on the Lotus 25's lead, leaving Jack to hold off Surtees and Hill. Ireland's efforts to catch this group failed as his BRP's ignition faltered and put him into the pits where Gregory, Settember and Raby had already called.

Bonnier, Ginther and Bandini were nudging, blocking and outbraking each other for sixth place with Amon sitting warily on their tails and wondering if Grand Prix racing really was a good idea. The two works Brabhams drew away from the Surtees/Hill duel, Bandini was getting the better of his more experienced adversaries, and Maggs had caught and passed Hall on the road, whereupon the tall Texan oilman latched onto the flying Cooper's tail and was towed through the field.

Taylor rejoined with a new fuel pump fitted as Clark howled by to complete lap 19, and Ireland rejoined with a woolly-sounding engine. Ten laps later Gurney appeared on his own and Brabham had blown up at Becketts in a steaming puff of blue smoke. Clark was 14 seconds clear of the black-helmeted Californian, and on lap 35 he had drawn out another second while the Brabham lay 12 seconds clear of the continuing BRM/Ferrari battle for third place. One minute behind this pair charged Ginther,

First time out with a yellow stripe on his sleek Lotus, Clark leads Brabham, Gurney, McLaren, Graham Hill, Surtees and the midfield slip-streaming pack along Hangar Straight in the 1963 Grand Prix.

Bandini and Bonnier, Amon had dropped back eighth, and Hall was ninth.

Taylor and Ireland stopped again, were stupidly push-started and found themselves disqualified. On lap 42 Bandini spun wildly at Stowe as his gear-change mounting broke just when he needed it. Clark flashed by to lap him, and as he rejoined Ginther and Bonnier were long gone.

At half-distance Clark had a 16½-second lead, but the Lotus was not as manageable as it could have been for he was running smaller section rear tyres to drop gearing slightly and so gain a little extra traction out of the slower corners. On the now oily track these smaller tyres saw the Scot working hard to remain neat and tidy, but his superiority was such that he had lapped everyone but Gurney, Hill and Surtees.

On lap 60 Gurney's engine erupted in a gout of smoke and hot oil into Stowe, and Clark was left 50 seconds clear of Hill who had got the better of Surtees. Bandini was charging hard to overcome his time deficit, while further back Anderson lost his eleventh place as his right calf was vibrated into cramp. He stopped at the pits, plunged his foot into a bucket of cold water – shades of 1926! – and continued after massage.

On lap 66 Bonnier coasted to a halt before Becketts as his Cooper's oil pressure zeroed, Amon made a precautionary stop for two gallons of fuel, and Siffert lost a well-deserved eighth place as his gearbox broke up past the pits. Hailwood inherited the place, but Maggs soon wrested it from him as he continued his fine comeback down in the field.

The race had been extended to eighty-two laps to ensure it ran the required two hours to qualify for Championship status, and Clark began cruising round in top gear to reduce his fuel consumption. A bag tank had kinked while being filled and there was doubt in the Lotus camp as his theoretical fuel requirement was only just squeezed in. At seventy-five laps he still held a 35 second lead over Hill, but as he swept round and round and came out of Woodcote for the last time to win his second consecutive British Grand Prix, and his fourth Championship round of this season, Hill's BRM stammered at Stowe as *its* pumps drew the last few cc from its drying fuel tanks. Surtees was by in a trice, shrieking home to steal second place while Hill limped in third and Ginther fourth in the sister car, a lap behind.

Clark, his car, Colin Chapman and the Team Lotus personnel packed onto a farm trailer for a memorable lap of honour, and with a piper playing 'Scotland the Brave' the new World Champion elect acknowledged the adulation of the crowds.

Five times winner of the British Grand Prix – Jim Clark.

Results

1 J. Clark (1.49 Lotus-Climax – Team Lotus) 2 hrs 14 mins 9.6 secs, 107.75 mph; **2** J. Surtees (1.47 Ferrari – SEFAC Ferrari) 2 hrs 14 mins 35.4 secs; **3** N.G. Hill (1.49 BRM – Owen Racing Organization) 2 hrs 14 mins 47.2 secs; **4** P.R. Ginther (1.49 BRM – Owen Racing Organization) 81 laps; **5** L. Bandini (1.49 BRM – Scuderia Centro-Sud) 81 laps; **6** J. Hall 1.49 Lotus-BRM – British Racing Partnership) 80 laps; **7** C. Amon (1.49 Lola-Climax – Reg Parnell) 80 laps; **8** M. Hailwood (1.49 Lotus-Climax – Reg Parnell) 78 laps; **9** A. Maggs (1.49 Cooper-Climax – Cooper Car Co) 78 laps; **10** Count C.G. de Beaufort (1.49 Porsche – Ecurie Maarsbergen) 76 laps; **11** M. Gregory (1.49 Lotus-BRM – Reg Parnell) 75 laps; **12** R. Anderson (1.49 Lola-Climax – DW Racing Enterprises Ltd) 75 laps; **13** J. Campbell-Jones (1.49 Lola-Climax – Tim Parnell) 74 laps.

FASTEST LAP   Surtees, 1 min 36.0 secs, 109.76 mph.

RETIREMENTS   B.L. McLaren (1.49 Cooper-Climax – Cooper Car Co), 7 laps, engine; A. Settember (1.49 Scirocco-BRM – Scirocco-Powell (Racing Cars)) 21 laps, ignition; T.P. Taylor (1.49 Lotus-Climax – Team Lotus) 24 laps, fuel pump; I. Ireland (1.49 BRP-BRM – British Racing Partnership) 27 laps, engine; J.A. Brabham (1.49 Brabham-Climax – Brabham Racing Organization) 28 laps, engine; I. Burgess (1.49 Scirocco-BRM – Scirocco-Powell (Racing Cars)), 37 laps, ignition; D.S. Gurney (1.49 Brabham-Climax – Brabham Racing Organization) 60 laps, engine; I. Raby (1.49 Gilby-BRM – Ian Raby Racing) 60 laps, gearbox; J. Bonnier (1.49 Cooper-Climax – R.R.C. Walker Racing Team) 66 laps, engine; J. Siffert (1.49 Lotus-BRM – Siffert Racing Team) 67 laps, gearbox.

1963 Grid

8 Brabham (Brabham-Climax BT7) (F1–2–63) 1:35.0	**1** Hill (BRM P57–5785) 1:34.8	**9** Gurney (Brabham-Climax BT7) (F1–1–63) 1:34.6	**4** Clark (Lotus-Climax 25 R4) 1:34.4

7 Maggs (Cooper-Climax T66) (F1–5–63) 1:36.0	**6** McLaren (Cooper-Climax T66) (F1–4–63) 1:35.4	**10** Surtees (Ferrari Dino 156/63 0001) 1:35.2

11 Ireland (BRP-BRM) 1:36.8	**5** Taylor (Lotus-Climax 25 R2) 1:36.8	**2** Ginther (BRM P57–5784) 1:36.0	**3** Bandini (BRM P57–5781) 1:36.0

19 Amon (Lola-Climax T4A BRGP44) 1:37.2	**12** Hall (Lotus-BRM 24 945) 1:37.0	**14** Bonnier (Cooper-Climax T66) (F1–2–63) 1:36.8

15 Settember (Scirocco-BRM) 1:40.8	**20** Hailwood (Lotus-Climax 24 942) 1:39.8	**22** Anderson (Lola-Climax T4BRGP43) 1:39.0	**25** Siffert (Lotus-BRM 24 950) 1:38.4

23 De Beaufort (Porsche 718) 1:43.4	**16** Burgess (Scirocco-BRM) 1:42.6	**26** Raby (Gilby-BRM) 1:42.4

24 Campbell-Jones (Lola-Climax Mk 4 BRGP42) 1:48.8	**21** Gregory (Lotus-BRM 24 'P1') 1:44.2

Non-arrivals: P. Hill and Baghetti, Nos 18 and 17 ATS; Nasif, No 27 De Tomaso
Reserve drivers listed: Arundell Nos 4 and 5 Lotus 25s; Fairman, Nos 17 and 18 ATS

1964 Brands Hatch

July 11, Brands Hatch, 80 laps of 2.65-mile circuit
approximately 212 miles

A new home was found for the Grand Prix in 1964 as the RAC decided to put their heads on the block and organize their own Grande Epreuve. They did the job very well, with help from the British Racing and Sports Car Club, key personnel from the other major British motor racing organizations, and from Motor Circuit Developments, who administered the race's new venue at Brands Hatch.

The Formula 1 circus came to the Kentish circuit with a rather more open start to the season behind them. Hill had won at Monaco with the BRM, for the second year running, Clark had cleaned up at Zandvoort and Spa, and then the Brabham team's legendary bad luck left them at Rouen where Gurney won the French, with Brabham third.

Team Lotus had lost their new number two driver, Peter Arundell when he suffered severe injuries in

the Formula 2 race at Reims, and for the Brands race Clark's Mark 33 monocoque car was joined by a 25 to be driven by Mike Spence. Hill and Ginther were in new monocoque BRM P261s, Brabham and Gurney had their latest spaceframe Brabhams, Surtees was joined by Bandini in revised Ferraris, the former's with a V8 engine, and McLaren had Phil Hill supporting him in the works Coopers. Two BRP-BRMs were entered for Ireland and Trevor Taylor, and other BRM V8 users were Hailwood and Amon in Parnell Lotus 25s, the American tourist Peter Revson in his Lola-bodied 24 run by the same organization, Bonnier in Walker's new Brabham, Siffert in his own sister car, and Raby in his newly-acquired ex-works prototype Formula 1 Brabham. Centro-Sud fielded two-red painted P57 BRMs for Maggs and Baghetti, Trintignant was having a last fling before retirement in his own P57 painted pale blue, and the works ran their experimental four-wheel drive research vehicle in practice for Dick Attwood. Bob Anderson's Brabham had a Climax V8 engine on carburettors, and two 1500 cc 4-cylinder cars with Ford twin-cam engines completed the entry; a Bob Gerard-entered Cooper for John Taylor, and a Willment-entered Brabham for the Australian Frank Gardner.

On the Thursday afternoon Taylor crashed his BRP heavily at Hawthorn's Bend when his foot slipped off the brake pedal, and Gurney ended the day with best lap in 1:38.4 to win one hundred bottles of Champagne. Brabham and Clark tied just 0.4 seconds slower, and on Friday a bruised Taylor appeared in BRP's Lotus-BRM 24 back-up car, Clark and Graham Hill both bettered Gurney's time and Anderson made everyone sit up and take notice as he got below 1:40.0 and among the fuel-injected works cars. Clark chose to race his spare Lotus 25.

The much-predicted crowd of 130,000-plus failed to materialize, as race-day dawned overcast and damp yet again. But the drizzle stopped early, the circuit dried, and with dull skies and a cool gentle breeze conditions were perfect for good racing.

For the first time the field was formed up on an American-style dummy grid, where the cars would be started, and from which they would roll forward onto the true grid, pausing only momentarily before the flag fell and unleashed them. Unfortunately, as the grid took off, Amon's clutch failed to bite, Siffert dodged left and cannoned into Gardner's ballasted F2

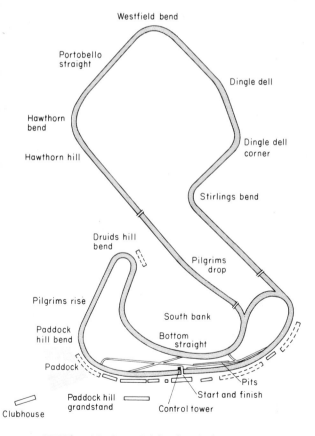

Westfield bend

Portobello straight

Dingle dell

Hawthorn bend

Hawthorn hill

Dingle dell corner

Stirlings bend

Druids hill bend

Pilgrims drop

Pilgrims rise

South bank

Paddock hill bend

Bottom straight

Paddock

Pits

Paddock hill grandstand

Start and finish

Clubhouse

Control tower

⊏⁼⁼⁼⊐ Grandstands erected for Grand prix

1964 Grid

The first Brands Hatch British Grand Prix start, 1964, with Clark already drawing ahead beyond the cloud of tyre smoke on pole position. Tail-ends seen clearly include (l-to-r) Magg's BRM, Taylor's Cooper-Ford, Revson's Lotus, Gardner's Brabham (about to hit Siffert's wheels) and Baghetti's BRM.

6
Gurney
(Brabham-Climax BT7)
(F1−1−63)
1:38.4

3
G. Hill
(BRM P261−2614)
1:38.3

1
Clark
(Lotus-Climax 25 R6)
1:38.1

7
Surtees
(Ferrari 158−0006)
1:38.7

5
Brabham
(Brabham-Climax BT7)
(F1−2−63)
1:38.5

8
Bandini
(Ferrari 156−0004)
1:40.2

19
Anderson
(Brabham-Climax BT11)
(F1−5−64)
1:39.8

9
McLaren
(Cooper-Climax T73)
(F1−1−64)
1:39.6

11
Ireland
(BRP-BRM)
(BRP−2−64)
1:40.8

16
Bonnier
(Brabham-BRM BT11)
(F1−4−64)
1:40.2

2
Spence
(Lotus-Climax 25 R4)
1:41.4

14
Hailwood
(Lotus-BRM 25 R7)
1:41.4

15
Amon
(Lotus-BRM 25 R3)
1:41.2

10
P. Hill
(Cooper-Climax T73)
(F1−2−64)
1:42.6

4
Ginther
(BRM P261−2613)
1:41.6

12
T. Taylor
(Lotus-BRM 24 945)
1:42.8

23
Raby
(Brabham-BRM BT3)
(F1−1−62)
1:42.8

20
Siffert
(Brabham-BRM BT11)
(F1−6−64)
1:42.8

22
J. Taylor
(Cooper-Ford T72)
(F1−3−64)
1:48.2

26
Gardner
(Brabham-Ford BT10)
(F2−4−64)
1:43.0

17
Maggs
(BRM P57−5785)
1:45.0

24
Revson
(Lotus-BRM 24 'P1')
1:43.4

18
Baghetti
(BRM P57−5784)
1:43.4

Non-starters: 21 Attwood (BRM P67), 1:45.2 − 25 Trintignant (BRM P57) 1:54.4.

Brabham which spun round drunkenly with its right-rear wheel torn off.

This minor drama naturally left the front-runners unaffected. Clark and Gurney jounced over the brow of Paddock Hill wheel-to-wheel, and held position up to the right-handed hairpin at Druids, where Clark had the advantage of being on the tighter line. Gurney was forced to snap back onto the Lotus' tail and Clark howled round the Bottom Straight and out into the country in a clear lead.

Gurney, Hill, Surtees and Brabham chased him hard, with McLaren leading the rest of the field, but on lap 3 Hill's BRM was second and Gurney peeled off into the pits with a dud ignition 'black box'. Amon was quickly out sans clutch, but Siffert was racing with a will and easily picked off Raby.

Hailwood bounded yards across the infield out of Bottom Bend, crushed a photographer's case and tore an oil-line beneath his Lotus' chassis. He gave up on lap 17, but had meanwhile soaked the circuit liberally with oil, and lap times were way down in consequence. McLaren went out with a broken gearbox on lap 7, and Gurney rejoined after losing many laps to take most of the sting out of the race.

Clark and Hill drew right away on their own and fought a gritty battle of skill and determination which saw them run first and second for the entire distance. Clark kept chipping away at his lap times while Hill's masklike concentration recalled memories of 1960. On lap 73 Clark did a record 1:38.8 lap which increased his lead to its peak of 7½ seconds. Then he

Results

1 J. Clark (1.49 Lotus-Climax – Team Lotus) 2 hrs 15 mins 7.0 secs, 94.14 mph; **2** N.G. Hill (1.49 BRM – Owen Racing Organization) 2 hrs 15 mins 9.8 secs; **3** J. Surtees (1.4 Ferrari – SEFAC Ferrari) 2 hrs 16 mins 27.6 secs; **4** J.A. Brabham (1.49 Brabham-Climax – Brabham Racing Organization) 79 laps; **5** L. Bandini (1.4 Ferrari – SEFAC Ferrari) 78 laps; **6** P. Hill (1.49 Cooper-Climax – Cooper Car Co) 78 laps; **7** R. Anderson (1.49 Brabham-Climax – DW Racing Enterprises Ltd) 78 laps; **8** P.R. Ginther (1.49 BRM – Owen Racing Organization) 77 laps; **9** M. Spence (1.49 Lotus-Climax – Team Lotus) 77 laps; **10** I. Ireland (1.49 BRP-BRM – British Racing Partnership) 76 laps; **11** J. Siffert (1.49 Brabham-BRM – Siffert Racing Team) 76 laps; **12** G. Baghetti (1.49 BRM – Scuderia Centro-Sud) 76 laps; **13** D.S. Gurney (1.49 Brabham-Climax – Brabham Racing Organization) 75 laps; **14** J. Taylor (1.49 Cooper-Ford – Bob Gerard Racing) 56 laps.

FASTEST LAP   Clark 1 min 38.8 secs, 96.56 mph.

RETIREMENTS   F. Gardner (1.49 Brabham-Ford – Race Proved by Willment) 0 laps, collision at start; B.L. McLaren (1.49 Cooper-Climax – Cooper Car Co) 8 laps, gearbox; C. Amon (1.49 Lotus-BRM – Reg Parnell Racing) 10 laps, clutch; M. Hailwood (1.49 Lotus-BRM – Reg Parnell Racing) 18 laps, engine; T.P. Taylor (1.49 Lotus-BRM – British Racing Partnership) 24 laps, driver; A. Maggs (1.49 BRM – Scuderia Centro-Sud) 38 laps, gearbox; I. Raby (1.49 Brabham-BRM – Ian Raby Racing) 38 laps, accident; P.J. Revson (1.49 Lotus-BRM – Revson Racing) 44 laps, plugs; J. Bonnier (1.49 Brabham-BRM – R.R.C. Walker Racing Team) 47 laps, brake pipe.

eased off and although Hill closed to within 3 seconds at the finish there was no chance of his catching the Lotus unless something went wrong with it. For the majority of the crowd this was a dull battle, but for the *cognoscenti* it was a minor classic of sustained effort and skill.

Surtees and Brabham battled for third place, with Bandini a lonely fifth after McLaren's retirement. Phil Hill led the midfield group, with Bonnier, Anderson, Ginther, Spence, Taylor, Ireland and John Taylor all nose to tail in his wake. After another interval came Baghetti, Siffert and Maggs, with Raby trailing.

Trevor Taylor went out overcome by cockpit heat and still shaken by his practice crash, and Bonnier, Phil Hill and Anderson broke clear until the Swede made a quick stop. Brabham stopped twice to convince himself his car was sound after finding it unaccountably sideways a couple of times, and his stops let Bandini by. He rejoined with Phil Hill and Anderson pushing hard, but left them behind, and it was while Clark and Hill were lapping the Cooper/Brabham duel that Clark drew away to break their performance stalemate.

On lap 66 Brabham took Bandini, and on lap 67 Phil Hill had got into his stride again after being passed and dropped by Anderson, and managed to repass the bright green Brabham. Ginther was leading his battle, but Ireland had fallen away with a misfire, and as the long race drew to its gritty, and unspectacular finish Clark lapped Bandini once more to put him two laps behind. It was the Flying Scotsman's third consecutive victory in his home event; with the last year of the 1½-litre Formula approaching, could he make it four?

Story of the race: Clark leading narrowly from Graham Hill as they dive under the second access bridge 200-yards short of Clearways Corner.

1965 Silverstone

July 10, Silverstone, 80 laps of 2.927-mile circuit
approximately 234 miles

Back to Silverstone for 1965 as this traditional venue began to alternate with Brands Hatch as the Grand Prix's regular home, and once more Clark arrived at the head of the World Championship standings with his Lotus. He had won the opening round in South Africa, Hill had completed his hat-trick at Monaco, and then it was Clark again in Belgium and France.

Team Lotus fielded a pair of their well-developed Mark 33s with Climax V8 engines for Clark and Spence. Brabham, Gurney and the rugged New Zealander Denny Hulme drove the dark-green and gold Brabham Racing Organization cars, and McLaren and the Austrian newcomer Jochen Rindt handled the now thoroughly eclipsed works Coopers. Clark and Gurney both had the latest 32-valve Coventry-Climax V8 engines available, but Lotus did not use their's until the last practice sessions, and the Brabham team not until the warming-up lap for the race itself.

Ferrari fielded a new flat-12-engined car for Surtees and a V8 for Bandini, while BRM had a promising newcomer named Jackie Stewart backing-up Hill in their P261 V8s. Stewart had won the non-Championship International Trophy race on this circuit earlier in the season.

The Japanese Honda concern ran a solitary transverse V12-engined car for Ginther, and Rob Walker had two Brabhams, with Climax V8 engine for Bonnier and BRM V8 for Siffert.

Clark stole pole position in the final session on Friday with a lap in 1 : 30.8 using the 32-valve engine, but Hill was just 0.2 seconds slower in the BRM, Ginther shrieked the white Honda round 0.3 seconds slower still, and Stewart completed the front row having equalled the Japanese car's time.

Gurney's 32-valve engine, fitted overnight, dropped two of them on the warming-up lap, and Brabham hastily handed his own car to the lofty American for the race. Promptly at 2 o'clock the race began under a light overcast sky, and Clark and Ginther shot away with the blaring Honda two lengths ahead by 'The Motor' Bridge. Ginther pinched out Clark against the inside wall at Copse, and the white V12 screamed down Hangar Straight still leading until Clark ducked out of its slipstream and dived ahead into Stowe. He scratched hard for the rest of that lap, using all the road and some of the grass out of Woodcote as he strove to break his opposition.

Ginther was swallowed by Hill and Surtees on lap 2, and while Hill could just hold the leading Lotus, Surtees was being outpaced and Ginther was coming back to repass. Stewart, Spence, McLaren and Hulme blurred by in a bunch, with Rindt and Gurney close behind. Bonnier led the privateers while Bandini thumped up onto the pit ramp completing that lap with his Ferrari's engine blown to pieces. Attwood followed him in to investigate a misfire, hit the ramp too fast and tore an under-chassis water pipe which had to be replaced.

Up front, Hill was fighting a losing battle to hold Clark, while Ginther's Honda was suffering its usual power-loss symptom after a demonic start. Stewart and Spence went by before the diminutive American came into the pits, but after a few more laps the Honda was out.

Gurney was having a hard time in Brabham's car, towering out of its confined cockpit into the slipstream with a handkerchief stuffed between his teeth to keep the wind from gagging him. At quarter-distance, twenty laps, Clark and Hill were first and second with little prospect of change, but Stewart was threatening Surtees' shrill flat-12 Ferrari for third, and Spence was on the BRM's tail. Hulme was sixth with McLaren, Rindt, Bonnier, Gurney, Siffert and Ireland next up.

Spence sliced by Stewart on lap 24, when Rindt spun at Becketts and rejoined behind Gurney. Siffert displaced Ireland, Hulme stopped abruptly when his car's alternator drive broke and its battery went flat, and Anderson was lagging with gearbox problems. Spence found he could draw away from Stewart as the BRM was not handling properly, and on lap 41 this very good Lotus number two nosed past Surtees to take third place. The Ferrari World Champion was back ahead after just one lap, Stewart's V8 was slightly off song, and he had settled back for a lonely fifth place.

Bonnier and Gurney took McLaren as he couldn't find a gear, and as he stopped for attention they disappeared into the distance. The Cooper mechanics could do nothing, so McLaren rejoined at the tail of

Shutters click, clutches bite and wheels spin as the 1965 Grand Prix leaves the line at Silverstone. Here on the front row are Stewart's BRM, Ginther's Honda, Graham Hill's BRM and — on its inevitable pole position, Clark's Lotus.

1965 Grid

4 Stewart (BRM P261–2617) 1:31.3	**11** Ginther (Honda RA272–1) 1:31.3	**3** Hill (BRM P261–2616) 1:31.0	**5** Clark (Lotus-Climax 33 R11) 1:30.8

7* Gurney (Brabham-Climax BT11) (F1–1–64) 1:31.9	**6** Spence (Lotus-Climax 33 R9) 1:31.7	**1** Surtees (Ferrari 1512–0007) 1:31.3

9 McLaren (Cooper-Climax T77) (F1–2–65) 1:32.8	**14** Hulme (Brabham-Climax BT7) (F1–1–63) 1:32.7	**2** Bandini (Ferrari 158–0006) 1:32.7	**7** Brabham* (Brabham-Climax BT11) 1:32.5

15 Bonnier (Brabham-Climax BT7) (F1–2–63) 1:33.5	**17** Gardner (Brabham-BRM BT11) (F1–4–64) 1:33.4	**10** Rindt (Cooper-Climax T77) (F1–1–65) 1:32.9

16 Siffert (Brabham-BRM BT11) (F1–6–64) 1:34.2	**18** Anderson (Brabham-Climax BT11) (F1–5–64) 1:34.1	**22** Attwood (Lotus-BRM 25 R3) 1:33.8	**23** Ireland (Lotus-BRM 25 R7) 1:33.6

20 Rhodes (Cooper-Climax T60) (F1–17–61) 1:39.4	**24** Raby (Brabham-BRM BT3) (F1–1–62) 1:36.0	**12** Gregory (BRM P57–5784) 1:35.9

*Gurney took over Brabham's car on the grid, his own car (8) broke its engine on warm-up lap – chassis F1–2–64

Non-arrivals: 12 R. Bucknum (Honda) – 19 P. Hawkins (Lotus-Climax 33 R8)

Non-starters: Rollinson (Cooper-Cosworth-Ford T76) 1:39.0, Gubby (Lotus-Climax 24 '943') 1:45.1

the field. Clark lapped Bonnier and Gurney on lap 50, the works Brabham taking advantage of Clark's brief tow to displace the Walker car. Hill was held up as he tried to lap Rindt, and then as Clark came out of Woodcote there was a slight but unmistakable 'popple' in his engine's exhaust note.

He had half a lap lead from Hill, but the BRM pit instantly signalled the news to their impassive number one and he drove harder to narrow the gap. Surtees had shaken-off Spence in the traffic, Rindt's engine broke on lap 63 and Clark began to run short of oil. He saw its pressure dipping as the oil surged through corners, and he began to coast through the bends, blaring the engine away up the straights as the oil pressure stabilised.

As Clark appeared, swishing through the turns and gunning the engine down the straights the estimated 115,000 crowd were on their feet, for Hill was knocking off 2 seconds a lap and hurling his BRM through the curves at near-impossible angles as its brakes deteriorated.

With five laps to go Clark was trying harder, nursing the engine when he dared, caning it when he could, and all the time the BRM's dayglo nose was drawing closer. On the seventy-ninth lap Clark's lead was 3.2 seconds and on the final lap he kept his foot down, Hill had a lurid slide at Copse and they burst out of Woodcote the same distance apart, first and second in the British Grand Prix for the second consecutive year.

Hill had set a new lap record of 1:32.2 on that last lap, but it had not been enough to dislodge the brilliant – and lucky – Scot.

Results

1 J. Clark (1.49 Lotus-Climax – Team Lotus) 2 hrs 5 mins 25.4 secs, 112.02 mph; **2** N.G. Hill (1.49 BRM – Owen Racing Organisation) 2 hrs 5 mins 28.6 secs; **3** J. Surtees (1.47 Ferrari – SEFAC Ferrari) 2 hrs 5 mins 53.6 secs; **4.** M. Spence (1.49 Lotus-Climax – Team Lotus) 2 hrs 6 mins 5.0 secs; **5** J.Y. Stewart (1.49 BRM – Owen Racing Organization) 2 hrs 6 mins 40.0 secs; **6** D.S. Gurney (1.49 Brabham-Climax – Brabham Racing Organization) 79 laps; **7** J. Bonnier (1.49 Brabham-Climax – R.R.C. Walker Racing Team) 79 laps; **8** F. Gardner (1.49 Brabham-BRM – Race Proved by Willment) 78 laps; **9** J. Siffert (1.49 Brabham-BRM – R.R.C. Walker Racing Team) 78 laps; **10** B.L. McLaren (1.49 Cooper-Climax – Cooper Car Co) 77 laps; **11** I. Raby (1.49 Brabham-BRM – Ian Raby Racing) 73 laps; **12** M. Gregory (1.49 BRM – Scuderia Centro-Sud) 70 laps; **13** R. Attwood (1.49 Lotus-BRM – Reg Parnell Racing) 63 laps; **14** K.J. Rindt (1.49 Cooper-Climax – Cooper Car Co) 62 laps*.
*Not running at finish, but classified as finisher.

FASTEST LAP   Hill, 1 min 32.2 secs, 114.29 mph.

RETIREMENTS   L. Bandini (1.47 Ferrari – SEFAC Ferrari) 3 laps, engine; P.R. Ginther (1.49 Honda – Honda Motor Co) 27 laps, ignition; D.C. Hulme (1.49 Brabham-Climax – Brabham Racing Organization) 30 laps, alternator belt; R. Anderson (1.49 Brabham-Climax – DW Racing Enterprises Ltd) 34 laps, gearbox; J. Rhodes (1.49 Cooper-Climax – Gerard Racing) 39 laps, ignition; I. Ireland (1.49 Lotus-BRM – Reg Parnell Racing) 42 laps, engine; K.J. Rindt 63 laps, engine, but classified as finisher.

Hunted and the Hunter – Clark's cutting-out Lotus understeers while Hill's virtually brakeless BRM oversteers wildly in its closing stages pursuit of the Scot.

1966 Brands Hatch

July 16, Brands Hatch, 80 laps of 2.65-mile circuit
approximately 212 miles

The first British Grand Prix to be run under the new 3-litre Formula was back at Brands Hatch, where the razzamatazz publicity machine was pumping out prophecies of 'The Return of Power'.

Unfortunately the sting was taken out of the race by the defection of Ferrari, whose new V12 was more than a match for its competitors during the early part of the year. Misfortune had knocked it out of the lead at Monaco, where Stewart won in a 2.1-litre BRM, and Reims, but Surtees had won the Belgian race in superb style, then had broken with the team at Le Mans.

The French GP had fallen to Brabham, driving his modestly-conceived but intensely practical Repco V8-engined car. It was the first-ever Grande Epreuve victory by a driver in a car carrying his own name, and with the Brabham's small size, useable range of power and fabled handling the team's prospects looked good as they came to the hilly, winding circuit in Kent.

Brabham had his Reims-winning BT19, and Hulme the latest BT20, while F3 star Chris Irwin was to drive their stand-by 2.7-litre Climax 4-cylinder car, similar to Anderson's latest acquisition.

Team Lotus had lost Clark briefly at Reims, where he was hit in the face by a bird during practice, but now he was recovered and he appeared with a brand-new Lotus 33 powered by a stop-gap 2-litre 32-valve Climax V8. Team-mate was Peter Arundell, recovered at last from his dreadful Reims F2 crash of 1964, and he had an older 33 with 2.1-litre BRM V8 power. The Owen Racing Organisation fielded two 2.1-litre Tasman BRM P261s for Hill and Stewart, and Cooper (under new management) ran two of their bulky Cooper-Maserati V12s for Surtees and Rindt. Gurney was running his own Anglo-American Racers' Eagle prototype with a 2.7 Climax engine, and McLaren's new racing team fielded their prototype Formula 1 car with a rather feeble Serenissima V8 engine fitted in place of its original linered-down Indy Ford unit.

Brabham and Hulme totally dominated practice, although Gurney put his good-handling Eagle beside them on the front row. These sessions were notable for the odd goings-on engendered by an MGM film unit trying to shoot scenes for Frankenheimer's stunningly awful film *Grand Prix*. Bonnier was running his old 1½-litre Brabham-BRM as a fake Ferrari, complete with dummy exhausts and red paint, and when this blew up a Climax version was substituted. Frankenheimer also paid Parnell a bag of gold to paint Spence's car red, while the driver was given a helmet in Ferrari driver Mike Parkes' colours!

More seriously, the racing tyre war was raging fiercely, and while the Brabhams and the Eagle excelled on their Goodyear covers, the BRMs toyed with Dunlops, Firestones and Goodyears, the Lotuses were on Firestones and it all became very complex and confusing.

Once again it was a dull overcast Saturday for the race, and the crowd was nowhere near the regular Silverstone attendance, however sanguine the BRDC's official estimates may have been in the past! Rain fell just before the start, then stopped abruptly, and a flurry of wheel changing saw most runners opting for all-weather or dry covers, although the works Coopers chose wet-weather Dunlops.

Brabham streamed off pole position to lead into Paddock Bend, with the Eagle pecking at his tail. Hulme was boxed-in on the surge up to Druid's, and Surtees side-swiped Hill to put a bend in the BRM's right-front suspension. Anderson started a lap late, and the tatty Shannon ebbed on the first lap to end Trevor Taylor's Grand Prix career.

The track was slick from the rain, and Rindt spun wildly after forcing past Gurney. Hulme was ensnared in mid-field after his poor start, while Brabham led an unabashed Rindt, then Gurney trying to stave-off Surtees, Clark and Hill having yet another of their great battles, then Stewart, McLaren, Hulme and Siffert.

The track was being squeegeed dry just as Gurney's engine coughed and put him out on lap 7, Rindt had been joined by Surtees in his pursuit of Brabham and Stewart caught and split the Clark/Hill duel to see if he could do more about the World Champion than his slightly handicapped number one.

At ten laps the Australian driver-constructor had already doubled Bondurant, Arundell, Lawrence and Bonnier. Stewart's V8 went off-song and he retired in the pits, Surtees had displaced Rindt as the course dried out but both Cooper-Maseratis were lurching and wallowing around as their tyres began to overheat. Hulme had taken sixth place as Stewart abandoned, and while he gained on Hill and Clark they were catching the Coopers.

1966 Grid

16
Gurney
(Eagle-Climax T2G–101)
1:35.8

6
Hulme
(Brabham-Repco BT20 F1-2-66)
1:34.8

5
Brabham
(Brabham-Repco BT19 F1-1-65)
1:34.5

1
Clark
(Lotus-Climax 33 R14)
1:36.1

3
Hill
(BRM P261–2616)
1:36.0

4
Stewart
(BRM P261–2614)
1:36.9

11
Rindt
(Cooper-Maserati T81 F1–3–66)
1:36.6

12
Surtees
(Cooper-Maserati T81 F1–6–66)
1:36.4

21
Anderson
(Brabham-Climax BT11)
(F1–5–64)
1:37.5

17
Spence
(Lotus-BRM 25 R13)
1:37.3

14
McLaren
(McLaren-Serenissima M2B/2)
1:38.5

7
Irwin
(Brabham-Climax BT22 F1-1-64)
1:38.1

20
Siffert
(Cooper-Maserati T81 F1–2–66)
1:38.0

18
Bonnier
(Brabham-Climax BT7)
(F1–2–63)
1:39.3

25
Bondurant
(BRM P261–2615)
1:38.9

23
T. Taylor
(Shannon-Climax Godiva)
1:41.6

19
Ligier
(Cooper-Maserati T81 F1–4–66)
1:41.4

22
J. Taylor
(Brabham-BRM BT11)
(F1–4–64)
1:40.0

2
Arundell
(Lotus-BRM 33 R11)
1:54.3

24
Lawrence
(Cooper-Ferrari T73)
(F1–2–64)
1:43.8

Non-arrivals: 8 Bandini – 9 Parkes (Ferraris) – 10 Amon (Cooper-Maserati)

Spence's Lotus-BRM dumped most of its oil on the track, but Brabham was bustling round quickly and neatly in a comfortable lead as the fourth-place bunch caught Rindt and Surtees. On lap 29 Hill and Clark appeared ahead of Rindt, and next time round they were second and third ahead of Surtees. One more lap and Hulme was past Rindt into fifth place, pushing his car's gold nose up alongside Surtees' cockpit going into South Bank with smoke pouring from a locked front wheel. This scene so surprised Surtees that he moved aside and Hulme shot through to take fourth place.

On lap 37 Hulme displaced Clark, and set-about Hill, passing him within three laps to take-up team position behind the leader. Hill and Clark continued racing as though for the lead, while the Coopers were still being fought manfully by Surtees and Rindt, with McLaren, Irwin, John Taylor, Ligier, Bondurant and Lawrence following on.

Clark's brake pedal was growing soft, and on lap 45 he had a fright as the pedal swooped down to its stop and he had to broadside the car to scrabble round the next corner. He crept into his pit, where the fluid reservoir was found to be empty, and it was hastily refilled and he tore back into the race with air bubbles in the system, behind the Coopers on the road, and one lap down.

Brabham and Hulme were cruising round 10 seconds apart and looking extremely comfortable, while Hill had settled for third and Surtees was finding corners more and more daunting. His works Cooper spun away from him on lap 55 and after a few more miles he bustled into the pits to retire, for its limited-slip differential had ceased to function.

Meanwhile Clark was flaying round the circuit, closing on Rindt and unlapping himself with five laps remaining. In these dying moments Hill was watching his oil pressure gauge like a hawk as it began to fluctuate through the corners, and he eased back a lot to preserve his engine. This allowed first Brabham, then Hulme, to lap him and the green and gold cars roared home to a remarkable 1–2 success by a whole lap from the strongest British opposition of the year. If only Ferrari had been there we might have seen a *proper* motor race.

The first 3-litre British Grand Prix gets away at Brands Hatch in 1966, with Brabham, Hulme, Clark and Gurney prominent on the charge up Paddock Hill.

The old rivals locked in combat yet again: Hill's BRM leading Clark's Lotus, with the damaged left-front rocker arm on the leading car visibly buckled along its upper surface.

Results

1 J.A. Brabham (2.99 Brabham-Repco – Brabham Racing Organization) 2 hrs 13 mins 13.4 secs, 95.48 mph; 2 D.C. Hulme (2.99 Brabham-Repco – Brabham Racing Organization), 2 hrs 13 mins 23.0 secs; 3 N.G. Hill (2.07 BRM-Owen Racing Organization) 79 laps; 4 J. Clark (1.99 Lotus-Climax – Team Lotus) 79 laps; 5 K.J. Rindt (2.98 Cooper-Maserati – Cooper Car Co) 79 laps; 6 B.L. McLaren (2.99 McLaren-Serenissima – Bruce McLaren Motor Racing Ltd) 78 laps; 7 C. Irwin (2.7 Brabham-Climax – Brabham Racing Organization) 78 laps; 8 J. Taylor (1.99 Brabham-BRM – David Bridges) 76 laps; 9 R. Bondurant (2.07 BRM – Bernard White) 76 laps; 10 G. Ligier (2.98 Cooper-Maserati – driver) 75 laps; 11 C. Lawrence (2.9 Cooper-Ferrari – J.A. Pearce Engineering) 73 laps; 12 J. Siffert (2.98 Cooper-Maserati – R.R.C. Walker Racing Team) 70 laps; 13 R. Anderson (2.7 Brabham-Climax – DW Racing Enterprises Ltd) 70 laps.

FASTEST LAP   Brabham 1 min 37.0 secs, 98.35 mph.

RETIREMENTS   T. Taylor (2.9 Shannon-Climax – Aiden Jones/Paul Emery) 2 laps, split fuel tank; D.S. Gurney (2.7 Eagle-Climax – Anglo-American Racers Inc) 9 laps, engine; M. Spence (1.99 Lotus-BRM – Reg Parnell Racing) 15 laps, oil pipe; J. Bonnier (1.49 Brabham-Climax – driver) 42 laps, clutch pipe; P. Arundell (1.99 Lotus-BRM – Team Lotus) 17 laps, gear linkage; J.Y. Stewart (2.07 BRM – Owen Racing Organisation) 17 laps, engine; J. Surtees (2.98 Cooper-Maserati – Cooper Car Co) 67 laps, differential.

1967 Silverstone

July 15, Silverstone, 80 laps of 2.927-mile circuit
approximately 234 miles

The second year of 3-litre Grand Prix racing was a pivotal one so far as the development of the class was concerned, for the Dutch Grand Prix on June 4 saw Clark and Hill giving dominant performances now as Lotus team-mates on the debut of their Cosworth-Ford V8 engined cars. Clark won the race, and the Lotus 49s were in a class of their own in Belgium and France although sidelined by mechanical failure.

The season had opened in South Africa with Pedro Rodriguez winning luckily for Cooper-Maserati, Hulme had won in Monaco, Gurney at Spa and Brabham on the Bugatti Circuit at Le Mans. The teams assembled at Silverstone prepared to see the Lotus 49s best for speed, but with the Brabham, Eagle, and Ferrari entries all ready to beat them on sustained performance.

The Brabham Racing Organization had their two F2-based BT24s with Repco engines and special long-range scuttle tanks for Brabham himself and Hulme, while Team Lotus fielded two 49s for Clark and Hill, with their ZF final drive casings strengthened since the distortion failures which had put them out in France. Gurney was joined by McLaren in a pair of Weslake V12-engined Eagles, while BRM were running three of their exotic H16-engined cars – the lightweight P115 for Stewart, and a pair of P83s for Spence and Irwin, the latter's being managed by Tim Parnell's organization. Parnell also had a 2.1 Tasman car for Piers Courage.

Cooper had a normal T81B Maserati V12 car for Rodriguez, put Alan Rees in their spare prototype and produced a brand-new and intensely ugly T86 on the second day of practice for Rindt. It was fitted with a 36-valve Heron-head Maserati V12 engine, and two private production T81s were fielded by Rob Walker for Siffert (the car carrying an affectionate Dymo-tape sticker with the name *Torrey Canyon*), and by Bonnier.

Surtees was running the immense and incredibly noisy V12 Honda, and another singleton entry came from Ferrari for Amon, with a 36-valve V12 engine. Ligier was running the ex-Hulme BT20 Brabham-Repco, Anderson had his 2.7 Brabham-Climax, David Hobbs was in White's Tasman BRM and the diminutive Swiss Silvio Moser was to drive a Cooper fitted with a 3-litre sports-racing ATS V8. Robin Darlington was listed to compete in a spaceframe McLaren-Climax V8, but had a road accident.

The Brabhams dominated the first day of practice, but on Friday the Lotus-Fords got going well until Hill suddenly felt his car behaving peculiarly and he was driving-in along the pit-lane when a rear radius arm broke away from the chassis at a bad weld and the car flicked sharp right into a wall, tearing off a wheel and radiators and damaging the monocoque. A spare chassis was complete at the Team Lotus base in Norfolk, so a hectic overnight session began to build it up into a race car for Hill on the morrow. Stewart and BRM were also in trouble, he was forced to take over Irwin's H16, Irwin took Courage's V8 and Courage became a spectator for the race.

With an enormous crowd estimated at 120,000 (those estimates again!) the Grand Prix field did a number of reconnaissance laps under an overcast but not threatening sky. Fuel range was marginal for this long race, and tanks were topped on the grid, Hill arriving at the last minute in his brand-new car to enormous applause.

The dummy grid rolled forward, their throttle blips tensed and relaxed, tensed, roared as the flag raised and then thundered as they all fled away with the Lotuses leading, Clark ahead of Hill, then Brabham, Amon, Gurney, Stewart, Hulme and the rest.

Hill lost second place to Brabham on lap 2 as he still had to acquaint himself with his car which had been set-up by guesswork. Spence boomed up the pit ramp with an electrical fire flickering behind his helmet. The Parnell mechanics hastily fitted a new transistor box to put his BRM back in the race.

As Clark drew away into another of his long Silverstone leads, Stewart was dropped by the second bunch who were fighting a torrid battle. Bonnier had started with a V11 and was out with a piston holed, and Rindt made several stops to convince himself that the smoke he could see in his mirrors came from nothing more vital than a leaking catch tank.

At ten laps Clark led from Hill who had settled back into second place by a hair's-breadth from

The 1967 start with the Repco-Brabhams of Hulme and Jack himself accompanying the Lotus-Fords of Hill and Clark off the front row. Surtees has set the Honda's tyres alight on row two while Amon is easing the Ferrari (8) off the line and Gurney's Eagle beak is just visible on the right. Spence's BRM H16 and McLaren's wheel-spinning Eagle-Weslake complete the scene.

1967 Grid

2 Hulme (Brabham-Repco BT24/2) 1:26.3	**1** Brabham (Brabham-Repco BT24/1) 1:26.2	**6** Hill (Lotus-Cosworth 49 R1) 1:26.0	**5** Clark (Lotus-Cosworth 49 R2) 1:25.3

7 Surtees (Honda RA 273—F102) 1:27.2	**8** Amon (Ferrari 312/0003) 1:26.9	**9** Gurney (Eagle-Weslake 104) 1:26.4

4 Spence (BRM P83-8303) 1:28.3	**30** McLaren (Eagle-Weslake 102) 1:28.1	**12** Rodriguez (Cooper-Maserati T81B F1-6-66) 1:27.9	**11** Rindt (Cooper-Maserati T86 F1-2-67) 1:27.4

20 Hobbs (BRM P261—2615) 1:30.1	**15** Irwin (BRM P261—2616) 1:29.6	**3** Stewart (BRM P83-8302) 1:28.7

17 Siffert (Cooper-Maserati T81 F1—2—66) 1:31.0	**19** Anderson (Brabham-Climax BT11) (F1—5—64) 1:30.7	**16** Courage* (BRM P261) 1:30.4	**14** Rees (Cooper-Maserati T81B F1-3-66) 1:30.3

18 Ligier (Brabham-Repco BT20 F1-2-66) 1:34.8	**22** Moser (Cooper-ATS T77) (F1—1—65) 1:32.9	**23** Bonnier (Cooper-Maserati T81 F1—5—66) 1:32.0

*Non-starter

Non-arrival: 21 R. Darlington (McLaren)

Brabham, Hulme, Amon and Gurney whose Eagle-Weslake was understeering badly. Hill left them all to close on his team-mate, and on lap 13 McLaren's Weslake V12 threw a rod. Hulme took third place from his Guv'nor and left him to battle with Amon in the lone Ferrari.

Stewart went out with transmission trouble on lap 20, and the two Lotuses were running alone but within themselves, way ahead of Hulme on his own, Brabham battling still with Amon and Gurney close behind.

Rindt's new Cooper made a disgusting noise and was parked at Copse, and on lap 26 Hill took over the lead from Clark. Gurney gave up with incurable clutch slip after eight more laps, by which time Hill had drawn 3 seconds clear of his team-mate while lapping backmarkers . . . like Surtees . . .

Brabham's BT24 had vibrated-off its mirrors so that the Australian – who reputedly never used them anyway – had a legitimate excuse for baulking Amon as the race rushed on. Only the Lotuses, the Brabhams, Amon and Rodriguez were left on the same lap, and the fourth-place duel was becoming really fierce with Amon catching stones, dust, oil and exhaust fumes as Brabham tore round fast enough to close on Hulme.

Rodriguez was lapped on the forty-seventh tour and then, on lap 55, a screw locating the inner end of the top-left rear suspension link dropped out of Hill's leading Lotus, the wheel skewed over and after a wild moment he raised his goggles to limp back to the pits. Within a minute the screw was replaced and he rejoined seventh, two laps down.

Clark was cruising round in an untroubled lead, Hulme had left Brabham and Amon once more and then, just ten laps after rejoining, Hill was accelerating out of Woodcote when the Ford V8's throaty bark cut with an abrupt 'Whumpf' and he coasted to a halt at Copse, with it broken internally.

As the third-place battle tore into Woodcote on its seventy-sixth lap Amon flicked the Ferrari's droop-snoot to the right of Brabham after feinting to his left, and he dived ahead right beneath the eyes of his over-joyed pit-crew.

Clark came home to win his fifth British Grand Prix victory by 12 seconds from Hulme who, thanks largely to his employer, finished 4 seconds clear of an exhausted Amon who had fought one of the toughest battles of his life.

Hill's philosophical reaction to his continued misfortune was typical. 'Hard luck Graham' cried a well-wisher in the paddock. 'Yeah, bugger innit' he smiled back.

But for Team Lotus it was a memorable day, and happily nobody could suspect that it was the last time we would see their truly Great Scot.

Results

1 J. Clark (2.99 Lotus-Cosworth – Team Lotus) 1 hr 59 mins 25.6 secs, 117.64 mph; **2** D.C. Hulme (2.99 Brabham-Repco – Brabham Racing Organization) 1 hr 59 mins 38.4 secs; 3 C. Amon (2.99 Ferrari – SEFAC Ferrari) 1 hr 59 mins 42.2 secs; 4 J.A. Brabham (2.99 Brabham-Repco – Brabham Racing Organization) 1 hr 59 mins 47.4 secs; 5 P. Rodriguez (2.99 Cooper-Maserati – Cooper Car Co) 79 laps; 6 J. Surtees (2.99 Honda – Honda Racing) 78 laps; 7 C. Irwin (2.07 BRM – R.H.H. Parnell) 77 laps; 8 D. Hobbs (2.07 BRM – Bernard White Racing) 77 laps; 9 A. Rees (2.99 Cooper-Maserati – Cooper Car Co) 76 laps; **10** G. Ligier (2.99 Brabham-Repco – driver) 76 laps.

FASTEST LAP   Hulme 1 min 27.0 secs, 121.12 mph.

RETIREMENTS   J. Bonnier (2.99 Cooper-Maserati – driver) 0 laps, engine; J. Siffert (2.99 Cooper-Maserati – R.R.C. Walker & J. Durlacher) 10 laps, engine; B.L. McLaren (2.99 Eagle-Weslake – Anglo-American Racers Inc) 14 laps, engine; J.Y. Stewart (2.07 BRM – Owen Racing Organization) 20 laps, transmission; K.J. Rindt (2.99 Cooper-Maserati – Cooper Car Co) 26 laps, gearbox; S. Moser (2.99 Cooper-ATS – Charles Vogele) 29 laps, oil-pressure; D.S. Gurney (2.99 Eagle-Weslake – Anglo-American Racers Inc) 34 laps, fuel feed/clutch; M. Spence (2.99 BRM – Owen/Parnell) 44 laps, ignition; N.G. Hill (2.99 Lotus-Cosworth – Team Lotus) 64 laps, engine; R. Anderson (2.7 Brabham-Climax – driver) 67 laps, engine.

'I didn't see ye Chris . . .': Brabham's mirrorless BT24 leads Amon's Ferrari in their torrid battle for third place, Silverstone '67.

1968 Brands Hatch

July 20, Brands Hatch, 80 laps of 2.65-mile circuit
approximately 212-miles

Jim Clark opened the 1968 season in dominant style by winning the South African Grand Prix on New Year's Day. It was the twenty-fifth World Championship race victory for the Scot, which broke Fangio's long-standing record of twenty-four, but it was to be his last, for in April he died in a piffling Formula 2 race at Hockenheim. Graham Hill picked up a shattered Lotus team, now racing under the red, white and gold colours of their new sponsoring tobacco company, and he gave them two consecutive victories in Spain and Monaco. The new McLaren cars came good in Belgium where Bruce himself scored a lucky win, and in the Dutch race Stewart won in the new Ken Tyrrell-entered French-built Matra with Ford power. The young Belgian, Jacky Ickx, won the French race at Rouen for Ferrari, and as the teams assembled once more at Brands Hatch several had reason to fancy their chances.

Gold Leaf Team Lotus entered two 49Bs for Hill and his new team-mate Jack Oliver, who had learned much of his racing on this very circuit. In addition Rob Walker's team were bolting together a brand-new 49B in the paddock, for Siffert to drive, and it was a miracle they were there at all . . . Earlier in the year Walker had acquired a Lotus 49, but Siffert had crashed it heavily in practice for the Race of Champions here at Brands Hatch. That evening, while the car was being dismantled in Walker's Dorking shop, the place caught fire and *everything* was destroyed. Walker managed to borrow temporary premises from the local Woolworths store, and with his partner Jack Durlacher the team was revived and an ex-Tasman Lotus 49 was rented to keep Siffert racing in the early part of the year.

Brabham and Rindt had new BT26 cars with quad-cam Repco engines which had so far proved fast but fiendishly unreliable, and Moser had one of the 1966 cars entered by Charles Vogele. Ferrari fielded two V12s for Amon and Ickx, Honda Racing their lone V12 for Surtees, and Matra Sports their own V12-engined car for Jean-Pierre Beltoise. Owen entered BRM P126s with new V12 engines for Rodriguez and Attwood, while Parnell ran a semi-works car for Courage. BRM V12 engines also appeared in the works Cooper T86 cars for Vic Elford and Robin Widdows, and in Bonnier's late-'67 McLaren M5A, while Gurney's faltering team ran a lone Eagle V12. Cosworth-Ford V8s powered the papaya-coloured

works McLarens for Bruce himself and Hulme, and the Tyrrell-managed Equipe Matra International arrived with their Matra-Ford hybrid for Stewart, who was forced to drive with a wrist in a plastic cast after cracking the scaphoid bone earlier in the year.

This had been a very wet season, and dull skies and a few spots of rain sent Ickx, Stewart, McLaren, Rindt and Rodriguez scurrying to fit rain tyres while the rest balanced the odds and took dries.

Oliver bucketed away into an immediate lead which lasted three laps before Hill dodged by, and although Oliver ran second quite comfortably his car was leaving an ominous stream of thin blue smoke. Siffert was running equally comfortably in third place, still getting to know his new Walker car, with Amon, Stewart and Surtees in his slipstream. Brabham's engine had failed on the opening lap, Gurney had hardly got moving off the grid when his engine faltered with a fuel pump problem, and Elford had been left on the dummy grid when his V12 engine refused to fire, later joining-in at the tail.

By ten laps Stewart was feeling the strain and began to fall back. As he fell further behind Amon he held up Surtees and although the Honda eventually rushed by it could not close with the leading group.

McLaren was treading warily on his wet-weather tyres, Hulme was feeling ill, Rindt was opposite-locking his wet-tyred car with wild abandon and Rodriguez was matching this performance slide for slide.

Gurney was out on lap 9 with incurable fuel system troubles, Bonnier had stopped for good, Attwood and Courage had their BRMs overheating, and Rodriguez brought in his unmanageable car to change tyres. Another V12 went out as Beltoise's howling Matra broke up internally.

The impressive Lotus procession up front broke on lap 27 as Hill wheeled abruptly off the Bottom Straight around the end of the pits and abandoned with a broken half-shaft which had wiped-out most of the right-rear wheel location. This left a rather startled Oliver leading the British Grand Prix again in his first Formula 1 season, and as his smoke trail had stopped it meant either the overfilling had levelled down or that there was no lubricant left . . .

He was lapping consistently, if not very quickly, at 1:30–1:31, and drawing away from Siffert who was being caught by Amon's Ferrari. Elford's BRM

1968 Grid

5
Amon
(Ferrari 312/0011)
1:29.5

9
Oliver
(Lotus-Cosworth 49B R2)
1:29.4

8
Hill
(Lotus-Cosworth 49B R5)
1:28.9

4
Rindt
(Brabham-Repco BT26/2)
1:29.9

22
Siffert
(Lotus-Cosworth 49B R7)
1:29.7

3
Brabham
(Brabham-Repco BT26/1)
1:30.2

14
Stewart
(Matra-Cosworth MS10–02)
1:30.0

24
Gurney
(Eagle 004)
1:30.0

2
McLaren
(McLaren-Cosworth M7A/3)
1:30.4

7
Surtees
(Honda RA301/F801)
1:30.3

10
Rodriguez
(BRM P133–01)
1:31.6

6
Ickx
(Ferrari 312/0009)
1:31.0

1
Hulme
(McLaren-Cosworth M7A/2)
1:30.4

11
Attwood
(BRM P126–03)
1:31.7

18
Beltoise
(Matra MS11/02)
1:31.6

16
Widdows
(Cooper-BRM T86B F1–1–68)
1:34.0

35
Elford
(Cooper-BRM T86B F1–4–68)
1:33.0

20
Courage
(BRM P126–01)
1:32.3

23
Bonnier
(McLaren-BRM M5A/1)
1:36.8

19
Moser
(Brabham-Repco BT20 F1–2–66)
1:35.4

Non-arrivals: 12 T. Lanfranchi (BRM P261) – 17 Bianchi (Cooper-Alfa Romeo T86) – 21 'Tom Jones' (Cooper-Maserati)

engine hurled a broken con-rod through its block out on the wooded back-stretch, and Widdows' engine began to stammer. Stewart was in nagging pain from his injured wrist, and was wilting with fatigue for the winding Brands Hatch circuit gave little chance for relaxation, physical or mental. Ickx and Hulme began to catch him, for fifth place, and then Surtees' howling fourth-place Honda had its wing-stays succumb to constant flexion and the whole empennage collapsed and eventually the wing itself planed off crazily into the air!

On lap 31 Ickx and Hulme caught Stewart, but the Belgian boy tried too hard on the uphill approach to Hawthorn's and while he was controlling a wild slide Hulme dodged by Stewart and they both shot away down the Portobello Straight. But Ickx caught and passed the Matra-Ford within a lap – he was annoyed with himself.

On lap 37 Amon displaced Siffert for second place, and tore round his next lap at a record 1:30.0 in an effort to break clear. But the determined Swiss, truly the 'greatest' of the late late-brakers , responded with a 1:29.8 on lap 40, 1:29.7 on lap 42 and completing lap 43 the blue and white Walker-Durlacher car was back into second place!

Oliver's afternoon of glory ended abruptly on the very next lap, as his Lotus belched a brief puff of smoke entering South Bank Bend and its final-drive unit collapsed with an horrendous screech and stench of hot metal.

Siffert blared delightedly by, and Rob Walker's famous Scots colours led a Grand Prix for the first time since Moss' performance early-on in the 1961 American race! While the rest of the field were virtually touring round Siffert and Amon raced on for the lead, very evenly matched although the Ferrari's left-rear tyre was virtually bald and the Lotus had a slight edge out of the slower corners.

Late excitement came on lap 54 as Rindt slammed past the pits with bright little flames along the left-side of the gearbox, where drips from a chafed fuel line had ignited. He realised the problem after two laps in which the airstream contained the blaze, then scrambled to a stop where alert fire marshals smothered it.

Siffert raced on with his heart in his mouth and his eyes on his mirrors, but he made no mistake, and the crowd rose vociferously to greet the popular Swiss driver's first-ever Grande Epreuve victory, and the end of a long drought for Rob Walker and his associates.

Over the crest at Paddock Hill in the 1968 race come the three Lotus 49Bs of Jack Oliver (9), Graham Hill (8) and Jo Siffert (22), with Surtees, Stewart and Amon close behind. The high-flying aerofoils were banned before the 1969 race.

Jackie Stewart drove a brave race at Brands Hatch in Ken Tyrrell's Matra. His right wrist was in a cast, the car's steering was heavy, and he finished sixth in a state of virtual collapse.

Results

1 J. Siffert (2.99 Lotus-Cosworth – R.R.C. Walker & J. Durlacher) 2 hrs 1 min 20.3 secs, 104.83 mph; **2** C. Amon (2.99 Ferrari – SEFAC Ferrari) 2 hrs 1 min 24.7 secs; **3** J. Ickx (2.99 Ferrari – SEFAC Ferrari) 79 laps; **4** D.C. Hulme (2.99 McLaren-Cosworth – Bruce McLaren Motor Racing) 79 laps; **5** J. Surtees (2.99 Honda – Honda Racing) 78 laps; **6** J.Y. Stewart (2.99 Matra-Cosworth – Equipe Matra International) 78 laps; **7** B.L. McLaren (2.99 McLaren-Cosworth – McLaren Motor Racing) 77 laps; **8** P. Courage (2.99 BRM-Parnell Racing) 72 laps; Running at finish but too far behind to be classified – S. Moser (2.99 Brabham-Repco – Charles Vogele) 52 laps.

FASTEST LAP Siffert, 1 min 29.7 secs, 106.35 mph.

RETIREMENTS J.A. Brabham (2.99 Brabham-Repco – Brabham Racing Organization) 0 laps, camshaft; J. Bonnier (2.99 McLaren-BRM – Ecurie Bonnier) 7 laps, engine; D.S. Gurney (2.99 Eagle-Weslake – Anglo-American Racers Inc) 8 laps, fuel pump; R. Attwood (2.99 BRM – Owen Racing Organization) 11 laps, radiator; J.P. Beltoise (2.99 Matra – Ecurie Matra Sports) 12 laps, oil-pressure; N.G. Hill (2.99 Lotus-Cosworth – Gold Leaf Team Lotus) 27 laps, universal joint; V. Elford (2.99 Cooper-BRM – Cooper Car Co) 27 laps, engine; R. Widdows (2.99 Cooper-BRM – Cooper Car Co) 36 laps, ignition; J. Oliver (2.99 Lotus-Cosworth – Gold Leaf Team Lotus) 44 laps, gearbox; P. Rodriguez (2.99 BRM – Owen Racing Organisation) 53 laps, timing chain; K.J. Rindt (2.99 Brabham-Cosworth – Brabham Racing Organization) 56 laps, fuel system fire.

1969 Silverstone

July 19, Silverstone, 84 laps of 2.927-mile circuit
approximately 245.87 miles

Jackie Stewart achieved full stature during the 1969 season which saw him approaching Clark's standards of consistent success. But whereas Graham Hill had been Clark's constant shadow, Stewart found his in Jochen Rindt.

Stewart's Tyrrell-prepared Matra-Fords were far more reliable than the Austrian's works Lotuses, and the Scot won in South Africa, Spain, Holland and France to become the first man to arrive for a British Championship round with four first places already to his name. The only failure for the Stewart Matra had come at Monaco, where its rear suspension broke, and Hill had gone by to win that classic an incredible fifth time.

The Silverstone entry was headed by Hill, the ageing World Champion, and Rindt who was now consistently outpacing him in their Gold Leaf Lotus 49Bs. John Miles was to drive one of their new four-wheel drive Mark 63s. Matra International fielded bulbous MS80s for Stewart and Beltoise, with the experimental spaceframe MS84 four-wheel drive car also on hand. McLaren ran their founder and Hulme in modified versions of the 1968 M7s, and their own four-wheel drive M9 was listed for Derek Bell. Jack Brabham had broken an ankle testing on the circuit, so his new driver, Ickx, had a choice of two Ford-powered BT26As. Ferrari entered two V12s for Amon and Rodriguez, but were in one of their regular sad and sorry troughs of misfortune, BRM had a new P139 for Surtees and an older P133 for Oliver, and then came the privateers.

Walker-Durlacher Racing were running their now well-used 49B for Siffert, and Frank Williams fielded his Ford-powered Brabham BT26 for the much-improved Courage. Bonnier was to run his newly-acquired Lotus 49B, but the works required it for their aces so he kindly consented to put some miles on their second four-wheel drive Mark 63! Colin Crabbe's Antique Automobiles team put Elford in a nicely-prepared side-tanked McLaren to complete the entry.

The new four-wheel drive Cosworth car should also have run, with Brian Redman driving, but it was withdrawn by the Ford engine manufacturers due to development problems and – in retrospect – to Keith Duckworth's far-sighted realisation that this wasn't the way to go . . .

Stewart crashed heavily at Woodcote during final practice when £100 awards were being made for the fastest lap at each half-hour during the two-hour period. He had taken the first £100 in 1:21.1, and then the second award at 1:20.6 which gave him pole position. Rindt replied with 1:21.4 and while trying to better this time for a third £100, the Scot kicked-up a piece of broken kerb with a front wheel, it slammed into his right rear tyre and caused a massive blow-out which spun the bright-blue MS80 into the earth bank opposite the race control building. Stewart skipped out unhurt, to take over Beltoise' MS80 in which he hastily got down to 1:21.2 for the race. Meanwhile Rindt took the final £100 award and pole position – in the quicker Matra's absence – at 1:20.8 in his Lotus 49B.

Raceday was warm but cloudy as a huge crowd packed into the historic circuit, although the organizers seemed to be mindful of their tax returns as they quoted '100,000' rather than the larger figures of previous years. Hill's engine broke while it was being warmed-up and the weary Lotus mechanics, who had been plagued by troubles with all their cars, set about changing it in less than three hours.

Rindt just beat Stewart into Copse and from that point on this pair of 'superstars' put on a spectacular display of flat-out Grand Prix racing, both cars torturing their broad shallow-treaded tyres through the turns as they achieved terrific yaw angles.

Down Hangar Straight on lap 1 it was Rindt leading from Stewart and Surtees who had made a terrific start in the new BRM, but as this trio braked into Stowe the Bourne car's nose collapsed onto the roadway and Surtees staggered to a crawl with a broken front wishbone.

Rindt led Stewart by the tiniest of margins for 6 laps, and then the Matra went through under braking into Stowe. This battle left Hulme floundering third, but performance is relative and he was ahead of McLaren, Rodriguez, Amon, Courage, Ickx (recovering ground after a bad start), Hill and Siffert. At the tail of the field Bell spun at Becketts and then retired the four-wheel drive McLaren from its only race appearance when a rear upright broke in Abbey Curve. Bonnier's Lotus 63 blew-up, and Ickx sliced his way from eighth to sixth between Amon and Rodriguez in the two Ferraris.

Beltoise was learning to drive the Matra MS84, and was trundling round disgustedly, as his team-

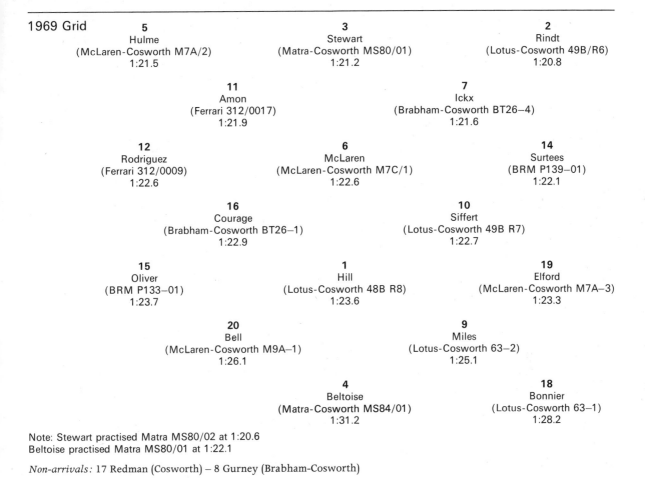

1969 Grid

5 Hulme (McLaren-Cosworth M7A/2) 1:21.5	**3** Stewart (Matra-Cosworth MS80/01) 1:21.2	**2** Rindt (Lotus-Cosworth 49B/R6) 1:20.8

11
Amon
(Ferrari 312/0017)
1:21.9

7
Ickx
(Brabham-Cosworth BT26–4)
1:21.6

12
Rodriguez
(Ferrari 312/0009)
1:22.6

6
McLaren
(McLaren-Cosworth M7C/1)
1:22.6

14
Surtees
(BRM P139–01)
1:22.1

16
Courage
(Brabham-Cosworth BT26–1)
1:22.9

10
Siffert
(Lotus-Cosworth 49B R7)
1:22.7

15
Oliver
(BRM P133–01)
1:23.7

1
Hill
(Lotus-Cosworth 48B R8)
1:23.6

19
Elford
(McLaren-Cosworth M7A–3)
1:23.3

20
Bell
(McLaren-Cosworth M9A–1)
1:26.1

9
Miles
(Lotus-Cosworth 63–2)
1:25.1

4
Beltoise
(Matra-Cosworth MS84/01)
1:31.2

18
Bonnier
(Lotus-Cosworth 63–1)
1:28.2

Note: Stewart practised Matra MS80/02 at 1:20.6
Beltoise practised Matra MS80/01 at 1:22.1

Non-arrivals: 17 Redman (Cosworth) – 8 Gurney (Brabham-Cosworth)

leader with Rindt in close touch rushed up behind him on the road. They caught him on lap 16, and in the confusion Stewart tried to go one side, Rindt the other, and it was the Austrian who emerged in the lead. Hulme was 23 seconds behind and McLaren 7 seconds behind him was being harried by Ickx's green-and-yellow Brabham. This battle for fourth place closed on Hulme, and on lap 21 both cars rushed by. Hulme bustled into his pit five laps later with an 'ignition fault', and retired with a broken camshaft.

With Hulme gone, Courage's dark-blue Brabham lay fifth, but only briefly, from Hill, Siffert, Amon and Rodriguez. On lap 28 Ickx barged past McLaren for third place but nobody could challenge Rindt and Stewart who were continuing a desperate high-speed battle of their own. When they caught up with the fifth-place tussle there was a hectic log-jam of cars, and Rindt got the best of the traffic to draw out 1½ seconds on his prime pursuer.

At forty-five laps the fifth-place stream broke-up as Amon's gearbox failed, and then Siffert lost fourth

gear, Rodriguez caught him in the general battle but on lap 61 his surviving Ferrari's engine failed and Siffert continued alone.

As the race ran into its closing stages Stewart began to press Rindt harder. Hill was getting the best of the fifth-place duel for although his Lotus' wings had been oddly adjusted and it handled indifferently, Courage had thumped a marker and torn one of his Brabham's nose fins half off. This was sufficient to upset its handling very considerably.

On lap 62 Stewart howled through Woodcote Corner in the lead, and as spectators leapt to their feet in the packed grandstands, Rindt sawed by and something was obviously wrong with the Lotus. One of the rear wing end-plates had come loose, and was fouling a rear tyre, and he swirled up onto the pit ramp where mechanics hastily wrenched the plate right off and he blared back into the race, some 34 seconds behind the Matra. Stewart held the gap constant until his engine began to stammer on left-handers because one of the fuel system's three Bendix pumps had failed. Rindt briefly gained a

Oversteer: Rindt and Stewart opposite-lock their cars out of Beckett's Corner during their ten-tenths battle for the 1969 Grand Prix at Silverstone.

second or so per lap, but then lap 76 saw Rindt's V8 cutting-out at Stowe as its pumps refused to scavenge the last few gallons from the tanks. Past the pits it cut completely, then banged back to life again, and somehow Rindt completed that lap, shot into the pits for a few gallons of fuel, and resumed morosely in fourth place. Courage dived by to lead Rindt round laps 81 and 82 but in response to urgent pit signals, Rindt recovered himself and slashed ahead again for the finish.

Hill and Siffert both made last-minute fuel stops with their Lotuses, and as Stewart howled across the line to score a well-deserved first victory in the British Grand Prix, Ickx's lapped Brabham died at Woodcote and *coasted* past the flag for second place. It had been a long and extremely fast motor race, Stewart's average being over 127 mph, and the pace had told on everyone at the finish, save Stewart and the Ken Tyrrell team's Matra-Ford.

Results

1 J.Y. Stewart (2.99 Matra-Cosworth – Matra International) 1 hr 55 mins 55.6 secs, 127.25 mph; 2 J. Ickx (2.99 Brabham-Cosworth – Motor Racing Developments) 83 laps; 3 B.L. McLaren (2.99 McLaren-Cosworth – Bruce McLaren Racing) 83 laps; 4 K.J. Rindt (2.99 Lotus-Cosworth – GLTL) 83 laps; 5 P. Courage (2.99 Brabham-Ford – Frank Williams Racing) 83 laps; 6 V. Elford (2.99 McLaren-Cosworth – Antique Automobiles) 82 laps; 7 N.G. Hill (2.99 Lotus-Cosworth – GLTL) 82 laps; 8 J. Siffert (2.99 Lotus-Cosworth – R.R.C. Walker & J.S. Durlacher) 81 laps; 9 J.P. Beltoise (2.99 Matra-Cosworth – Matra International) 78 laps; 10 J. Miles (2.99 Lotus-Cosworth – GLTL) 75 laps.

FASTEST LAP   Stewart 1 min 21.3 secs, 129.61 mph.

RETIREMENTS   J. Surtees (2.99 BRM – Owen Racing Organization) 1 lap, collapsed front suspension; D. Bell (2.99 McLaren-Cosworth – Bruce McLaren Racing) 5 laps, suspension; J. Bonnier (2.99 Lotus-Cosworth – Ecurie Bonnier/GLTL) 6 laps, engine; J. Oliver (2.99 BRM – Owen Racing Organization) 20 laps, transmission; D.C. Hulme (2.99 McLaren-Cosworth – Bruce McLaren Racing) 27 laps, ignition; C. Amon (2.99 Ferrari – SEFAC Ferrari) 45 laps, gearbox; P. Rodriguez (2.99 Ferrari – SEFAC Ferrari) 61 laps, engine.

1970 Brands Hatch

July 18, Brands Hatch, 80 laps of 2.65-mile circuit
approximately 212 miles

The RAC's normally highly-successful organization of the British Grand Prix began its sorry slide into controversy and muddle in 1970. The season started with the club being patted on the back for agreeing to give every entry a start, whereas strict field limits and qualifying were standard practice at most Championship rounds.

A large entry was attracted, and the race looked set to be a classic battle between the Cosworth-Ford V8 brigade and the new generation of increasingly competitive 12-cylinder cars from Ferrari, Matra-Simca and BRM.

Brabham had scored an immensely popular win in the opening Championship round, in South Africa, and Stewart had been a lucky winner of the Spanish race in his new Tyrrell-entered March. Brabham had lost Monaco on the last corner to Rindt in an obsolete Lotus, and then the Austrian used the revolutionary new Lotus 72 to score two consecutive victories in Holland and France. In Belgium meanwhile, Rodriguez had scored a runaway win for BRM. It was the first non-Ford Grand Prix victory since Ickx's French win in 1968.

But this upsurge in competition had been marred by two major tragedies, for Bruce McLaren had been killed at Goodwood while testing a Can-Am sports car, and Piers Courage had died in Williams' new De Tomaso during the Dutch Grand Prix.

Lotus ran two wedge-shaped, torsion-bar suspended Mark 72s at Brands, for Rindt and Miles, and added their standby 49C for the fast-rising Brazilian star, Emerson Fittipaldi. This was to be his Formula 1 debut, and he had soared into this works drive from Formula Ford within a year. Brabham had his new monocoque-chassised BT33 for himself, and a similar car sponsored by the German magazine *Auto Motor und Sport* for the former Porsche sports car ace Rolf Stommelen. A third car was mentioned for Tim Schenken, but money was too short. McLaren were continuing bravely after their grievous loss, and they entered four cars. Hulme was driving despite unhealed burns on his hands sustained during practice at Indianapolis, and in McLaren's place was Gurney, both using the latest M14 cars. Peter Gethin should have driven an older M7 but a shortage of Ford engines kept him out. The fourth McLaren was another M7 modified to carry an Alfa Romeo V8 sports car engine, to be driven by Andrea de Adamich.

March 701s appeared in the works flame-red STP-backed colours for Amon and Siffert, while the American additive company ran their own sister car for Indianapolis driver Mario Andretti. Tyrrell's two dark-blue cars were to be driven by Stewart and his new French team-mate, Francois Cevert, while a sixth 701 was run by Crabbe's Antique Automobiles outfit for the works' new find, Ronnie Peterson.

Surtees was giving his own marque its Formula 1 debut with the neatly-made, all-new TS7, but an engine shortage made him scratch an entry for Trevor Taylor in the McLaren M7C which he had used in the early races of the year. Williams ran his early De Tomaso for Brian Redman, and private Lotus 49s came from the Walker team for Graham Hill (the 1968 car converted to C-specification), and from American enthusiast Pete Lovely – a normal B-Type. Hill was still walking only with difficulty after his United States Grand Prix crash late the previous year, but he had already finished in the points at Kyalami and in Spain.

Finally, among the Cosworth-Ford users, Bonnier made a mysterious entry for a McLaren which the works didn't know he had – and which never appeared – and Moser's Bellasi special was withdrawn after an apparent disagreement with the organisers over starting money. It was reported that the RAC had now decided to pay only the first twenty qualifiers, which was in contravention of the Geneva Agreement between race organizers and entrants. The problem was ironed-out but Moser stayed away from the only race of the year which could guarantee him a start.

The 12-cylinder entry was headed by Ferrari, with two of their latest flat-12 312Bs for Ickx and Swiss newcomer Clay Regazzoni. Matra had been acquired by the Simca subsidiary of America's Chrysler Corporation, and their wailing V12 was now showing true promise in new MS120 chassis. Beltoise was joined in the French team by Henri Pescarolo. BRM completed the field with three new P153 cars for Oliver, Rodriguez and their Canadian paying customer, George Eaton.

Practice saw two defections. The De Tomaso broke a hub-shaft in an apparent design failure which persuaded Williams to withdraw. Stommelen crashed heavily at Clearways in his Brabham, damaging it too badly to stand a chance of starting the race.

Rindt took pole position with a 1:24.8 lap on Thursday, knocking a second off Brabham's Race of Champion's record set in March. On Friday the Australian equalled Rindt's time, and Ickx completed the front row, only 0.3 seconds lower. The first five cars were under the lap record, but all the Marches were in terrible handling difficulty. Stewart had won the non-Championship race in March with his car, but only when Brabham made a last-minute stop, and now he was again keeping his car in touch only by sheer heroics.

Raceday was bright and sunny for a change, and official crowd figures claimed 'a record 57,500' which put new light on earlier estimates . . . A small fuel leak on Cevert's March ignited on the way down to the pit area, but it was quickly smothered and repaired, while poor De Adamich had one of his car's brimming fuel bags split, and it could not be replaced in time for him to start. Brabham was worried about his fuel consumption and had his tanks topped-up after the warming-up lap, while Peterson complained of a 'funny-feeling' clutch pedal.

Ickx and Brabham raced away into Paddock wheel-to-wheel, and the Ferrari dived through on the grass verge to lead out of Druids and away round that first lap, from the turquoise-and-gold Brabham, Rindt, Oliver, Hulme, Regazzoni, Stewart, Beltoise, Miles and the rest. Hill was right in the pack from a scintillating back-row start.

The leading trio battled away from Oliver, who in turn was clear of Hulme. Rodriguez shuddered into the BRM pit on lap 5 complaining of a rear-end vibration, and both rear wheels were changed. Four laps later he was in again, but nothing untoward could be found so he rejoined, way behind.

Ickx looked like running away with the race, but as he flashed into Paddock Bend for the seventh time the Ferrari decelerated abruptly with its differential breaking-up. Simultaneously Rindt and Brabham arrived at the crest of the hill with the Lotus' wedge nose forcing Brabham wide, and in the dip this startled duo flashed by the Ferrari for the lead. Rindt led down from Druids, and the race was over for the next sixty-one laps as the Austrian couldn't pull clear of the Australian, and Brabham was content to follow, watch, and wait. It was the 1964 Hill/Clark battle all over again, and was not much to look at, though a fine demonstration of consistent, concentrated control.

Eaton's BRM lost its oil pressure and retired, while the leading pair left the lonely Oliver. Hulme was being caught by a battling group consisting of Regazzoni, Stewart and Beltoise, and it wasn't until lap 13 that Stewart barged past the Ferrari at Druids with two wheels over the inside kerb. Beltoise followed him through at South Bank, but the Swiss hung on

determinedly. Pescarolo passed Miles for eighth place as the number two Lotus stopped with misfiring, and after a few more miles retired with a damaged camshaft. Further back, Siffert, Hill, Gurney, Cevert, Amon and Surtees were involved in torrid battles, passing and repassing each other all round the circuit.

At quarter-distance the fourth-placed battle had caught Hulme, and Andretti was eighth with one of the March's front fins torn off. Pescarolo had stopped to change a punctured tyre, and the next two laps saw both Siffert and Andretti abandon as brackets used to raise their March's roll-centre at the rear proved too weak, and broke. Beltoise's Matra left the fourth-place battle with a puncture, a new wheel was badly fitted, and he pulled in again on the next lap. He felt ill with a head-cold, had now lost too much time, so gave up on the spot.

Peterson was running seventh now, benefiting from retirements and having led both works Marches throughout practice and the race, while lap 32 saw Regazzoni in front of Stewart and challenging Hulme hard. The Tyrrell March was handling dangerously as the circuit became slippery with oil and rubber, and fell away in sixth place.

Hill stole Peterson's place as the yellow March slowed with an inoperative clutch (the fluid had leaked away) and later made a pit stop which revived it for just three laps. Surtees was now making progress and he displaced Hill from seventh, going well in his brand-new car. The red TS7 was handling beautifully on Brands' now slick surface, and was catching Stewart's March while holding-off the leaders who were trying to lap it. Then Surtees abandoned abruptly as his oil pressure disappeared and the Ford engine rattled its bearings.

Stewart stopped to change a punctured tyre, fluid dripping from a melting clutch-line ignited on the exhaust and that put the blue March out. Oliver's lonely drive in third place ended at the bottom of Paddock Hill when the BRM's engine failed, leaving Rindt still leading Brabham, Hulme and Regazzoni duelling for third, Hill and Amon for fifth. Fittipaldi was making consistent progress from the back despite a broken exhaust, and was having a minor battle with Cevert. Rodriguez, way behind, understeered into the bank at Druids.

With eleven laps to go Brabham had the measure of Rindt, his car was more secure on the slick surface, and he shot by out of South Bank Bend. His next lap at 1:25.9 dropped the Lotus, and in four laps he

Two wheels on the grass at Druid's Hairpin as Ickx tries to slip his Ferrari inside Jack Brabham's new BT33 at the start of the 1970 race at Brands Hatch. Rindt, Oliver and Hulme look on.

1970 Grid

3
Ickx
(Ferrari 312B/003)
1:25.1

17
Brabham
(Brabham-Ford BT33/2)
1:24.8

5
Rindt
(Lotus-Cosworth 72C/2)
1:24.8

9
Hulme
(McLaren-Cosworth M14D/1)
1:25.6

23
Oliver
(BRM P153–04)
1:25.6

1
Stewart
(March-Cosworth 701/4)
1:26.0

6
Miles
(Lotus-Cosworth 72B/1)
1:25.9

4
Regazzoni
(Ferrari 312B/002)
1:25.8

7
Beltoise
(Matra-Simca MS120/03)
1:26.5

26
Andretti
(March-Cosworth 701/3)
1:26.2

27
Peterson
(March-Cosworth 701/8)
1:26.8

8
Pescarolo
(Matra-Simca MS120/01)
1:26.7

10
Gurney
(McLaren-Cosworth M14A/1)
1:26.6

22
Rodriguez
(BRM P153–05)
1:26.9

2
Cevert
(March-Cosworth 701/7)
1:26.8

11
De Adamich*
(McLaren-Alfa Romeo M7D/1)
1:27.1

16
Amon
(March-Cosworth 701/1)
1:27.0

24
Eaton
(BRM P153–03)
1:26.9

15
Siffert
(March-Cosworth 701/5)
1:28.0

20
Surtees
(Surtees-Cosworth TS7/001)
1:27.7

29
Lovely
(Lotus-Cosworth 49B R11)
1:30.3

14
Hill
(Lotus-Cosworth 49C R7)
1:28.4

28
Fittipaldi
(Lotus-Cosworth 49C R10)
1:28.1

*Non-starter due to fuel tank leak

Non-arrivals: 12 Gethin (McLaren-Cosworth) – 19 Schenken (Brabham-Cosworth) – 21 T. Taylor (McLaren-Cosworth) –
30 Bonnier ('McLaren') – 31 Moser (Bellasi-Cosworth)
Non-starter: 25 Redman (De Tomaso-Cosworth)

drew an incredible 10 seconds ahead. Amon won his battle with Hill for fifth place as the Lotus' clutch pedal broke loose, while Regazzoni lost touch with Hulme in a sideways moment at Druids while trying to barge past.

Brabham flashed neatly round those last few laps, Rindt had settled for second, and the forty-six-year-old veteran blared into his last lap 14 seconds in the lead of his last British Grand Prix. Eyes turned to the bridge at Clearways from which he would pop to take the flag, but then he was overdue . . . and Rindt blasted into view first with the Brabham creeping along behind!

The astonished Austrian took the flag to win in a sensational repeat of his last-corner victory over Brabham at Monaco, and Jack coasted across the line second having run out of fuel at Stirling's Bend. Hulme was third, exhausted and in agony from his burned hands, 0.2 seconds ahead of Regazzoni. Amon was fifth and Hill a fine sixth for a man with his physical handicap, an obsolete car, and just a half-inch of oil left in its dry-sump tank.

Rindt couldn't believe his luck as he took his place on the victory float, while a black-faced Brabham slouched dejectly in the pits with his speechless team. But the 1970 British Grand Prix had still more sensation to come . . . 90 minutes after the finish, Rindt was disqualified!

Scrutineer Cecil Mitchell found that the Lotus' rear wing struts were bent, and he decided that with the struts straight the upper edge of the wing would be $1\frac{1}{2}$ cms above the maximum legal height. Had the car started the race with bent struts; had they been bent by air-pressure during the race, or had someone bent them deliberately after the finish to render the wing legal?

Since the standard struts were angled anyway it would have made little real difference to the wing, and some farcical measuring and re-measuring went on in the unevenly-surfaced scrutineering bay. The wing was dismantled and rebuilt, measurements were averaged and found to be correct. Then Mitchell decided the wing had been re-assembled incorrectly and so it was torn down and rebuilt once more.

All this time the World's news-wires were singing with retractions of the British Grand Prix result, while Chapman, Rindt and Lotus team manager Peter Warr were closeted with the stewards. Brabham correctly remained aloof and withdrawn from all this hoo-haa, and after $3\frac{1}{2}$-hours haggling, the results were confirmed, with Rindt the winner.

Unfortunately, something of a pattern was being set for the future . . .

Results

1 K.J. Rindt (2.99 Lotus-Cosworth – GLTL) 1 hr 57 mins 2.0 secs, 108.69 mph; 2 J.A. Brabham (2.99 Brabham-Cosworth – Motor Racing Developments) 1 hr 57 mins 34.9 secs; 3 D.C. Hulme (2.99 McLaren-Cosworth – Bruce McLaren Racing) 1 hr 57 mins 56.4 secs; 4 G. Regazzoni (2.99 Ferrari – SEFAC Ferrari) 1 hr 57 mins 56.8 secs; 5 C. Amon (2.99 March-Cosworth – March Engineering) 79 laps; 6 N.G. Hill (2.99 Lotus-Cosworth – R.R.C. Walker Racing with Brooke-Bond Oxo) 79 laps; 7 F. Cevert (2.99 March-Cosworth – Elf-Tyrrell) 79 laps; 8 E. Fittipaldi (2.99 Lotus-Cosworth – GLTL) 78 laps; 9 R. Peterson (2.99 March-Cosworth – Antique Automobiles) 72 laps; 10 P. Lovely (2.99 Lotus-Cosworth – Pete Lovely Volkswagen Inc) 69 laps.

FASTEST LAP   Brabham 1 min 25.9 secs, 111.06 mph

RETIREMENTS   J. Ickx (2.99 Ferrari – SEFAC Ferrari) 7 laps, differential; G. Eaton (2.99 BRM – Yardley-BRM) 11 laps, oil-pressure; J. Miles (2.99 Lotus-Cosworth – GLTL) 16 laps, engine; J. Siffert (2.99 March-Cosworth – March Engineering) 20 laps, suspension bracket; M. Andretti (2.99 March-Cosworth – STP) 22 laps, suspension bracket; J.P. Beltoise (2.99 Matra-Simca – Equipe Matra) 25 laps, wheel; H. Pescarolo (2.99 Matra-Simca – Equipe Matra) 24 laps, accident; J. Surtees (2.99 Surtees-Cosworth – Team Surtees) 52 laps, oil-pressure; J.Y. Stewart (2.99 March-Cosworth – ELF-Tyrrell) 53 laps, clutch line; J. Oliver (2.99 BRM – Yardley-BRM) 55 laps, engine; P. Rodriguez (2.99 BRM – Yardley-BRM) 59 laps, accident; D.S. Gurney (2.99 McLaren-Cosworth – Bruce McLaren Racing) 61 laps, overheating.

Not a man to be out-braked, Clay Regazzoni in his first F1 season slams the door at Druid's on Stewart's largely unmanageable Tyrrell-entered March.

1971 Silverstone

July 17, Silverstone, 68 laps of 2.927-mile circuit
approximately 199 miles

Money has always been a vital factor in all forms of motor sport but during the early 'seventies it became *the* over-riding factor in shaping the face of Grand Prix racing. By 1971 the British Grand Prix represented such a huge annual investment that the RAC, its supporting clubs and their normal sponsors could not support the pressures being exerted by the increasingly-powerful Formula 1 Constructors' Association and its interests.

At that time the International Wool Secretariat was searching for a suitable prestige event with which to promote its 'Woolmark' image, and they joined forces with *The Daily Express* (which had its usual job of priming the public) and the RAC in staging the Woolmark British Grand Prix. Evidence of their interest was spread all over Silverstone, on marshals' clothing, hoardings, dolly girls, car stickers . . . most things which moved, and everything which didn't. Despite their support the RAC could only afford twenty-five starters, and the race was round six of a Championship season which had seen Andretti and Ickx win two Grands Prix for Ferrari, and Stewart slaying the 12-cylinder cars with his brand-new Tyrrell-Ford in Spain, Monaco and France. In fact at the French circuit at Paul Ricard, Stewart was so fast along the main straight that Ferrari and Matra supporters began talking darkly of 3.2-litre Cosworth engines, and of alcohol-laced fuels. In fact the French scrutineers there tapped a sample of the Tyrrell's ELF fuel at the pressure gauge, and had to admit it was a true brew, just like everybody else's . . .

Tyrrell had two of their new cars, for Stewart and Cevart. McLaren ran two of their latest M19s for Hulme and Gethin, and added an older M14 to give Oliver another chance in Formula 1 (he had been dropped by the works teams at the end of 1970). Since Jack Brabham's retirement his partner Ron Tauranac had continued their Motor Racing Developments team, and he was running a new BT34 for Hill and an older BT33 for Schenken. Lotus still had not fully recovered from the death of Rindt on the eve of almost certainly clinching his World title at Monza the previous September, but they had a Mark 72 for their new number one, Fittipaldi, and the experimental four-wheel drive turbine-powered 56B for his Swedish team-mate, Reine Wisell. An older 72 had been sold to South African driver Dave Charlton, and he was present with the car in his sponsoring Lucky

Strike tobacco company's colours. March had three of their curious-looking 711s with pylon-mounted elliptical front wings for Peterson, 'Nanni' Galli and De Adamich (with an Alfa Romeo engine), while customer cars were run by Williams for Pescarolo and by the stock-broker consortium of Clarke-Mordaunt-Guthrie for former F3 and F2 charger Mike Beuttler. Rob Walker with the Brooke-Bond-Oxo foods combine was supporting Surtees in his own new TS9, while sister cars (all works-prepared) were to be driven by Derek Bell and Stommelen, the first backed by the Hago wire company, and the latter by his German magazine and the Eifelland caravan concern.

The proper Grand Prix racing teams of Ferrari SpA SEFAC, British Racing Motors and Equipe Matra faced this phalanx of Ford-powered kit cars. Ickx and Regazzoni were in the latest 312B2s for the Italian team, and Siffert was alone in a front-line BRM P160 following the tragic death of Rodriguez in a piffling little German sports car race the previous weekend. New Zealander Howden Ganley drove what was really a third-string BRM P153, while Matra-Simca's raucous MS 120Bs were being handled this season by Amon and Beltoise.

After racing on the brightly-shining, brand-new facility at Ricard the return to Silverstone's windy airfield was a regression to stark reality although the weather was kind and the packed hospitality tents behind the crowded Formula 1 paddock gave a garden-party atmosphere.

Grand Prix racing at this period was becoming frantically competitive, and Regazzoni took pole on the same time as Stewart, with Siffert completing the front-row, only 0.1 seconds slower. Just two fleeting seconds covered the first fourteen cars!

Enormous queues led to Silverstone from all parts of Northamptonshire and Buckinghamshire on race-morning, as the usual huge crowd packed into the circuit. Just 50 minutes before the Grand Prix was due to start, Tyrrell's mechanics found that the oil scavenge pump on Stewart's engine was not working because a torque-setting screw had dropped out. With great difficulty this was replaced, and the torque set by guesswork before the car blared away on its warming-up lap. Charlton finished his preliminary lap with oil smoke belching from his engine.

As the field rolled forward from the dummy grid,

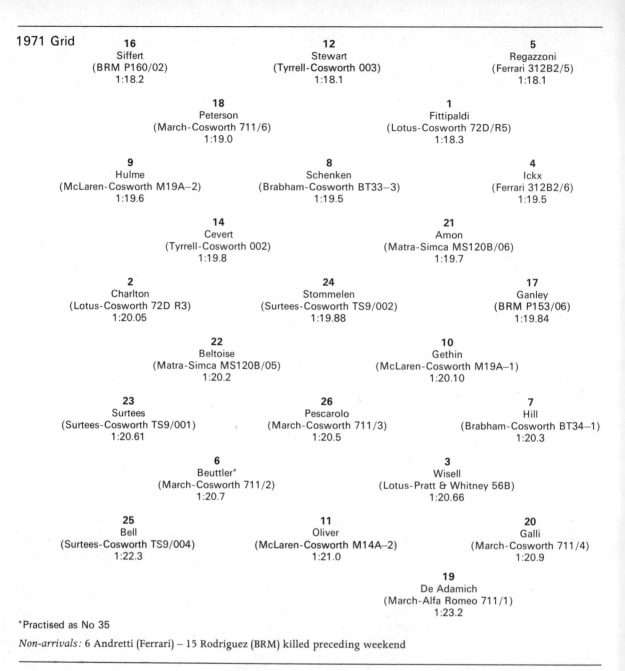

1971 Grid

16
Siffert
(BRM P160/02)
1:18.2

12
Stewart
(Tyrrell-Cosworth 003)
1:18.1

5
Regazzoni
(Ferrari 312B2/5)
1:18.1

18
Peterson
(March-Cosworth 711/6)
1:19.0

1
Fittipaldi
(Lotus-Cosworth 72D/R5)
1:18.3

9
Hulme
(McLaren-Cosworth M19A—2)
1:19.6

8
Schenken
(Brabham-Cosworth BT33—3)
1:19.5

4
Ickx
(Ferrari 312B2/6)
1:19.5

14
Cevert
(Tyrrell-Cosworth 002)
1:19.8

21
Amon
(Matra-Simca MS120B/06)
1:19.7

2
Charlton
(Lotus-Cosworth 72D R3)
1:20.05

24
Stommelen
(Surtees-Cosworth TS9/002)
1:19.88

17
Ganley
(BRM P153/06)
1:19.84

22
Beltoise
(Matra-Simca MS120B/05)
1:20.2

10
Gethin
(McLaren-Cosworth M19A—1)
1:20.10

23
Surtees
(Surtees-Cosworth TS9/001)
1:20.61

26
Pescarolo
(March-Cosworth 711/3)
1:20.5

7
Hill
(Brabham-Cosworth BT34—1)
1:20.3

6
Beuttler*
(March-Cosworth 711/2)
1:20.7

3
Wisell
(Lotus-Pratt & Whitney 56B)
1:20.66

25
Bell
(Surtees-Cosworth TS9/004)
1:22.3

11
Oliver
(McLaren-Cosworth M14A—2)
1:21.0

20
Galli
(March-Cosworth 711/4)
1:20.9

19
De Adamich
(March-Alfa Romeo 711/1)
1:23.2

*Practised as No 35

Non-arrivals: 6 Andretti (Ferrari) – 15 Rodriguez (BRM) killed preceding weekend

---

the RAC's Dean Delamont faltered with the Union Jack as he noticed excessive creeping. Regazzoni rolled forward, dabbed the brakes and stopped, while on the penultimate row Oliver actually started, stopped, was bunted from behind and smashed into the back of Hill's Brabham, which put them both out before the race had begun! Tauranac later protested Oliver's start, and the luckless McLaren driver was reprimanded and fined £50.

As this drama was enacted Delamont dropped the flag properly, Regazzoni blasted off into an imme-

diate lead, with Ickx on his tail from row three, then Stewart, Siffert, Schenken, Peterson and Hulme.

The first four blasted away on their own, and on lap 2 Stewart led Siffert's white BRM past Ickx and two laps later the Scot outbraked Regazzoni into Stowe. Next time round Siffert slipped into second place at Copse, and although he howled away from the two Ferraris he could not hold Stewart who simply bulleted away into an increasing lead.

Hulme could not maintain the pace in seventh place, and Fittipaldi passed him in the Lotus and

then went after Schenken and Peterson, picking-off the Brabham on lap 13 and closing with the blue-helmeted Swede in his red March.

At that stage Stewart was 4 seconds clear of Siffert, but the BRM's Firestone tyres induced severe vibration through the corners, his wing adjustment slipped, and the big-hearted Swiss was being forced to ease his pace. He lost 2 seconds in a lap to Stewart, and on the seventeenth time round Regazzoni retook second place, 14 seconds behind the meteoric Tyrrell.

Charlton had just missed Hill's crippled Brabham as he puffed into the pits to retire ending the first lap, and De Adamich and Gethin made stops on lap 19, one with throttle problems on the Alfa engine, and the other to complain of wild oversteer in his McLaren. Cevert stopped with a broken fuel pressure gauge soaking him in petrol, and lost two laps, Beuttler went out with fluctuating oil pressure, and Bell abandoned with a sheared radius rod bracket. On lap 32 Hulme abandoned with engine failure, and three laps later Amon was out when a valve dropped, wrecking his expensive French V12. Stommelen's visor had been smashed by a stone thrown-up from Pescarolo's back wheels, Gethin lost more time with a puncture on lap 36, and while Stewart rushed round in a Clark-like exhibition of sheer virtuosity, interest centred on the fourth-place battle between Ickx,

The majestic sweep of Woodcote Corner early on in the 1971 Grand Prix with the twin Ferraris of Regazzoni and Ickx about to be caught by Stewart's wide-nosed Tyrrell and Siffert's BRM. Schenken's Brabham and Peterson's March are next up.

Peterson, Fittipaldi (who had started eleventh) and Schenken.

The Swede and the Brazilian took it in turns to attack Ickx, and then moved up a place as on lap 38 he headed for the pits with a chunking left-front tyre. His flat-12 had been cutting out in corners, and while the punctured tyre was hastily changed, Ickx discussed his problems with Forghieri and then shrieked back into the race, down in thirteenth place. He fought his way back up to ninth on lap 51, when he bounded up the pit ramp and straight into the paddock with no oil pressure and the engine tightening-up.

Siffert's engine began to misfire just as Regazzoni eased back and the BRM had started to close the gap. Tyre vibration had sheared the ignition coil bracket behind his head, and after a stop to fix it, Siffert rejoined way down the field. Regazzoni's race ended when he thumped into the pits on lap 48 with his left-front Firestone tyre breaking up, and as the engine was restarted there was no oil pressure so the second Ferrari went out.

This very fast race was taking its toll, and Stewart was left with a 38 seconds lead over Peterson, Schenken with a sticky gearbox and Fittipaldi whose Lotus was beginning to jump out of fourth gear. Ganley should have inherited fifth place after a good drive in his old BRM, but as Regazzoni retired so the New Zealander skewed into the pits with a puncture. While the wheel was being changed Pescarolo, Stommelen and Surtees howled by.

With only five laps to run Schenken's gearbox broke up at Abbey Curve, and as he began the long walk home, Fittipaldi blared by as the last runner on the same lap with Stewart.

So the Scot hammered out of Woodcote to his second British Grand Prix victory, by over half-a-minute. Pescarolo was being pressed hard by Stommelen for fourth place, but the Frenchman held it to the line by just 0.5 seconds.

Stewart's average was a record-breaking 130.48 mph, and it was the shortest British Grand Prix thus far, having lasted just $1\frac{1}{2}$ minutes longer than the standard football match. It was really a rather sad – though still exciting – shadow of the great races which Silverstone had seen, particularly that classic of exactly twenty-years before, but there was no diminishing Stewart's performance in the Tyrrell. In fact the scrutineers paid his team the ultimate accolade, by being present when the engine was stripped to check its capacity! It *was* 2993 cc and legal.

Unchallengeable: J.Y. Stewart in the Elf-Tyrrell 003 on his way to scoring one of his record Grande Epreuve victories in this car. After the Silverstone win the scrutineers paid Tyrrell the ultimate accolade – they checked 003's engine capacity!

Results

1 J.Y. Stewart (2.99 Tyrrell-Cosworth – ELF-Team Tyrrell) 1 hr 31 mins 31.5 secs, 130.48 mph; 2 R. Peterson (2.99 March-Cosworth – STP March) 1 hr 32 mins 7.6 secs; 3 E. Fittipaldi (2.99 Lotus-Cosworth – GLTL) 1 hr 32 mins 22.0 secs; 4 H. Pescarolo (2.99 March-Cosworth – Frank Williams Racing Cars) 67 laps; 5 R. Stommelen (2.99 Surtees-Cosworth – AMS Eifelland-Team Surtees) 67 laps; 6 J. Surtees (2.99 Surtees-Cosworth – Brooke Bond Oxo-Rob Walker) 67 laps; 7 J.P. Beltoise (2.99 Matra-Simca – Equipe Matra) 66 laps; 8 H. Ganley (2.99 BRM – Yardley-BRM) 66 laps; 9 J. Siffert (2.99 BRM – Yardley-BRM) 66 laps; 10 F. Cevert (2.99 Tyrrell-Cosworth – ELF-Team Tyrrell) 65 laps; 11 G. Galli (2.99 March-Cosworth – STP March) 65 laps; 12 T. Schenken (2.99 Brabham-Cosworth – Motor Racing Developments) 63 laps*.
*Retired, but covered sufficient distance to be classified. R. Wisell ('3.0' Lotus-Pratt & Whitney – GLTL) 57 laps and A. De Adamich (2.99 March-Alfa Romeo – STP March) 56 laps, were still running at finish but too far behind to be classified.

FASTEST LAP   Stewart 1 min 19.9 secs, lap 45, 131.88 mph.

RETIREMENTS   N.G. Hill (2.99 Brabham-Cosworth – Motor Racing Developments) 0 laps, startline collision; J. Oliver (2.99 McLaren-Cosworth – Bruce McLaren Motor Racing) 0 laps, startline collision; D. Charlton (2.99 Lotus-Cosworth – GLTL) 1 lap, engine; M. Beuttler (2.99 March-Cosworth – Clarke-Mordaunt-Guthrie) 21 laps, oil-pressure; D. Bell (2.99 Surtees-Cosworth – Team Surtees) 23 laps, suspension; D.C. Hulme (2.99 McLaren-Cosworth – Bruce McLaren Motor Racing) 32 laps, engine; C. Amon (2.99 Matra-Simca – Equipe Matra) 35 laps, valve; G. Regazzoni (2.99 Ferrari – SEFAC Ferrari) 48 laps, oil-pressure; J. Ickx (2.99 Ferrari – SEFAC Ferrari) 51 laps, engine; P. Gethin (2.99 McLaren-Cosworth – Bruce McLaren Motor Racing) 53 laps, engine; T. Schenken, 63 laps, gearbox.

1972 Brands Hatch

July 15, Brands Hatch, 76 laps of 2.65-mile circuit
approximately 201.4 miles

The Wool Secretariat found their trade collapsing at the end of 1971, and were unable to take up their option on the British Grand Prix for the following year. In their place the John Player tobacco company decided to extend their motor racing interest from Lotus cars to the Grand Prix, and the Club executive in Belgrave Square allowed them to take the British Grand Prix into their corporate promotional plans.

The old Gold Leaf Team Lotus image was scrapped, and in its place the team cars were sprayed black-and-gold, and known purely as John Player Specials. All marks identifying them as Lotuses were to be removed, and this was part of a remarkable Player promotional philosophy which allowed no dilution of their own 'corporate persona'. They extended this policy to the Grand Prix, replacing its traditional, perfectly honourable and geographically accurate 'British' tag, with the 'John Player' name.

Two things were remarkable about this change. One was that the RAC acquiesced in such a thing at all. Did they need the money that badly? 'We never dreamed so many people would be upset' they said. The other was that a company such as Player should insist upon such a title, to the extent of tackling journalists who still talked of 'The British Grand Prix' and insisting that they mend their ways!

Meanwhile Stewart and Tyrrell had won in Argentina, Hulme and McLaren in South Africa, and Beltoise and BRM at Monaco in the rain. Fittipaldi had come good for *Lotus* in Spain, and repeated this success in Belgium, while Stewart was a lucky victor in France, where he made his come-back after missing a race due to an ulcer.

Now Tyrrell came to Brands Hatch with three cars for Stewart and Cevert, the reigning Champion having a choice of his 1971 model or the latest 005. Lotus had a choice of three revised Mark 72s for Fittipaldi and his new team-mate Dave Walker, while a third entry for Brands Hatch protege Tony Trimmer did not materialise. McLaren were to run updated M19s for Hulme and his new American team-mate Peter Revson, who had last raced in a British Grand Prix on this circuit in 1964. A third entry for Redman did not appear, following a practice crash in France.

There were five Marches entered, including the works 721Gs for Peterson and his paying number two Niki Lauda, a raw Brazilian named Carlos Pace in

Williams' much-raced 711, and Beuttler in his backers' latest 721G. Stommelen also had a 721, dressed in strange bodywork and masquerading as the 'Eifelland-Ford', while another Brands protege named Ray Allan had March plans fall through.

Bernie Ecclestone, of 'fifties Connaught fame, had bought the old Brabham team, and fielded two new BT37s and the old BT34 for Hill and two South Americans, Carlos Reutemann from the Argentine and Emerson Fittipaldi's brother Wilson. Team Surtees had three TS9Bs in variegated sponsors' colours for Hailwood, Schenken and De Adamich, while Charlton's old Lotus 72, Pescarolo's new Williams-built 'Politoys' and Francois Migault's amateur-built Connew special completed the long list of Cosworth runners.

The 12-cylinder brigade were headed by Ferrari, with up-dated 312B2s for Ickx and Arturo Merzario, who was making his F1 debut in place of Galli, who had been co-opted to drive the new Tecno flat-12. A third Ferrari for Andretti was scratched. BRM had lost their way with Siffert's tragic death on this circuit the previous October, and now with American tobacco sponsorship they were struggling to run a five car team. Sadly Helmut Marko had been partially blinded by a stone while racing one of their cars in France, and so he was obviously out of this race, while they also dropped Wisell and took on Oliver as a Brands Hatch specialist for another one-off return to Grand Prix racing. Beltoise and Gethin drove the other P160s for the Bourne circus, while Matra had two of their latest MS 120s but only one driver, Amon, as their Formula 1 programme was on the wane.

Stewart bent his new car in practice when its suspension failed after a lap in 1:22.4, and then it was left to Ickx to steal pole on the new 2×2 grid at 1:22.2 from Fittipaldi on 22.6. Hulme played himself in during practice for he had done a backward somersault in his CanAm McLaren in America the previous weekend! The Connew's suspension collapsed on the bumps, and Peter Connew withdrew it, but Migault *had* just qualified.

Ickx had scored a runaway win here in the BOAC 1000 Kms sports car race, and now he shrieked off the line to take an immediate lead from Fittipaldi and Beltoise – bursting through from row three. The BRM effectively held up the rest of the field while the Ferrari and Lotus howled away, and the Tecno had a

1972 Grid

8
E. Fittipaldi
(Lotus-Cosworth 72D R7)
1:22.6

5
Ickx
(Ferrari 312B2/5)
1:22.2

1
Stewart
(Tyrell-Cosworth 003)
1:22.9

19
Revson
(McLaren-Cosworth M19A–1)
1:22.7

11
Beltoise
(BRM P160/01)
1:23.4

22
Schenken
(Surtees-Cosworth TS9B/006)
1:23.2

3
Peterson
(March-Cosworth 721G/3)
1:23.7

21
Hailwood
(Surtees-Cosworth TS9B/005)
1:23.5

27
Reutemann
(Brabham-Cosworth BT37/2)
1:23.8

6
Merzario
(Ferrari 312B2/7)
1:23.7

2
Cevert
(Tyrrell-Cosworth 002)
1:23.9

18
Hulme
(McLaren-Cosworth M19C/1)
1:23.9

14
Oliver
(BRM P160/04)
1:24.4

25
Pace
(March-Cosworth 711/3)
1:24.0

12
Gethin
(BRM P160/03)
1:24.5

9
Walker
(Lotus-Cosworth 72D R6)
1:24.4

30
Galli
(Tecno T/002)
1:25.1

17
Amon
(Matra-Simca MS120C/04)
1:24.6

23
De Adamich
(Surtees-Cosworth TS9B/004)
1:25.2

4
Lauda
(March-Cosworth 721G/4)
1:25.1

28
W. Fittipaldi
(Brabham-Cosworth BT34/1)
1:25.5

26
Hill
(Brabham-Cosworth BT37/1)
1:25.2

29
Charlton
(Lotus-Cosworth 72D R3)
1:25.6

31
Beuttler
(March-Cosworth 721G/1)
1:25.6

24
Pescarolo
(Politoys-Cosworth FX3/1)
1:27.4

33
Stommelen
(Eifelland-March-Cosworth 721/4)
1:26.3

Non-starter: Migault, No. 34 Connew-Cosworth, 1:30.3

tyre burst in the general jostling down the pack and trailed into its pit for a wheel-change at the end of the opening lap.

On lap 3 Stewart cut past Revson to do something about Beltoise. De Adamich bounced off Walker and crashed at Dingle Dell, while the Lotus toured in to its pit for an inspection before continuing, and on lap 7 Stewart dived past Beltoise and took off after the leaders. Revson and Schenken were next past the obdurate Frenchman, Gethin's V12 blew up, and on lap 7 Pescarolo had something break in the new Politoys and he crashed heavily at Dingle Dell, partially blocking the track but climbing out unscathed. The Tecno possibly punctured a tyre on some of this debris, for on lap 12 Galli thundered into the bank at Clearways as it suddenly got away from him.

Beltoise regained fifth place as Schenken ran onto the verge, and behind them raced a bunch including Hailwood, Cevert, Peterson, Reutemann and Pace, and after a gap came Oliver, Merzario and Hulme.

Fittipaldi found he could close on Ickx around Druids and the Bottom Straight but then the Ferrari would haul away from him on the faster section out into the woods though it was burning oil. Beltoise's BRM began to behave oddly and he eased-off, stopping on lap 22 just as Hill rejoined after a stop with a punctured tyre and as Charlton gave up with gearbox trouble.

Next time round, the leaders became enmeshed with Walker while trying to lap him, and in an instant Stewart closed up, Ickx braked late into Druids and caught Fittipaldi off-balance, and while the Brazilian was controlling a slide, Stewart dived through and away after the Ferrari.

Lap after lap saw the field howling round in dull procession, until Hailwood's gearbox failed and dropped him back from sixth to tenth then out of the race on lap 31. Simultaneously Merzario rushed in with a puncture and rejoined with a will, and three laps later the leaders doubled the unhappy Amon, struggling along with his unwilling Matra.

As they blared away under South Bank Bridge Fittipaldi slotted neatly in front of Stewart, and in mid-field Reutemann and Pace touched and both stopped to examine their cars. Oliver abandoned out in the woods when his BRM's left-rear lower radius rod pulled away from the suspension upright, and as Ickx began to slow, so Fittipaldi left Stewart and closed with the Ferrari. Revson was a safe fourth, with Schenken comfortably on his tail, then Cevert, Peterson and Hulme who was about to be lapped like Amon behind him.

By lap 47 the McLaren number one was a lap behind, and the leading trio were tightly bunched. The Ferrari had lost too much oil from a split cooler, and two laps later Ickx shut-off and retired. Schenken lost a certain fourth as he spun at Druids, stalled, and coasted downhill to restart his engine, which he was able to do but only after Cevert, Peterson and Hulme had streamed by. A lap behind came Merzario, still charging hard and passing Revson on the road as he strove to atone for his delay.

Hill had crashed at Paddock while being lapped by the leaders ('. . . from a gentleman to a twit in a tenth of a second . . .' was his lucid summary). Then on lap 61 Cevert ran onto the loose at the same point and thudded to a stop just short of the abandoned Brabham, which let Peterson inherit fourth. Schenken's Surtees halted abruptly as its rear suspension came unscrewed and allowed the wheels to steer, so Amon found himself suddenly presented with sixth place after a really miserable afternoon's drive. Merzario was right behind.

Fittipaldi and Stewart were firmly placed first and second, with neither showing any edge on the other, and Revson was a steady third with Peterson's March popping and banging as its fuel ran low. Hulme was displaced by Amon as the New Zealander came to life, and as Peterson tore into Paddock Bend with only one lap to go his engine died as he was changing down. Stuck in neutral the March careered over the brow far too fast, ran wide onto the grass and bounced off Cevert's Tyrrell to come to rest against Hill's Brabham.

So Fittipaldi came home to win his sponsor's race, with only Stewart and Revson on the same lap at the finish. Amon was an amazed and delighted fourth, followed by a tired Hulme and an exuberant Merzario.

While Emerson Fittipaldi was enjoying the fruits of his first British Grand Prix victory, his elder brother Wilson was walking-in from the back of the circuit after a last-minute shunt when his Brabham's suspension failed. On the lap of honour brother Emerson's winning car had a tyre deflate . . . he had all the luck in that family!

Results

1 E. Fittipaldi (2.99 Lotus-Cosworth – JPTL) 1 hr 47 mins 50.2 secs, 112.06 mph; 2 J.Y. Stewart (2.99 Tyrrell-Cosworth – ELF-Team Tyrrell) 1 hr 47 mins 54.3 secs; 3 P.J. Revson (2.99 McLaren-Cosworth – Yardley-Team McLaren) 1 hr 49 mins 02.7 secs; 4 C. Amon (2.99 Matra-Simca – Equipe Matra) 75 laps; 5 D.C. Hulme (2.99 McLaren-Cosworth – Yardley-Team McLaren) 75 laps; 6 A. Merzario (2.99 Ferrari – SEFAC Ferrari) 75 laps; 7 R, Peterson (2.99 March-Cosworth – STP-March) 74 laps*, 8 C. Reutemann (2.99 Brabham-Cosworth – Motor Racing Developments) 73 laps; 9 N. Lauda (2.99 March-Cosworth – STP-March) 73 laps; 10 R. Stommelen (2.99 March-Cosworth – Team Eifelland Caravan) 71 laps; 11 J.P. Beltoise (2.99 BRM – Marlboro-BRM) 70 laps; 12 W. Fittipaldi (2.99 Brabham-Cosworth – Motor Racing Developments) 69 laps*; 13 M. Beuttler (2.99 March-Cosworth – Clarke-Mordaunt-Guthrie-Durlacher) 69 laps.

* Classified though not running at finish.

FASTEST LAP   Stewart, laps 58 and 60, 1 min 24.0 secs, 113.57 mph.

RETIREMENTS   A. De Adamich (2.99 Surtees-Cosworth – Ceramica Pagnossin-Team Surtees) 3 laps, accident; P. Gethin (2.99 BRM – Marlboro-BRM) 5 laps, engine; H. Pescarolo (2.99 Politoys-Cosworth – Team Williams-Motul) 7 laps, accident; G. Galli (2.99 Tecno – Martini Racing Team) 9 laps, accident; D. Charlton (2.99 Lotus-Cosworth – Lucky Strike Racing) 19 laps, gearbox; M. Hailwood (2.99 Surtees-Cosworth – Brooke Bond-Oxo-Rob Walker – Team Surtees) 30 laps, gearbox; J. Oliver (2.99 BRM – Marlboro-BRM) 36 laps, suspension; C. Pace (2.99 March-Cosworth – Team Williams-Motul) 38 laps, differential; N.G. Hill (2.99 Brabham-Cosworth – Motor Racing Developments) 47 laps, accident; J. Ickx (2.99 Ferrari – SEFAC Ferrari) 48 laps, oil loss; D. Walker (2.99 Lotus-Cosworth – JPTL) 58 laps, suspension; F. Cevert (2.99 Tyrrell-Ford – ELF-Team Tyrrell) 60 laps, accident; T. Schenken (2.99 Surtees-Cosworth – Team Surtees) 63 laps, suspension; W. Fittipaldi, 69 laps, suspension/accident; R. Peterson 74 laps, low on fuel/accident.

'Sponsorship' is written all over Fittipaldi's winning Lotus as it hurtles into Paddock Bend.

1973 Silverstone

July 14, Silverstone, 67 laps of 2.927-mile circuit
approximately 196.1 miles (plus two laps 'false start'!)

Back to Silverstone for the sixteenth time, where once again 'British Grand Prix' was officially a taboo term to describe the now traditional jamboree of speed which included all kinds of supporting races, stunts and demonstrations in addition to the comparatively brief blurr of noise, colour and spine-tingling speed which Grand Prix racing had become.

The Formula 1 circus had a packed programme of no less than fifteen Championship-qualifying races to follow this season, and the British event was the ninth of them. Fittipaldi's black Lotus 72s had won in Argentina, Brazil and Spain, while Stewart had responded to win in South Africa, Belgium, and then Monaco where he equalled Jimmy Clark's long-standing record of twenty-five Grande Epreuve victories. Hulme won the new Swedish round for McLaren, and then Peterson came good in France where his car hung together long enough to give him his long-deserved first Grand Prix victory. So to Silverstone, where the Championship battle between Stewart and Fittipaldi was to continue, and where the Scot had won the International Trophy race earlier in the year in a classic dice with Peterson, run partly in a snowstorm!

Lotus fielded four 72s so that both their aces, Fittipaldi and Peterson, should have a choice of two cars. Tyrrell fielded his regular 006/2 for Stewart and the identical 006 for Cevert, while the Yardley-backed McLarens were all chisel-nosed M23s for Hulme and Revson as usual and for the very promising but very wild South African Jody Scheckter having his third Grand Prix ride for the team.

Ecclestone's MRD outfit fielded three of their triangular-section BT42 cars, for Wilson Fittipaldi, Reutemann and De Adamich, the Italian's car being run as a works-prepared private entry backed by Ceramica Pagnossin. In addition an old BT37 was entered by the Hexagon used car dealership for the capable Ulsterman, John Watson, unfortunately being sprayed in their chocolate livery. The new Universal Oil Products-backed Shadow team appeared with DN1 cars for Oliver and American sports car king George Follmer in the works' jet-black colours, while a third Shadow was raced by Hill in Embassy cigarette-packet livery, as a private entry. Surtees had three of his latest TS14A cars, for Hailwood, Pace and the German saloon car driver Jochen Mass whose car was plain and pristine white, with

just Ford Cologne to support his entry.

The two Williams-built Iso-Marlboro cars were to be driven by Ganley and the New Zealand Formula 5000 pilot, Graham McRae, while a flock of Marches completed the list of Ford-engined runners. The works STP 721G had been totally rebuilt to the latest 1973 specifications with deformable structures protecting the fuel tanks against impact damage, and it was to be driven for the first time by a very promising newcomer from Formula 3 and Formula 2 named Roger Williamson, who was backed by Leicester builder and Donington racing car museum founder Tom Wheatcroft. The stockbroker consortium's similar car was entered for Beuttler, and two newly-built but generally similar 731s were fielded by the youthful Lord Alexander Hesketh's private team for James Hunt, and by Lec Refrigeration for David Purley, son of that company's chief. Wealthy Liechtensteiner Rikky von Opel had Mo Nunn's one-off Ensign.

By this time the Ford brigade were truly dominant, for Ferrari had lost their way completely, Matra-Simca had pulled-out to concentrate on sports car racing, and BRM were a shambles with obsolete machinery cluttering the Bourne works. Ickx appeared with the ill-handling and overweight new Ferrari 312B3, there were three ancient BRM P160s for Regazzoni, Beltoise and Lauda, and Amon had a choice of two Martini-supported Tecno flat-12s, one designed by New Zealander Alan McCall, and the other a nice-looking new car produced by Amon's associate Gordon Fowell.

Practice came to life late on the Friday as Peterson put on a truly electrifying display of ten-tenths driving. His beautiful black-and-gold Lotus barreled through the long sweep of Woodcote Corner on a ballistic trajectory, going like an artillery shell, bobbing and yawing as it hammered between the pits and main grandstands at well over 140 mph. Through the faster curves at Chapel and Abbey he was equally spectacular, and took pole with a record 1:16.3 lap.

On a more mundane level, Purley crashed at Becketts and damaged the March too badly to race, while Hunt's car which had impressed in Monaco and France was quite quick, and Williamson's inexplicably slow.

The twenty-eight cars formed-up on the dummy grid before a packed Silverstone house, but oil falling

1973 Grid

8
Revson
(McLaren-Cosworth M23–2)
1:16.5

7
Hulme
(McLaren-Cosworth M23–1)
1:16.5

2
Peterson
(Lotus-Cosworth 72 R6)
1:16.3

1
E. Fittipaldi
(Lotus-Cosworth 72 R5)
1:16.7

5
Stewart
(Tyrrell-Cosworth 006/2)
1:16.7

10
Reutemann
(Brabham-Cosworth BT42/3)
1:17.4

6
Cevert
(Tyrrell-Cosworth 006)
1:17.3

30**
Scheckter
(McLaren-Cosworth M23–3)
1:16.9

19
Regazzoni
(BRM P160/09)
1:17.5

21
Lauda
(BRM P160/08)
1:17.4

11
W. Fittipaldi
(Brabham-Cosworth BT42/2)
1:18.1

23**
Hailwood
(Surtees-Cosworth TS14A/04)
1:18.0

27
Hunt
(March-Cosworth 731/3)
1:17.6

24**
Pace
(Surtees-Cosworth TS14A/03)
1:18.3

31**
Mass
(Surtees-Cosworth TS14A/01)
1:18.3

25
Ganley
(Williams-Cosworth IR/02)
1:18.6

20**
Beltoise
(BRM P160/01)
1:18.4

18*
Purley
(March-Cosworth 731/2)
1:18.4

9**
De Adamich
(Brabham-Cosworth BT42/4)
1:19.1

3
Ickx
(Ferrari 312B3/010)
1:18.9

29
Watson
(Brabham-Cosworth BT37/2)
1:20.1

14**
Williamson
(March-Cosworth 721G/4)
1:19.5

28
Von Opel
(Ensign-Cosworth MN01)
1:19.2

16**
Follmer
(Shadow-Cosworth DN1/5A)
1:20.3

15
Beuttler
(March-Cosworth 721G/2)
1:20.1

26
McRae
(Williams-Cosworth IR/01)
1:20.8

12
Hill
(Shadow-Cosworth DN1/3A)
1:20.5

17**
Oliver
(Shadow-Cosworth DN1/4A)
1:20.3

22
Amon
(Tecno-McCall PA123/6)
1:21.0

*Non-starter
**Cars eliminated in early multiple accident, missing from the grid at restart

Mayhem on the first lap; at left (behind bridge pier) Williamson pin-wheels through the air, Beuttler (15) finds a way past Scheckter (just slammed straight by Hailwood's disintegrating Surtees), while De Adamich's demolished Brabham careers towards the bank with Beltoise, Mass and Wilson amid the smoke. Seconds later Roger Williamson's shattered March frames the whole incredible race-stopping scene.

from around the catch-tank of Oliver's Shadow just off the Woodcote line passed un-noticed. As the flag fell, Peterson flashed away ahead of Stewart, while Lauda's BRM jerked convulsively then stopped as its left-hand half-shaft snapped. Oliver thumped into its tail from the back of the grid, and his Shadow snuffled away after the field with its front-end considerably damaged, while Lauda's car subsided with its left-rear wheel missing!

Stewart dived inside Peterson at Becketts as the Lotus skated wide on its cold tyres, and then he scratched as hard as he could round the rest of the lap to storm out of Woodcote in a huge lead. Next into the corner was Peterson, whose car was oversteering badly, then the exuberant Scheckter whom Hulme had just waved-by into the curve.

The woolly-headed youngster seared into Wood-cote on a knife-edge, ran straight through Oliver's oil patch and began to slide wide, wider and *wider* . . . The white-and-papaya McLaren flicked broadside on the grass, broad tyres fountaining stones and dust high into the air, then surged broadside across the track as Hulme, Cevert, the remarkable Hunt, Revson and Regazzoni hurtled alongside. With a crump of folding metal and glass-fibre it bounced off the pit-wall and rolled back with Scheckter waving both arms to warn the pack. He was too late.

Revson clipped-off his team-mate's rear wing, which planed-back and removed Hunt's engine air-box, and very nearly his head. Pace dived for the pit-wall gap, changed his mind and snapped broad-side to block-off Beltoise's BRM. As the Frenchman desperately braked De Adamich thundered into his tail in the new Brabham, cannoning the BRM clean over Pace's car as the whole melee of cars careered wildly to the left side of the track, collecting Hailwood and Mass on the way. Williamson tried to pass under the pit-wall, was pinched into it and pin-wheeled through the air to climb out unharmed beyond the 'Motor' Bridge. Hill's rear suspension was re-arranged by Follmer's works Shadow, and Von Opel's Ensign crushed its nose cone. As Stewart beat down into

Woodcote to complete his second lap the track was virtually blocked, and at the last moment he spotted red flags and skidded to a stop with locked wheels just short of the carnage, Peterson and the rest skittering to a halt in his wake . . .

From this desperate scene of drifting dust, blue rubber smoke, billowing clouds of extinguishant, bouncing wheels and showers of shattering glass-fibre and metal, emerged all the drivers except De Adamich, who was trapped in his Brabham by the ankles, one of which had been broken. Rescuers spent some 40 minutes gingerly cutting the calm Italian clear, and meanwhile desperate work was going on in the pits to resurrect the less badly damaged cars, although the whole Surtees team was beyond help, as was Beltoise's BRM, Follmer's Shadow, Williamson's March and of course Scheck-ter's McLaren which had started it all.

It was well into the afternoon before the track was cleared, everyone had settled down, De Adamich was in hospital and the surviving cars formed up in their original grid positions for the restart. Lauda's BRM had been repaired with a new drive-shaft, Hill's Shadow had its rear suspension rebuilt, and Hunt's white March had a yellow airbox fitted which had been borrowed from the Beuttler team.

At 3.36 the restart was flagged away for the full

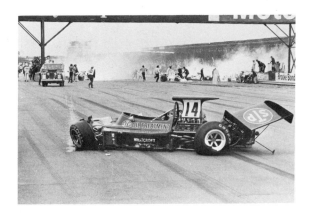

sixty-seven-lap distance, and Peterson blared away once more while Lauda took advantage of the vacant grid position in front of him where Scheckter had been and hammered through into second place down towards Copse. This time Stewart's Becketts ruse was blown, and Peterson held-off Lauda by a tight line and rocketed down the Hangar Straight. Braking into Stowe Stewart performed a classical job of taking second place from Lauda, and he rapidly caught Peterson whose car was still oversteering too much despite tweaks during the enforced interval.

Diving back down into Stowe for the seventh time Stewart lined-up inside Peterson, but as he changed-down he found second gear instead of fourth and locked the Tyrrell's rear wheels. In an instant it had flicked through the markers onto the old runway, missed a photographer by what seemed inches to Stewart but was in fact yards, half-spun back onto the circuit and then arced away deep into the cornfields! He could just see Peterson, Fittipaldi, Lauda, Revson, Hulme, Hunt, Cevert, and Reutemann as they roared by over the corn, and then he had to wait for Regazzoni, Ickx, then Ganley and Wilson Fittipaldi to go by before he could rejoin. The Tyrrell's nose was crumpled and full of crops, and after three slow laps in thirteenth place he came into the pits as the water temperature climbed. After attention, he rejoined a lap down but between Hulme in fourth place and Hunt on the road.

Lauda had fallen back as his early pace overheated his tyres, and Revson took third place and began to get the measure of Fittipaldi who was trying to keep the smooth-driving American away from his team-mate in the lead, but Revson was wanting to travel so

fast and Peterson was slowing so much with continued oversteering problems that the second place battle couldn't help but close on him.

The gap was down to 2.2 seconds when light rain began to slatter across the course, and then on lap 37 Fittipaldi faltered and stopped at Abbey with a drive-shaft joint failure. Revson was free to chase after Peterson, and as the Swede began some lurid slides on the dampened track surface the McLaren driver closed up and went by on lap 39 to grab the lead.

Meanwhile the thin field had slimmed even further as McRae gave up with a sticking throttle after just one lap, Amon's Tecno had stammered out of the race with fuel pressure problems, Hill's repaired Shadow had stopped when the steering rack came loose and Watson retired with a seized metering unit after several pit-calls.

Hunt and Hulme closed with Peterson in a developing battle for the points, though the New Zealander was handicapped by an overheating right-front tyre. This bunch were close enough to Revson to keep him running hard, and on lap 56 Hunt dived alongside Peterson into Becketts but was shut off firmly by the Swede. This piece of pushing and shoving gave Hulme the chance to outfumble Hunt into Chapel Curve and then McLaren were looking for a 1–2 finish as 'The Bear' closed with Peterson.

Meanwhile Wilson Fittipaldi's Brabham had an oil line pull apart and coated the pits straight and the entry to Copse Corner with lubricant, and spoiled the area where Hulme was thinking he had his best chance of taking the Lotus.

Hunt was really going to work in Hesketh's modified March, and he set fastest lap at 1:18.6, 0.9

Even the great make mistakes: Stewart spun out of contention with Peterson at Stowe Corner, slithering across the infield, fish-tailing back onto the circuit in front of Lauda and Fittipaldi and then gunning his way to safety down among the cornstalks!

Results

1 P.J. Revson (2.99 McLaren-Cosworth – Yardley-Team McLaren) 1 hr 19 mins 18.5 secs, 131.75 mph; **2** R. Peterson (2.99 Lotus-Cosworth – JPTL) 1 hr 29 mins 21.3 secs; **3** D.C. Hulme (2.99 McLaren-Cosworth – Yardley-Team McLaren) 1 hr 29 mins 21.5 secs; **4** J. Hunt (2.99 March-Cosworth – Hesketh Racing) 1 hr 29 mins 21.5 secs; **5** F. Cevert (2.99 Tyrrell-Cosworth – ELF-Team Tyrrell) 1 hr 29 mins 55.1 secs; **6** C. Reutemann (2.99 Brabham-Cosworth – Motor Racing Developments) 1 hr 30 mins 03.2 secs; **7** G. Regazzoni (2.99 BRM – Marlboro-BRM) 1 hr 30 mins 30.2 secs; **8** J. Ickx (2.99 Ferrari – SEFAC Ferrari) 1 hr 30 mins 35.9 secs; **9** H. Ganley (2.99 Iso-Marboro-Cosworth – Williams Racing) 66 laps; **10** J.Y. Stewart (2.99 Tyrrell-Cosworth – ELF-Team Tyrrell) 66 laps; **11** M. Beuttler (2.99 March-Cosworth – Clarke-Mordaunt-Guthrie Durlacher) 65 laps; **12** N. Lauda (2.99 BRM – Marlboro-BRM) 63 laps; **13** R. von Opel (2.99 Ensign-Cosworth – Team Ensign) 61 laps.

FASTEST LAP   Hunt lap 63, 1 min 18.6 secs, 134.06 mph.

RETIREMENTS   J. Oliver (2.99 Shadow-Cosworth – Nicholls Advanced Vehicle System-Shadow Cars) 0 laps, startline collision; A. De Adamich (2.99 Brabham-Cosworth – Ceramica Pagnossin), R. Williamson (2.99 March-Cosworth – STP March), Follmer (2.99 Shadow-Cosworth – Nicholls Advanced Vehicle System-Shadow Cars), J.B. Beltoise (2.99 BRM – Marlboro-BRM), M. Hailwood, C. Pace and J. Mass (2.99 Surtees-Cosworths – Brooke-Bond-Oxo-Team Surtees) plus J. Scheckter (2.99 McLaren-Cosworth – Team Yardley McLaren) all eliminated in 1st lap multiple collision. G. McRae (2.99 Iso-Marlboro-Cosworth – Frank Williams Racing Cars Ltd) 0 laps, throttle; C. Amon (2.99 Tecno – Martini Racing Team) 6 laps, fuel-pressure; N.G. Hill (2.99 Shadow-Cosworth – Embassy Racing) 24 laps, loose steering rack; J. Watson (2.99 Brabham-Cosworth – Hexagon of Highgate/MRD) 26 laps, seized metering unit; E. Fittipaldi (2.99 Lotus-Cosworth – JPTL) 36 laps, drive-shaft; W. Fittipaldi (2.99 Brabham-Cosworth – Motor Racing Developments) 44 laps, oil pipe.

seconds slower than Stewart's April record, on lap 63. Under glowering but dry skies Revson came hurtling into Woodcote for the sixty-seventh time, and howled under the chequered flag to win this unusual motor race, while under 3 seconds behind came Peterson, Hulme and Hunt fanned across the road and throwing everything into this last corner. Peterson slid wildly through to hold second by 0.2 seconds from Hulme who was 0.4 seconds ahead of Hunt, and the Lotus all but got away from Peterson on the exit. He backed-off sharply and almost collected Hulme up his tail before the pits!

As Revson began his traditional lap of honour on the farm trailer, the weather broke, and nine minutes after the flag Silverstone was awash under heavy rain. It had been a strange race, but stranger ones were to follow . . .

James Hunt, who shone in Lord Hesketh's well-developed March 731 despite the handicap of uncompetitive Firestone tyres.

1974 Brands Hatch

July 20, Brands Hatch, 75 laps of 2.65-mile circuit
approximately 198.75 miles

The sponsoring company continued their hopeless attempt to erase 'British' from the Grand Prix race at Brands Hatch this season, but with their help the RAC were successful in attracting a huge entry, from which all those who could qualify within 130 per cent of the fastest practice time would be allowed to start.

There were no less than thirty-eight Cosworth-Ford cars in the paddock, plus six 12-cylinders, and extra pits were added to the midfield row to accommodate them all. Peterson had been joined by Ickx in the Lotus team, still carrying black livery, and since Stewart had retired and poor Cevert had been killed in America, Scheckter and Patrick Depailler were to handle the new Tyrrell 007s. McLaren had won Marlboro backing from BRM, and had updated M23s for Hulme and Emerson Fittipaldi, while a third M23 was managed by a Yardley-backed team within the works organization, and this was to be driven by Hailwood. Reutemann and Pace shared the works BT44 Brabhams, while Watson had an older BT42 entered and prepared by Paul Michaels' Hexagon equipe, and a fourth BT42 was prepared with Radio Luxembourg money for the Brands Hatch management's latest protege-cum-publicity gimmick – Signorina Lella Lombardi, who had saloon and Formula 5000 racing experience.

Works Marches were to be driven by the grizzled Italian, Vittorio Brambilla, and by the young Hans-Joachim Stuck, son of the pre-war Auto Union stormer, while a newcomer from Formula 3 named Mike Wilds had scraped together the cash to hire Hesketh's old March 731 in a forlorn attempt to qualify. The new Shadow DN3s were to be driven by Welshman Tom Pryce and Frenchman Jean-Pierre Jarier, while Surtees' waning fortunes depended upon Derek Bell and Mass in a pair of works TS15s, while the Finnish sports car driver Leo Kinnunen hired a sister car. Williams fielded Merzario and the Dane Tom Belso in two of his machines, backed by Marlboro and by the Italian Iso-Rivolta luxury car concern, and Australian Vern Schuppan was running Mo Nunn's Ensign, supported by Theodore 'Teddy' Yip, a Singapore businessman. Schenken was running Tauranac's new Trojan T101,

Hunt had the very promising new Hesketh 308, and Ganley was saddled with the hopeless Japanese Maki F101 produced for its first race by an obscure Tokyo outfit with more enthusiasm and money than good sense. John Nicholson, the Cosworth-Ford engine tuner, fielded his neat Lyncar which acted virtually as research vehicle for his small company, and Purley yet another Cosworth-engined 'special' – Ray Jessop's Token. Hill's Embassy team fielded two Lola T370s for the race, driven by the ageing and slowing ex-World Champion himself and by Guy Edwards, who had a wrist in plaster following a Formula 5000 shunt at Mallory Park the previous weekend, and who gave-up his place to Peter Gethin after a few painful practice laps.

The 12-cylinders came from the Ferrari team, almost unrecognisable now compared to their sorry state at Silverstone the previous year, who had the latest and very potent 312B3s for Lauda and Regazzoni. Brand-new BRM P201s with tragically obsolescent, much-burst and much re-patched V12 engines after their sole new unit died, were fielded by the French Motul fuels-backed Bourne team for Beltoise and Pescarolo, while team-mate Migault struggled along with their much-bent, much straightened, P160.

Not surprisingly, the nine non-qualifiers after practice were Purley, Bell, Belso, Lella Lombardi who had performed her function of drumming-up public interest, Schuppan, Nicholson, Ganley, Wilds (who was unfortunate after a hectic rebuild job on the March) and Kinnunen.

The first ten qualifiers ran within the old lap record of 1:20.8 set by Fittipaldi in the 1972 Victory race, but only the front row cars of Lauda and Peterson cracked the 1:20.0 barrier, by 0.3 seconds each. Back in the field Migault qualified with a fast and brave time in his ancient BRM, Hulme was hopelessly slow in this his last driving season, and Schenken just scraped into the race 2.7 seconds slower than Lauda on pole.

Raceday was dry and sunny, and Lauda made an impeccable start to flash into Paddock Bend's downhill sweep ahead of Scheckter, Regazzoni, a rather

---

Non-qualifiers: 42, Purley (Token RJ/02) 1:22.7 – 18 Bell (Surtees TS16/03) 1:22.7 – 21 Belso (Williams IR/02) 1:23.3 – ▶
208 Lombardi (Brabham BT42/3) 1:23.3 – 22 Schuppan (Ensign MN02) 1:23.4 – 29 Nicholson (Lyncar) 1:23.6 – 25
Ganley (Maki F101) 1:23.7 – 35 Wilds (March 731/3) 1:24.1 – 43 Kinnunen (Surtees TS16/01) 1:25.6

1974 Grid

1
Peterson
(Lotus-Cosworth 72 R8)
1:19.7

12
Lauda
(Ferrari 312B3/015)
1:19.7

7
Reutemann
(Brabham-Cosworth BT44/1)
1:20.2

3
Scheckter
(Tyrrell-Cosworth 007/1)
1:20.1

24
Hunt
(Hesketh-Cosworth 308/1)
1:20.3

16
Pryce
(Shadow-Cosworth DN3/3A)
1:20.3

5
E. Fittipaldi
(McLaren-Cosworth M23–8)
1:20.5

11
Regazzoni
(Ferrari 312B3/014)
1:20.3

4
Depailler
(Tyrrell-Cosworth 007/2)
1:20.8

9
Stuck
(March-Cosworth 741/1)
1:20.7

2
Ickx
(Lotus-Cosworth 72 R5)
1:21.2

33
Hailwood
(McLaren-Cosworth M23–1)
1:21.2

37
Migault
(BRM P160/09)
1:21.4

28
Watson
(Brabham-Cosworth BT42/2)
1:21.3

17
Jarier
(Shadow-Cosworth DN3/2A)
1:21.6

20
Merzario
(Williams-Cosworth IR/04)
1:21.6

10
Brambilla
(March-Cosworth 741/2)
1:21.6

19
Mass
(Surtees-Cosworth TS16/02)
1:21.6

8
Pace
(Brabham-Cosworth BT44/2)
1:21.7

6
Hulme
(McLaren-Cosworth M23–6)
1:21.7

26*
Hill
(Lola-Cosworth T370/HU2)
1:21.9

27*
Gethin
(Lola-Cosworth T370/HU3)
1:21.7

15
Pescarolo
(BRM P201/01)
1:22.2

14
Beltoise
(BRM P201/02)
1:22.1

23
Schenken
(Trojan-Cosworth T103)
1:22.4

*Gethin took over Hill's car at start, when his own car's engine failed on warming-up lap, Hill taking spare

slow-off-the-mark Peterson, and the rest. The potent Ferrari streaked around that opening lap and had 2 seconds in hand across the timing line, leaving Scheckter and the rest floundering in its wake.

The scene looked set for the kind of Ferrari-dominated race which we had seen in Spain, save for Scheckter managing to leave Regazzoni yard by yard in the second wailing 312B3. Way back in the field Gethin abandoned the race, as his own Lola had blown-up on the reconnaissance lap, he had hastily taken over Hill's car and its cockpit was far too big for the diminutive Formula 5000 ace. Barely in control, he took the wise course and gave up before he hurt anybody.

So the race developed, with Lauda storming away into an imperious lead while Scheckter fell back, but ran clear of Regazzoni who was clearly holding-up Peterson. Reutemann, Fittipaldi, Pryce, Stuck, Ickx and Hailwood howled by, with Hunt leading the rest until a rear suspension bolt sheared on the Hesketh at South Bank and the much-publicised 'English white hope' spun out of contention with just two-and-a-half laps completed!

Both Regazzoni and Peterson were forced into their pits by punctures, after the exuberant Stuck crashed heavily at Dingle Dell and strewed debris across the track. Hailwood was duelling with Ickx until the McLaren spun at Hawthorns, stalled and would not restart, while Merzario's engine had failed, Depailler's seized and Jarier was about to be lapped by the charging Pryce when he pulled into the pits with a chassis failure. The Welshman had the same problem, for a sub-frame tube in the Shadow's tail had fractured, and while it affected the handling it also distorted the gear-linkage and confined him to fourth and fifth. He adapted his driving admirably to suit this strange state of affairs and ran home well into seventh place.

It was a dull race as Lauda reeled off the laps with nobody looking like challenging him. Fittipaldi and Ickx fought past Regazzoni for third and fourth places, and then with twenty laps to go Lauda found himself in an unexpected slide and began to study his rear tyres carefully in his mirrors. Sure enough, the distinctive concave profile of a deflating Goodyear was visible on the right-rear wheel, and he eased back progressively as control became more difficult. He had been driving very neatly, keeping his fragile tyres off the kerbs and verges, but had probably picked-up something from Stuck's crashed car.

Scheckter was closing rapidly, and it was like 1970 all over again as the Ferrari supporters clapped hands to their heads in horror, and Tyrrell fans went wild with joy. The Ferrari pit signalled frantically to their young Austrian ace that they had a replacement wheel and tyre ready for a quick stop, but he foolishly

Ferrari's unlucky circuit: Brands Hatch again saw a Ferrari failure in 1974 when Niki Lauda stayed out too long with a deflating tyre on his leading 312B3. Here he locks over into Druid's, as Scheckter's Tyrrell appears over the brow.

preferred to plod on, even after Scheckter howled by past the pits and away into an increasing lead on lap 70.

One lap later Fittipaldi rushed past, and still the relatively inexperienced Lauda soldiered on. Now he had left it far too late, even if he did change his mind and stop, but then the tyre made his decision for him and flew to pieces out in the country on the seventy-fourth and penultimate lap.

So the Ferrari bumped into its pit, where Ferrari's sports-car trained mechanics had a new wheel fitted in record time. Lauda exploded away towards the pit exit, but there a great unruly scrum of sponsors' girls, photographers, honorary officials and even a Ford Cortina course car blocked the way, all assembled to watch Scheckter take the flag and oblivious to the possibility of any last-minute pit stop! As the Tyrrell screamed by to win, a well-meaning marshal saw Lauda accelerating towards this human barrier. He knew the chequer was out and grabbed a red flag from a nearby rack, and stopped Lauda with it. This was the normal way of closing the pit-lane during practice, once the chequered flag was out, but now Lauda dutifully halted instead of blaring his engine, nudging the crowd aside and storming out to finish. Thus the Championship leader was denied the chance of completing another lap, which would have given him fifth place and two more points. Instead he abandoned his car in the pit lane, and was simply classified ninth, two laps behind the winner, while Fittipaldi, Ickx, Regazzoni, Reutemann and Hulme took the points-scoring places from second to sixth.

Lauda leapt from his car close to tears, but later admitted to making a duff decision while righteously outraged at the organisational disaster which trapped him in the pit-lane. Ferrari team manager Luca di Montezemolo and engineer Forghieri were equally outraged, and after long discussions with the shame-faced RAC stewards they announced their intention to appeal against the official results direct to the FIA in Paris.

On September 13 the appeal was heard, with Ferrari claiming fifth place for their man, while Ecclestone of Brabham and Mayer of McLaren counter-claimed to preserve fifth and sixth places, and their accompanying points, for Reutemann and Hulme. It was just like a law-court and the FIA panel decided that the RAC were remiss in allowing a red flag to be shown to Lauda, falsely indicating that the race had been 'stopped' at that point, rather than 'finished' by the chequered flag. The RAC had to bear all expenses. Lauda consequently gained his two points, and he certainly deserved them, but this piece of bureaucratic result-juggling has left a very bad taste, for while the RAC's unbelievable incompetence deserved the severest censure, Lauda could not be guaranteed to have completed any last lap which he might have been allowed to start. Anything could have happened to him, from collision to solo-crash, but that was the way the 1975 British Grand Prix came to an end, months after it had been flagged away. Surely things could only improve in 1975 . . .?

Chaos: with Lauda trapped in the pit-lane by a milling mob of humanity and a parked course car Jody Scheckter wins the Grand Prix for Tyrrell.

Results

1 J. Scheckter (2.99 Tyrrell-Cosworth – ELF-Team Tyrrell) 1 hr 43 mins 02.2 secs, 115.73 mph; **2** E. Fittipaldi (2.99 McLaren-Cosworth – Texaco-Marlboro-McLaren) 1 hr 43 mins 17.5 secs; **3** J. Ickx (2.99 Lotus-Cosworth – JPTL) 1 hr 44 mins 03.7 secs; **4** G. Regazzoni (2.99 Ferrari – SEFAC Ferrari) 1 hr 44 mins 09.4 secs;** **5** C. Reutemann (2.99 Brabham-Cosworth – Motor Racing Developments) 74 laps;** **6** D. Hulme (2.99 McLaren-Cosworth – Texaco-Marlboro-McLaren) 74 laps; **7** T. Pryce (2.99 Shadow-Cosworth – Don Nicholls Advanced Vehicle Systems-Shadow Cars) 74 laps; **8** C. Pace (2.99 Brabham-Cosworth – Motor Racing Developments) 74 laps;** **9** N. Lauda (2.99 Ferrari – SEFAC Ferrari) 73** laps; **10** R. Peterson (2.99 Lotus-Cosworth – JPTL) 73 laps; **11** J. Watson (2.99 Brabham-Cosworth – Hexagon of Highgate) 73 laps; **12** J.P. Beltoise (2.99 BRM – Motul-BRM) 73 laps; **13** N.G. Hill (2.99 Lola-Cosworth – Embassy-Racing) 69 laps; **14** J. Mass (2.99 Surtees-Cosworth – Fina-Team Surtees) 68 laps; **15** H. Pescarolo (2.99 BRM – Motul-BRM) 64 laps*; **16** F. Migault (2.99 BRM – Motul-BRM) 63 laps.

*Not running at finish, although classified.

**After two inquiries, Lauda was promoted to 5th place, demoting provisional 5th, 6th, 7th and 8th place finishers.

FASTEST LAP   Lauda lap 25, 1 min 21.1 secs, 117.63 mph.

RETIREMENTS   P. Gethin (2.99 Lola-Cosworth – Embassy Racing) 1 lap, J. Hunt (2.99 Hesketh-Cosworth – Hesketh Racing) 2 laps, suspension; T. Schenken (2.99 Trojan-Cosworth – Trojan Racing) 7 laps, suspension; V. Brambilla (2.99 March-Cosworth – Beta-March) 17 laps, fuel-pressure; A. Merzario (2.99 Iso-Marlboro-Cosworth – Williams Racing) 26 laps, engine; P. Depailler (2.99 Tyrrell-Cosworth – ELF-Team Tyrrell) 35 laps, engine; H.-J. Stuck (2.99 March-Cosworth – March Engineering) 36 laps, accident; J.-P. Jarier (2.99 Shadow-Cosworth – Nicholls Advanced Vehicles Systems-Shadow Cars) 45 laps, suspension; M. Hailwood (2.99 McLaren-Cosworth – Team Yardley McLaren) 57 laps, spun and stalled; H. Pescarolo (2.99 BRM – Motul-BRM) 65 laps, engine.

1975 Silverstone

July 19, Silverstone, 67 laps of 2.932-mile circuit
approximately 196.44 miles
(Race result issued at 55 laps approximately 161.26 miles after red flag shown)

It was a relief to return to the wide-open spaces of Silverstone after the overcrowded organisational disasters of Brands Hatch, but for this race the historic airfield course had changed its character. The pits had been completely rebuilt, the paddock was no longer the instructive free-for-all it had been, with good views of the teams at work for the paying customer, and the superfast sweep at Woodcote was no more. In its place was a cow-pat of asphalt and sleepers, round which the circuit zig-zagged right-left-right to form a chicane to slow the cars past the

main grandstands. Nine onlookers had been killed in a crash during the Spanish Grand Prix, and the idea of a car tumbling out of control at Woodcote and ending-up among the stands had become just too conceivable for comfort. The chicane was quick and quite interesting, but it was not the spine-chilling Woodcote which had enthralled the crowds for so many years.

The entry was headed by reigning Champion Fittipaldi, joined by Mass in the latest versions of McLaren's long-lived and successful M23 design. Scheckter and Depailler were in their updated Tyrrell 007s, Reutemann and Pace in the Brabham BT44Bs now sponsored tastefully by the Martini aperitif concern. Brambilla and Stuck appeared with the two main March 751s, while similar cars ran for the Italian girl Lombardi who had found herself starting Grand Prix races during the season with her Italian Lavazza-backed car, and the American Mark Donohue whose backer Roger Penske had bought a March after it proved consistently quicker in private testing than their own design Penske-Ford. Lotus were in a sorry state this season, with Peterson out of the hunt in the now totally obsolete 72s, and for this race – still the Lotus sponsor's showcase – the tall blonde Swede was accompanied by newcomers Jim Crawford and Brian Henton. Shadow had two of their now very competitive DN5s for Pryce and Jarier, the quiet and very talented Welshman having given the UOP-supported team their first Formula 1 win earlier in the year at Brands Hatch. Surtees were running their obsolete and uncompetitive works TS16 for Watson, while David Morgan rented their standby TS16 with finance from the Southern Organs musical instrument concern which had come to the fore in recent years with blanket sponsorship in club racing. Williams entered two of his latest specials for French Formula 2 star Jacques Laffite and his compatriot Jean-Pierre Jabouille, but the latter entry was withdrawn before practice began as Williams was short of engines, having broken two in France.

Graham Hill had announced his long overdue retirement just before this meeting, after a record 17 British Grand Prix drives, and his new GH1 Hill-Fords were to be driven by newcomer Tony Brise, who had made a brilliant Formula 1 debut in Spain, and by the Australian Alan Jones. Hunt was in Hesketh's 308B, although the team's very striking

8 Pace (Brabham-Cosworth BT44B/2) 1:19.50	**16** Pryce (Shadow-Cosworth DN5/2A) 1:19.36
11 Regazzoni (Ferrari 312T/024) 1:19.55	**12** Lauda (Ferrari 312T/023) 1:19.54
3 Scheckter (Tyrrell-Cosworth 007/6) 1:19.81	**9** Brambilla (March-Cosworth 751/3) 1:19.63
7 Reutemann (Brabham-Cosworth BT44B/1) 1:20.04	**1** E. Fittipaldi (McLaren-Cosworth M23/9) 1:19.91
2 Mass (McLaren-Cosworth M23–6) 1:20.8	**24** Hunt (Hesketh-Cosworth 308B/2) 1:20.14
27 Andretti (Parnelli-Cosworth VPJ4/001) 1:20.36	**17** Jarier (Shadow-Cosworth DN5/4A) 1:20.33
10 Stuck (March-Cosworth 751/2) 1:20.46	**23** Brise (Hill-Cosworth GH1/1) 1:20.41
5 Peterson (Lotus-Cosworth 72 R9) 1:20.58	**28** Donohue (March-Cosworth 751/5) 1:20.50
18 Watson (Surtees-Cosworth TS16/05) 1:20.83	**4** Depailler (Tyrrell-Cosworth 007/4) 1:20.60
22 Jones (Hill-Cosworth GH1/3) 1:21.19	**21** Laffite (Williams-Cosworth FW/04) 1:21.01
29 Lombardi (March-Cosworth 751/1) 1:21.60	**15** Henton (Lotus-Cosworth 72 R5) 1:21.26
39 W. Fittipaldi (Copersucar-Cosworth FD/03) 1:21.67	**19** Morgan (Surtees-Cosworth TS16/02) 1:21.65
32 Nicholson (Lyncar-Cosworth) 1:22.86	**6** Crawford (Lotus-Cosworth 72 R8) 1:21.86

Non-qualifiers: 31 Wunderink (Ensign MN/04) 1:25.02 – 35 Fushida (Maki F101/02) 1:26.61

new 308C was shown to press and public during this meeting. Andretti had the new Vel's Parnelli Team USA VPJ4 which had been designed by Maurice Phillippe, the ex-Lotus draughtsman responsible for the original Mark 72s. Wilson Fittipaldi was in his own car, backed by the Brazilian Copersucar sugar consortium, Dutchman Roelof Wunderink was to drive the Ensign with support from a Dutch burglar-alarm manufacturer, Nicholson had the Lyncar and the Japanese driver Hiroshi Fushida was trying his luck with the erstwhile Maki F101.

Only two 12-cylinder cars were to race, but the flat-12 Ferrari 312Ts for Lauda and Regazzoni had dominated Ford V8 opposition for much of the season. The lone Stanley-BRM, for Bob Evans, was withdrawn 'for development'; the luckless Bourne concern having been wound-up late in 1974 and its assets being acquired by Louis Stanley, for many years the 'guiding force' behind the company's ill-fortune.

Throughout practice the weather was very unsettled, with showers and sunny spells chasing across the rolling countryside, and on the Thursday a violent thunder-storm crashed its way across the circuit and lightning damage cut off all power for some time. Fastest time in the four sessions fell to Scheckter, Pace, Pryce, and then Pace again, but the quiet, remote Welshman stole pole position to great rejoicing amongst his supporters and the Shadow team. His 1:19.36 lap, was followed by Pace's 1:19.50, with Lauda and Regazzoni sitting menacingly on the second row of the 2×2 grid, within 0.05 seconds of the Brazilian Brabham driver. One second covered the first dozen cars, while only Wunderink and Fushida failed to qualify.

The most enormous crowd assembled on that Saturday morning, with thousands finding car-parks packed and all vantage points occupied if they arrived much later than 9 am! Literally miles of traffic jams developed in a manner reminiscent of 1948, yet the official estimate claimed 77,000-odd as 'a record . . .' This proved either that the RAC-Silverstone press service had a short memory, *or* that the 100,000-plus estimates of recent recall were wild exaggerations . . .

Yellow flags were to fly at the chicane on the first lap, and it was impressed upon the drivers that anyone overtaking under them would be severely penalised. The organisers would brook no repeat of the 1973 debacle, and in fact it was a clean start, with Pace whipping away from Pryce, the Ferraris, Scheckter, Hunt, Fittipaldi E., Andretti, Brise, Reutemann, Mass, Brambilla and the rest.

After four meteoric laps the leading septet had broken away, and Regazzoni elbowed ahead of Pryce then dived inside Pace on lap 13 into the new chicane. He emerged in the lead, waved-on by a

'Emmo' on his way to his second British Grand Prix success, in the McLaren M23 – a far cry from the cars used by his South American predecessors who won in 1951, 1954 and 1956 . . .

large part of the enthusiastic crowd with whom the uncomprising Swiss had always been a popular figure.

Reutemann's engine had failed on lap 5, Laffite's gearbox came apart next time round, the unfortunate Peterson had his engine break on lap 8 and Lombardi made a string of early pit-stops in a vain attempt to cure misfiring, finally abandoning on lap 19.

Brise's progress from midfield had been exciting to watch, particularly through the chicane where he was outbraking everyone who let him, including Andretti. He was gaining on the leading group when a wheel came loose and he was forced briefly into the pits.

Fittipaldi had taken Hunt for sixth place, but nobody could hold Regazzoni who was driving as hard as he knew to build-up an early time cushion. Unfortunately a brief shower wetted the far side of the circuit, and the Ferrari spun wildly at Stowe, bending its wing mount on one of the proliferating wire catch-fences and losing its lead. As 'Regga' rushed into the broad new pit-lane for attention, Pryce, Pace and the rest had long gone in the lead, and the Welshman was rushing round until lap 21 when he spun into the fencing at Becketts and was thumped on the head by a flying fence-pole.

Scheckter had stolen the lead from Pace, but the rain decided him to stop for a change of tyre, and the Brabham howled back into the lead past the pits. Lauda and more runners followed Scheckter's example as heavy rain swept across the course, but Pace, Fittipaldi Hunt and Mass pressed-on, balancing their charges delicately over the slippery surface with their slick tyres.

Lauda's stop went wrong as he took off with one wheel insecure, and it came adrift before the end of the pit-lane, whereupon his crew scampered down to him and tried again. He did a slow lap, came in again to be sure, and then rejoined. Scheckter had gone back into seventh place, inherited fifth as stops were made, and charged after the pussy-footing leaders with all the confidence that wet-weather tyres could give. The Tyrrell caught the leaders one by one, and streaked away into a long lead on lap 27 while they slipped and slithered in his wake. Jarier had stopped his Shadow for wet tyres and he too was soaring through the field into second place. But not for long . . . the wind had blown the rain away and was now drying the circuit rapidly . . .

Both Scheckter and Jarier drove through every puddle they could see to cool their soft-compound tyres. If they could keep them together long enough they might just gain enough time to stop and change back to dries, and on lap 32 Scheckter blared down the pit-lane with Jarier out on the track and passing into the lead. Mass, Hunt and Fittipaldi were taking turns to tow each other in the pursuing dry-tyred group, and as the sun came out Jarier dived for the pits and Hunt shot into the lead!

Mass's nose-cone had come adrift so he stammered into the pits holding the glass-fibre panelling with one hand to have it replaced, and when the race stabilized once more Hunt was leading from Fittipaldi and Pace, with Scheckter well behind in fourth place and Jarier miles away a lonely fifth.

The Hesketh's crisp exhaust note flattened abruptly as a tail-pipe broke away, and this robbed Hunt of just sufficient power to allow first Fittipaldi and then Pace to blaze past. Brambilla and Donohue in their Marches had been battling away in midfield and displaced Jarier, and Mass had rejoined eighth, the last unlapped runner.

Fifty laps gone and the skies were blackening beyond Stowe and Club as a strong wind swept dense rain clouds towards the circuit. Ending lap 54 Jarier lost control out of the Woodcote chicane, and the Shadow slammed through the catch-fences below the main grandstand with astonishing force. A fence post

split the Frenchman's helmet wide open and put him in hospital with concussion, while another somersaulted into the paying seats and slightly hurt a woman spectator. So much for the 'modern safety measures . . .'

Really heavy rain was now hammering down from Stowe to Woodcote and on to Copse, and all the dry-tyred runners were thinking seriously of investing in a set of wets. Scheckter picked-off Hunt's ailing Hesketh on lap 53 as rain enveloped the circuit, and in his efforts to keep in touch the Englishman spun and dropped well back, but still held fourth place.

Into lap 56 Fittipaldi strode cautiously past the pits, with the twice-lapped Regazzoni between him and Pace on the road, then Scheckter all alone, and Hunt even more isolated. Brambilla was next into the chicane, but he flicked right into the pit-lane and trundled down for a tyre change as Donohue and Mass went by into fifth and sixth. These leading cars were jumbled-up among lapped traffic which included Brise, Jones, Watson, Morgan, Wilson Fittipaldi, Nicholson, Andretti, Lauda, Depailler and Henton, and the far side of the circuit was beginning to flood under a tropical downpour.

Pace spun back behind Scheckter at Becketts, and while Fittipaldi and Regazzoni blipped their slithering cars through Stowe and Club at about 30 mph, all hell broke out at both corners as dry-tyred cars aquaplaned helplessly towards the catch-fences and banks. At Stowe, Mass steered into the right-hander but his car simply speared straight-on into the fencing, with Donohue following him in. Mass' car was drivable, but it took the young German too long to realise it, and his split-second chance to make it a McLaren 1–2

Used Formula 1 machinery lying amongst the torn down catch fences at Club Corner. Crawford's Lotus 72, Pace's Brabham, the Copersucar, Hunt's Hesketh, Scheckter's Tyrrell and Morgan's Surtees are recognisable, while Wilson himself in the flame-proof overalls seems to be praying. His prayers were answered . . . little brother was safe, and won.

was missed. Depailler slithered round the back of the catch fences, accelerated to rejoin the circuit, and spun yards into the corn instead! Watson slithered off here too.

Down at Club near-tragedy saw Brise beat down the catch-fences in a heavy accident which tore his helmet off inflicting concussion and facial injuries, while Howard Tilden, the chief marshal there, was felled by following cars which careered and cannoned helplessly through the torn-down fencing. Scheckter destroyed the front of his Tyrrell against the bank, started to climb out, saw other cars revolving through the downpour and ducked back inside while they thudded into and around his wreck. Hunt, Pace, Morgan, Henton, Wilson Fittipaldi and Nicholson all smashed into this area, and flying pieces slightly hurt at least one of the amazed spectators.

After the 1973 accident Dean Delamont and the RAC had wisely initiated a system of special area observers whose sole job was to contact race control should a major incident away from control's field of vision make it advisable to stop the race. Chris Tooley, the Club observer, was in no doubt as car after car plumed into the wreckage of others, and he called 'Priority – stop the race'. The red flag went out at Woodcote, and flags flurried into action back round the circuit from there.

Fittipaldi had stopped at the pits to fit wet tyres, and rejoined just as the race was stopped, completing one final lap past all the muck and mayhem. Jones, Andretti, Lauda, Brambilla and Regazzoni emerged wet and disconsolate from Woodcote, the Ferraris touring into the pits while the others joined Fittipaldi who parked at Copse.

The whole race had stumbled to a premature halt, and with two-thirds of the distance completed – indeed, only ten laps to go – International regulations precluded a restart, and allowed whatever result the stewards decided to count for full World Championship points.

Here the RAC scored again, for while the CSI laid down no International procedure for such a fracas, the British club had a national rule which published positions at the end of the lap preceding a red-flag incident as the race result. Tom Binford, from Indianapolis, was the FIA steward of the meeting, and this was standard practice at the Speedway, so the 1975 British Grand Prix result appeared with the first and sixth-place finishers the only points-scorers actually mobile at the end of the day!

Perhaps it was better for all concerned that the British Grand Prix had disappeared after 1971, for this 1975 'snafu' was the biggest and best yet! Even the fabled British sense of humour had finally been stretched beyond its limit, just like the technology of the modern Grand Prix car . . .

Results

1 E. Fittipaldi (2.99 McLaren-Cosworth – Marlboro Team Texaco) 1 hr 22 mins 05.0 secs, 120.04 mph; 2 C. Pace (2.99 Brabham-Cosworth – Martini Racing) crashed 56th lap; J. Scheckter (2.99 Tyrrell-Cosworth – ELF-Team Tyrrell) crashed 56th lap; 4 J. Hunt (2.99 Hesketh-Cosworth – Hesketh Racing) crashed 56th lap; 5 M. Donohue (2.99 March-Cosworth – First National City Bank) crashed 56th lap; 6 V. Brambilla (2.99 March-Cosworth – Beta Team March) *completed* 56 laps; 7 J. Mass (2.99 McLaren-Cosworth – Marlboro Team Texaco) crashed 56th lap; 8 N. Lauda (2.99 Ferrari – SEFAC Ferrari) *completed* 55 laps; 9 P. Depailler (2.99 Tyrrell-Cosworth – ELF-Team Tyrrell) crashed 55th lap; 10 A. Jones (2.99 Hill-Cosworth – Embassy Racing) *completed* 55 laps; 11 J. Watson (2.99 Surtees-Cosworth – Team Surtees) crashed 55th lap; 12 M. Andretti (2.99 Parnell-Cosworth – Vel's Parnelli Jones Racing) *completed* 55 laps; 13 G. Regazzoni (2.99 Ferrari – SEFAC Ferrari) *completed* 55 laps; 14 J.-P. Jarier (2.99 Shadow-Cosworth – UOP Shadow Racing) crashed 54th lap; 15 A. Brise (2.99 Hill-Cosworth – Embassy Racing) crashed 54th lap; 16 B. Henton (2.99 Lotus-Cosworth – JPTL) crashed 54th lap; 17 J. Nicholson (2.99 Lyncar-Cosworth – Pinch Plant Ltd) crashed 52nd lap; 18 D. Morgan (2.99 Surtees-Cosworth – Team Surtees/National Organs) crashed 51st lap*; 19 W. Fittipaldi (2.99 Copersucar-Cosworth – Copersucar Fittipaldi) crashed 51st lap*.

*Amid all this carnage, judged too far behind 'to be classified as finishers'!

FASTEST LAP   G. Regazzoni (2.99 Ferrari – SEFAC Ferrari) lap 16, 1 min 20.9 secs, 130.47 mph.

RETIREMENTS   C. Reutemann (2.99 Brabham-Cosworth – Martini Racing) 5 laps, engine; J. Laffite (2.99 Williams-Cosworth – Williams Ambrozium H7 Racing) 6 laps, gearbox; R. Peterson (2.99 Lotus-Cosworth – JPTL) 8 laps, engine; L. Lombardi (2.99 March-Cosworth – Lavazza March) 19 laps, engine; T. Pryce (2.99 Shadow-Cosworth – UOP Shadow Racing) 21 laps, accident; J. Crawford (2.99 Lotus-Cosworth – JPTL) 29 laps, accident; H.-J. Stuck (2.99 March-Cosworth – Lavazza March) 46 laps, accident.

Fittipaldi looks suitably amazed at his good fortune on the winner's rostrum for the 1975 Grand Prix. Behind team manager Teddy Mayer stands HRH The Duke of Kent, whose father had attended the Donington Grand Prix, thirty-seven years previously.

1976 Brands Hatch

July 18, Brands Hatch, 76 laps of 2.61-mile circuit
approximately 198.36 miles

For the 1976 season over £300,000 was invested in Brands Hatch circuit improvements which were hastily but magnificently completed in time for the venue's seventh British Grand Prix meeting. Gone was the ramshackle pit row and remote, steeply inclined paddock, to be replaced by a glittering line of pit-garages, a vast expanse of concrete pit road and a special Formula 1 paddock adjacent to the pits themselves. The circuit had been remodelled to enlarge its infield for all this building, and emerged marginally shorter.

To recoup some of their outlay Motor Circuit Developments went to town with pre-race promotions, including a charity 'Grand Prix Night of the Stars' in London's Albert Hall early in GP week. Their enterprise paid-off, with over 100,000 spectators attending the three-day meeting and a genuine 77,000 appearing for race day itself. They saw a remarkable event – fully in keeping with the British GP's recently established reputation . . . !

Early in the season Ferrari's well-developed 312T2 cars had seemed invincible. James Hunt's McLaren had beaten an off-colour Lauda in Spain only to be disqualified for a technical infringement. Tyrrell's startling new six-wheelers had placed first and second in Sweden, and in France Hunt won fair and square after both Ferraris uncharacteristically failed. His Spanish success had then been reinstated by an FIA Tribunal, and so the articulate and immensely popular Englishman came to Brands as favourite to humble Ferrari once more.

The Maranello team produced a brand-new 312T2 for their Austrian World Champion, and a slightly older but essentially similar machine for Regazzoni. Hunt and Mass were looking for McLaren's third British GP victory in four years with their M23s, and two Tyrrell P34 six-wheelers were present for Scheckter (first here in '74) and Depailler. Andretti and Gunnar Nilsson drove Lotus 77s, from which the sponsor's brand names had been removed in deference to a sensitive Government, while Brabham-Alfa Romeos were entered for Reutemann and Pace. Four March 761s appeared, for Peterson, Stuck, Merzario and Brambilla. Watson was in the latest Penske PC4, while Amon was proving his continued class in the startlingly quick Ensign. Emerson Fittipaldi was struggling patriotically with his brother's Copersucar, and the declining Shadow team fielded two cars

for Pryce and an unhappy Jarier. He wanted to drive the V12 Matra-engined Ligier alongside Laffite, but his contract was binding. Two Surtees TS19s appeared for Jones and Lunger, the Williams-Wolf team ran a single car for Ickx and a flock of privateers completed the field, including two girls – former English ski team captain Divina Galica in an ancient Surtees and Lombardi in a Brabham. Both were clearly no-hopers, though loved by the media.

Practice saw Hunt stealing the Champers for quickest time in the first session, and Lauda pipping him imperiously for pole position on the Saturday. Non-qualifiers were Ickx (having a handicapped season), Mike Wilds' hastily contrived Shadow and the two driver persons.

Lauda chose to start from the outside of the front row and *most* of the grid was rearranged accordingly, fastest on the left. Niki blasted away perfectly to leave Hunt hanging fire as Regazzoni walloped through from the second row, hugging the inside line into Paddock Bend. He was blamed for subsequent events, but TV film shot from the top of the hill suggests that Lauda also shouldered across, perhaps thinking it was Hunt charging up inside him.

The result was mayhem as Regazzoni's Ferrari crushed its left-hand radiator sponson against Lauda's right-rear wheel. The Austrian tore clear but his team-mate broadsided right in front of the pack! Hunt just failed to clear the Ferrari, careering up onto two wheels as rear tyres met. Amon miraculously dived through a narrowing gap under the bank but Laffite buried his Ligier deep into it. And then that was all . . .

In a terrific display of Grand Prix driving the rest of the massed pack surged clear, and chased away after Lauda. Regazzoni limped into the pits, having gushed livid green coolant all round the circuit, Hunt abandoned behind the new Paddock with a broken steering arm, and only the Ligier remained at Paddock Bend where a scattering of dust and stones lay on the track.

Just as spectators were thinking 'What a shame, Hunt, Regga and Laffite are out of it', red flags appeared on the startline in response to Paddock Observer Tony Salmon's priority call. The race was stopped 'due to debris on the track', and Lauda, Depailler and Andretti led the pack weaving to a halt between pits and grandstand.

1976 Grid

1
Lauda
(Ferrari 312T2/028)
1:19.35

11
Hunt
(McLaren-Cosworth M23/8)
1:19.41

5
Andretti
(Lotus-Cosworth 77/1)
1:19.76

2
Regazzoni
(Ferrari 312T2/027)*
1:20.05

4
Depailler
(Tyrrell-Cosworth P34/2)
1:20.15

22
Amon
(Ensign-Cosworth MN05)
1:20.27

10
Peterson
(Matra-Cosworth 761/3)
1:20.29

3
Scheckter
(Tyrrell-Cosworth P34/3)
1:20.31

35
Merzario
(March-Cosworth 761/4)
1:20.32

9
Brambilla
(March-Cosworth 761/1)
1:20.36

28
Watson
(Penske-Cosworth PC4-01)
1:20.41

12
Mass
(McLaren-Cosworth M23/6)
1:20.61

26
Laffite
(Ligier-Matra JS5/02)*
1:20.67

6
Nilsson
(Lotus-Cosworth 77/2)
1:20.67

7
Reutemann
(Brabham-Alfa Romeo BT45/3)
1:20.99

8
Pace
(Brabham-Alfa Romeo BT45/1)
1:21.03

34
Stuck
(March-Cosworth 761/2)
1:21.20

18
Lunger
(Surtees-Cosworth TS19/03)
1:21.30

19
Jones
(Surtees-Cosworth TS19/02)
1:21.42

16
Pryce
(Shadow-Cosworth DN5/5B)
1:21.84

30
Fittipaldi
(Copersucar-Cosworth FD04/03)
1:22.06

32
Evans
(Brabham-Cosworth BT44B/1)
1:22.47

24
Ertl
(Hesketh-Cosworth 308/3)
1:22.75

17
Jarier
(Shadow-Cosworth DN5/4B)
1:22.72

25
Edwards
(Hesketh-Cosworth 308/2)
1:22.76

38
Pescarolo
(Surtees-Cosworth TS19/01)
1:22.76

*After the original first corner accident, Regazzoni drove 312T/026 and Laffite JS5/01 in the restarted race.

Non-qualifiers: 13 Galica (Surtees TS16/05) 1:25.24 – 20 Ickx (Williams FW05/03) 1:23.32 – 33 Lombardi (Brabham BT44B/2) 1:27.08 – 40 Wilds (Shadow DN3B/5) 1:25.66.

Now came the question of who should restart? The Stewards decided that no competitors who failed to complete that first lap would be eligible, no spare cars would be allowed, but that the original opening lap should be forgotten and the race restarted to run its full distance. If it had been restarted to run the *remainder* of the distance it would have been logical to exclude those cars disabled by the accident, but now the row began.

Hunt, Regazzoni and Laffite all appeared on the grid in their spare cars, and while the commentator described the scene, with all three being ordered out of the race, a swelling roar of disapproval boomed from 77,000 jeering throats. If the race had continued this would never have happened, Hunt's misfortune would have been accepted as an occupational hazard, but now England's hero was to be sidelined by bureaucracy.

Nobody seemed to recall the telling precedent of the 1973 restart, from which Lauda's BRM led away after having been left on the original grid with only three wheels on the car!

Undoubtedly the Stewards were taken aback by the crowd's vociferously hostile reaction, virtually unprecedented at a British race. While they wavered McLaren's mechanics worked furiously to repair the damaged M23's steering, and ecstatic cheers greeted its reappearance on the grid as Hunt slid down into the cockpit and his spare was returned to its garage. Now the Stewards capitulated, it was evident that Hunt had been moving at the precise moment the red flag had been shown, and therefore he was eligible to restart by the letter of the law. One wonders why more sober consideration of the law had not been made before the original decision was reached?

Ferrari and Ligier elected to start their spare cars anyway and argue it out afterwards, and from the flag the second British GP of the year saw Lauda, Hunt, Regazzoni, Amon and the rest streaming cleanly through Paddock Bend and up to Druids. Having brilliantly avoided trouble first time round, the tail-enders now fell over each other. Edwards

abandoned his battered Hesketh on the infield, while up at the Hairpin Peterson and Depailler met, and Stuck crashed in avoidance. Andretti was left on the grid!

Amon's engine was off-tune, and the race settled down with Lauda storming round ahead of a simmering James Hunt – pained by a damaged thumb – a rather muted Regazzoni, Scheckter, Brambilla and Peterson. Andretti took off over two laps late after a spark-box change, and dropped out smartly with engine failure. Amon was losing water which eventually cooked his engine, so the gallant Ensign challenge folded. Laffite and Regazzoni had their 'illegal entries' fail under them which seemed to be saving the Stewards some post-race deliberation, while Brambilla overheated his left-front tyre and had to stop for a wheel-change, eventually retiring when a suspension pick-up pulled out after a bump with Peterson.

Merzario has always liked Brands Hatch and he closed on Peterson in fifth place, and inherited it as the Swede stopped to change a wheel in an identical tyre failure to Brambilla's. Peterson was beset by a series of stops after bouncing off his team-mate at Druids. From lap 15 to lap 37 when Regazzoni's oil pressure zeroed the leader board showed Lauda leading Hunt, Regazzoni, Scheckter, Merzario and Nilsson. Watson had shattered the Penske's nose on Merzario's March on lap 8 and rejoined nineteenth after a pit stop. His charge through the field became a major feature of the race as he won some places, was presented with others as mechanical misfortune struck those ahead of him, and soared towards the leaders. He lost eighth place in a spin at Druids, rejoining eleventh behind Reutemann and the Surtees. Merzario's March threw a drive shaft on lap 40 to promote the bearded Ulsterman to tenth place, and on lap 47 he displaced Jones to tackle the battling duo of

The British GP's annual pile-up; first lap, first bend. Hunt (11) is back on four wheels, Regazzoni sits quietly steaming in mid-track while Laffite (26) is still airborne.

Pryce and Nilsson in Shadow and Lotus respectively.

Meanwhile Lauda had been holding around six seconds lead from Hunt until the Ferrari's gearbox began to play tricks, on occasion, selecting fifth instead of third. Hunt loomed closer, driving at his hardest and best. On lap 35 he flayed round the circuit in 1:20.38 for a new fastest lap. On lap 38 he lowered it to 20.35. Lap 41 – Lauda streaked round in 19.91. Lap 44 – Hunt had it again at 19.82!

With the huge crowd willing him on Hunt suddenly found the elusive Ferrari slowing early into the corners as Lauda searched carefully for an accurate down-change. On lap 45 the McLaren nudged alongside into Druids' Hairpin, and emerged from behind the trees in the lead!

Lauda settled back to protect his second place, for Hunt was charging away remorselessly in the McLaren, drawing out a long and increasing lead. Scheckter's third place looked as secure as Lauda's second, and as Pryce's Shadow misfired and Nilsson's Lotus blew-up to end a courageous drive so Watson was given fourth place when he looked set to take it on merit. Now only ten cars were still running.

Hunt charged on to become the first English winner of the British GP since Peter Collins' memorable – but sadly soon overshadowed – success for Ferrari in 1958. As the huge crowd gave Hunt a deliriously happy reception so Lauda toured across the line a relieved second and still safely ahead in the World Championship chase; Scheckter was third, Watson an immensely popular and impressive fourth, ahead of Pryce, Jones, Fittipaldi and the rest.

Then the protests began, as Ferrari, Tyrrell and Copersucar all objected to Hunt's restart. After hearing eye-witness accounts of the Paddock Bend incident Tyrrell and Copersucar withdrew their protests, accepting that Hunt had been mobile at the moment the red flag was shown and therefore was eligible to take the restart. Ferrari, led by lawyer Montezemolo, were not so sure and decided to take the matter to appeal. They remembered the last GP race at Brands Hatch, and openly considered the British organisers to be quite incapable of running a World Championship motor race.

It was fifty years from that first Grand Prix at Brooklands . . . fifty years, a different world, and a different sport away – but *what* fantastic entertainment this great British sporting institution had become . . .

Results

1 J.S.W. Hunt* (2.99 McLaren-Cosworth – Marlboro Team McLaren), 1 hr 43 mins 27.61 secs, 115.19 mph; **2** N. Lauda (2.99 Ferrari – SpA Ferrari SEFAC), 1 hr 44 mins 19.66 secs; **3** J. Scheckter (2.99 Tyrrell-Cosworth – ELF Team Tyrrell), 1 hr 44 mins 35.84 secs; **4** J. Watson (2.99 Penske-Cosworth – Citibank Team Penske), 75 laps; **5** T. Pryce (2.99 Shadow-Cosworth – Shadow Racing) 75 laps; **6** A. Jones (2.99 Surtees-Cosworth – Durex Team Surtees) 75 laps; **7** E. Fittipaldi (2.99 Copersucar-Cosworth – Copersucar-Fittipaldi) 74 laps; **8** H. Ertl (2.99 Hesketh-Cosworth – Hesketh Racing) 73 laps; **9** C. Pace (2.99 Brabham-Alfa Romeo – Martini Racing) 73 laps; **10** J.-P. Jarier (2.99 Shadow-Cosworth – Shadow Racing) 70 laps.

FASTEST LAP Hunt, 1 min 19.82 secs, 117.71 mph, on lap 44.

RETIREMENTS G. Edwards (2.99 Hesketh-Cosworth – Penthouse Rizla Racing), 0 laps, collision; H.J. Stuck (2.99 March-Cosworth – March Racing) 0 laps, accident; J. Mass (2.99 McLaren-Cosworth – Marlboro Team McLaren) 1 lap, clutch; M. Andretti (2.99 Lotus-Cosworth – JPTL) 4 laps, engine; C. Amon (2.99 Ensign-Cosworth – Team Ensign) 8 laps, water loss; H. Pescarolo (2.99 Surtees-Cosworth – Team Norev) 16 laps, fuel pressure; V. Brambilla (2.99 March-Cosworth – Beta Team March) 22 laps, suspension pick-up failure; B. Evans (2.99 Brabham-Cosworth – RAM Racing), 24 laps, gearbox; J. Laffite (2.99 Ligier-Matra – Ligier Gitanes) 31 laps, rear suspension pick-up failure/disqualified; G. Regazzoni (2.99 Ferrari – SpA Ferrari SEFAC) 36 laps, engine/disqualified; A. Merzario (2.99 March-Cosworth – Ovoro Team March) 39 laps, engine; C. Reutemann (2.99 Brabham-Alfa Romeo – Martini Racing) 46 laps, oil pressure; P. Depailler (2.99 Tyrrell-Cosworth – ELF Team Tyrrell) 47 laps, engine; B. Lunger (2.99 Surtees-Cosworth – Chesterfield Team Surtees) 55 laps, gearbox; R. Peterson (2.99 March-Cosworth – March Racing) 60 laps, fuel pressure, engine; G. Nilsson (2.99 Lotus-Cosworth – JPTL) 67 laps, engine.

* Subsequently disqualified by an FIA Appeal hearing in Paris, 24 September 1976. All other finishers elevated one place.

Hunt dives through on the inside of Lauda at the top of Druid's on lap 45

The Rewards

In 1926, the RAC invited entries for their first Grand Prix, asking fees of £50 for one car, or £120 for a three-car team. No single entrant was allowed to field more than five cars (or so they said), and in return for this fee the Club offered no less than £1,000 prize money for first place, £300 for second and £200 for third.

At that time, manufacturers were used to paying for their racing. In 1924 Sunbeam spent the present-day equivalent of some £280,000 to run three cars in just two Grand Prix races, but while the construction of such cars had once been a speculative investment, the currency of Grand Prix success had been sadly debased by the mid-'twenties. Formerly, success had reaped huge rewards. When Sunbeam dominated the 1912 *Coupe de l'Auto* race, and finished 3–4–5 in the concurrent Grand Prix de l'ACF, the company followed up with a profit of 80 per cent on their share capital. From 1910–13 Sunbeam's profits trebled, and it was largely thanks to their racing success.

Unfortunately, as Grand Prix racing proliferated, so did the motor car itself. The percentage of buyers attracted by racing success was a modest drop in the ocean for most manufacturers. But for some, like Louis Delage, and Louis Coatalen of Sunbeam-Talbot-Darracq, the urge to enter racing was irresistible. Eventually it ruined them both.

When the German state-backed teams became dominant in the 'thirties, times had changed. Now major works teams could expect to be paid for investing money in motor sport, and they demanded considerable appearance money and expenses. When Fred Craner attracted them to Donington Park in 1937 and 1938 he had to dig deep into the Derby and District Motor Club's coffers to raise the necessary capital.

Donington's prize list seemed meagre when compared to the Brooklands awards of the preceding decade, but of course the team's starting fees were hidden, and now they were out-going from the Club rather than in-coming. First prize was £250, plus a year's tenure of the Donington Trophy (with replica). Second to fifth places received £120, £75, £50 and £25 respectively, plus a Donington statuette. A Donington plaque consoled any runner able to complete seventy laps within the time allowance.

When the RAC revived their own race at Silverstone in 1948, only the major Continentals and per-haps a few favoured 'names' from home could expect starting money or expenses. First place carried £500 prize money, second £300 and third £200, while fourth to tenth places were rewarded on a sliding scale: £100, £75, £50, £40, £30, £25 and £20. RAC plaques went to all finishers, and for the 1950 race they were joined by the revived Mervyn O'Gorman Trophy, and the Fred G. Craner Memorial Trophy.

Mervyn O'Gorman had been a prominent Committee Member of the pre-war Brooklands Automobile Racing Club, and his classical gilded trophy had originated in the dark ages. Now it was to go to the race winner, while the Craner Trophy was destined for the best British finisher at the wheel of a British car.

Poor Fred G. Craner had died suddenly in January 1949, at the early age of 54, and in succeeding years his Trophy suffered a wretched series of affronts. When the BRDC took over the race in 1952 their programme referred to the 'Fred C. Craner' Trophy, and transposed its photograph with that of O'Gorman's. This C. instead of G. business persisted for several years, and in 1965 poor Fred's Cup became known as the 'Fred Cramer Trophy' in the Silverstone programme.

In 1972 the old, unfashionable Mervyn O'Gorman Trophy was retired, to be replaced by a modern Trophy donated by the race's commercial sponsors, but the 'Fred Craner Trophy', without that difficult middle initial, survived one more season, to disappear in 1973, just as an award to the first British car-and-driver combination began to have meaning once more.

The cash awards remained largely unaltered over the years, even in 1955 when the race went to Aintree. While *The Daily Express* had been presenting a cup each year to be awarded outright to the Silverstone winner, now *The Daily Telegraph* performed that function at the Liverpool circuit, and then in 1957 for the Grand Prix d'Europe, the BARC slashed their starting money inducements, and with support from the Aintree management put up horse-race style money instead; 2,500 guineas for the winner, 1,500 guineas for second, 1,000 guineas for third and 500 guineas for fourth. A further 200 guineas was awarded for the first 90 mph lap, and the Aintree Automobile Racing Company put up a £100 Trophy to be won outright. This was the first time that the first prize money alone exceeded the RAC's original 1926 figure.

Silverstone replied in 1958 with a scale of £750, £350, £125, £80, £50, £40, £30, £20 for the first eight places, and in 1959 the Aintree organizers again mystified Continental entrants with guinea prizes, starting at 1,000 for first place.

Not until 1965 was Silverstone prize money jacked-up from £750 to £1,000, and then at Brands Hatch in 1970 the Formula 1 Manufacturers' murky machinations showed their unmistakable thumbprint. Awards were listed in Swiss Francs, beginning with 1,000 SF (converted to £96 10s 6d) for pole position. For the race itself, a sliding payments scale made awards at twenty, forty, sixty laps and the finish, the interim payments beginning at 4,000SF (£386 2s 0d] for the leader. The overall winner trousered 20,000SF (£1,930 10s 0d], and another scale extended payments down to twentieth place. Lap-charting took on a whole new dimension! That 1970 event was heralded as 'Britain's most expensive race', with a £70,000 budget for the whole meeting, £32,000 of which went to the Grand Prix field.

Back at Silverstone for 1971, just the prize money for the meeting totalled £39,259. In 1972 the RAC announced 'In accordance with the decision of the CSI a prize fund of 420,000 Swiss Francs will be distributed according to the race order at nineteen, thirty-eight, fifty-seven and seventy-six laps'.

By 1973 awards at seventeen, thirty-four and fifty-one laps and the finish saw payments of £665.33 for the leader down to £43.33 for twentieth place, with final prize monies of £3,405 for the winner, sliding to £170 for twentieth place. Now, to run twentieth throughout the British Grand Prix would yield £343.32, or £43.32 more than the second-place Alfa Romeo won in 1950, and nearly £100 more than Rosemeyer and Nuvolari received for *winning* at Donington pre-war!

By 1975 Formula 1 financing was considered far too technical a matter for public eyes, and these words enshrouded the subject for all time: 'The financial budget for the . . . Grand Prix is £85,962.50 and will be paid in total to the Formula 1 Association for distribution to the entrants'.

Few of the thousands who paid to fight their way into Silverstone would think they saw value for that kind of money, but then, times do change, and the 1926–27 crowds at Brooklands should really have thought so too . . .

Appendix: The Drivers

*Race winners

Abecassis, George (GB) 1949
Adamich, Andrea de (I) 1971–3
Allison, Cliff (GB] 1958
Amon, Chris (NZ) 1963–5, 1967–73, 1976
Anderson, Bob (Rh) 1963–7
 Killed, Silverstone, 1967
Andretti, Mario (US) 1970, 1975–6
Ansell, Geoffrey (GB) 1948–9
Ansell, R.E. (GB) 1948–9
Arundell, Peter (GB) 1966
Ashdown, Peter (GB) 1959
Ashmore, Fred (GB) 1949
Ashmore, Gerry (GB) 1961
*Ascari, Alberto (I) 1948, 1951–4
 Killed, Monza, 1955
Aston, Bill (GB) 1952
Attwood, Richard (GB) 1964–5, 1968

Baghetti, Giancarlo (I) 1961, 1963–4
Bainbridge, G.H. (GB) 1948
Bandini, Lorenzo (I) 1961, 1963–6
 Killed, Monaco GP, 1967
Baring, A.A. (GB) 1949
Baron, Arthur (GB) 1936
Baumer, Walter (D) 1938
 Killed in action, 1939–45
Beaufort, Carel G. de 1961–3
 Killed, Nurburgring, 1964
Beauman, Don (GB) 1954
 Killed, Wicklow, 1955
Becke, A.W.K. von der (NL) 1935
Begue, René Le (F) 1936
Behra, Jean (F) 1953–8
 Killed, AVUS, 1959
Bell, Derek (GB) 1969, 1971
Bell, Peter (GB) 1948
Beltoise, Jean-Pierre (F) 1968–74
*Benoist, Robert (F) 1926–7
 Executed, Buchenwald, 1944
Beuttler, Mike (GB) 1971–3
Bianchi, Lucien (B) 1960–1, 1968
 Killed, Le Mans, 1969
Bianco, Gino 1952
'Bira, B.' (Si) 1935–7, 1948–50, 1953–4
Bolster, John (GB) 1949
Bondurant, Bob (US) 1966
Bonetto, Felice (I) 1951, 1953
 Killed, Carrera PanAmericana, 1953

Bonnier, Jo (S) 1958–69
 Killed, Le Mans 24-Hrs, 1972
Bordino, Pietro (I] 1927
 Killed, Alessandria, 1928
Bourlier, Edmond (F) 1926–7
*Brabham, Jack (AUS) 1955–68, 1970
Brambilla, Vittorio (I) 1974–6
Brandon, Eric (GB) 1952
Brauchitsch, Manfred von (D) 1937–8
Briault, D.L. (GB) 1936
Brise, Tony (GB) 1975
 Killed, plane crash, 1975
Bristow, Chris (GB) 1959
 Killed, Belgian GP, 1960
*Brooks, Tony (GB) 1956–61
Brown, Alan (GB) 1952–4
Bucci, Clemar (ARG) 1954
Bueb, Ivor (GB) 1957–9
 Killed, Clermont, 1959
Burgess, Ian (GB) 1958–63

Campbell, Malcolm (GB) 1926–7
 Died, 19
Campbell-Jones, John (GB) 1963
Cantoni, Heitel (I) 1952
Caracciola, Rudolf (D) 1937
Carriere, René (F) 1936
Castellotti, Eugenio (I) 1955–6
 Killed, Modena, 1957
Cevert, Francois (F) 1970–3
 Killed, Watkins Glen, 1973
Chamberlain, Jay (US) 1962
Charlton, Dave (SA) 1971–2
Chiron, Louis (F) 1927, 1948–51
Claes, Johnny (B) 1949–52
*Clark, Jim (GB) 1960–7
 Killed, Hockenheim, 1968
Clarke, T.G. (GB) 1936
*Collins, Peter (GB) 1952–8
 Killed, German Grand Prix, 1958
Comotti, Gianfranco (I) 1948
Connell, I.F. (GB) 1936, 1938?
Conelli, Count Carlos (I) 1927
Cotton, Billy (GB) 1938, 1949
Courage, Piers (GB) 1967–69
 Killed, Dutch Grand Prix, 1970
Crawford, Jim (GB) 1975
Crook, Anthony (GB) 1952–3

Crossley, Geoffrey (GB) 1950

Daigh, Chuck (US) 1960
Davis, S.C.H. (GB) 1927
Depailler, Patrick (F) 1974–6
Divo, Albert (F) 1926
Dobbs, H.G. (GB) 1935–6
Dobson, Arthur
Dobson, Austin
Don, Kaye (GB) 1936
Donohue, Mark (US) 1975
    Killed, Osterreichring, 1975
Downing, Ken (GB) 1952
Dreyfus, René (F) 1938
Driscoll, Pat (GB) 1935
Dubonnet, André (F) 1926

Eaton, George (C) 1970
Eccles, A.H. Lindsay (GB) 1935
Edwards, Guy (GB) 1974, 1976
Elford, Vic (GB) 1968–9
Emery, Paul (GB) 1956
Ertl, Harald (A), 1976
Etancelin, Phillippe (F) 1948–51
Evans, Bob (GB), 1976
Evans, Dennis (GB) 1936
Evans, Kenneth (GB) 1936
Everitt, W.G. (GB) 1935
Eyston, George (GB) 1926–7

Fagioli, Luigi (I) 1950
    Killed, Monaco, 1952
Fairfield, Pat (SA) 1935
Fairman, Jack (GB) 1953, 1955–61
Falkner, M.F.L. (GB) 1936
*Fangio, Juan-Manuel (ARG) 1950–1, 1953–7
Farina, Giuseppe (I) 1950–3
    Killed on road, 1966
Fischer, Rudi (CH) 1952
*Fittipaldi, Emerson (BRA) 1970–6
Fittipaldi, Wilson (BRA) 1972–3, 1975
Fletcher, 1938
Flockhart, Ron (GB) 1954, 1956, 1959
    Killed, plane crash 1962
Folland, Dudley (GB) 1948
Follmer, George (US) 1973
Fotheringham-Parker, Philip (GB] 1949, 1951
Fry, Joe (GB) 1950
    Killed, Blandford, 1950
Featherstonhaugh, 'Buddy' 1935

Galli, Giovanni (I) 1971–2
Gallop, Clive (GB) 1926
Ganley, Howden (NZ) 1971, 1973
Gardner, Frank (AUS) 1964–5
Gaze, Tony (AUS) 1952

Gerard, Bob (GB) 1948–51, 1953–4, 1956–7
Gereini, Gerino (I) 1958
Gethin, Peter (GB) 1971–2, 1974
Ghika, Prince 1927
Gilbey, S.J. (GB) 1948
Ginther, Richie (US) 1961–5
Giraud-Cabantous, Yves (F) 1949–50
Godia-Sales, Francesco (E) 1956
*Gonzales, J. Froilan (ARG) 1951, 1953–4, 1956
Gould, Horace (GB) 1954–7
*Graffenried, Baron E. de 1949–50, 1952
Greene, Keith (GB) 1959–62
Gregory, Masten (US) 1959–63, 1965
Gubby, Brian (GB) 1965
Gurney, Dan (US) 1960–70
Gendebien, Olivier (B) 1956, 1960

Hailwood, Mike (GB) 1963–4, 1972–4
Halford, Bruce (GB) 1956
Halford, Frank (GB) 1926
Hamilton, Duncan (GB) 1948–9, 1951–3
Hampshire, David (GB) 1948–50
Handley, Wal (GB) 1935
    Killed, 1939–45
Hanson, Robin (GB) 1937–8
Harrison, Cuth (GB) 1948–50
Harvey, Maurice (GB) 1926–7
Hasse, Rudolf (D) 1937–8
    Killed in action, 1944
Hawthorn, Mike (GB) 1952–8
    Killed on road, 1959
Hall, Jim (US) 1963
Henton, Brian (GB) 1975
Herrmann, Hans (D) 1959
Hill, Graham (GB) 1958–74
    Killed, plane crash, 1975
Hill, Phil (US) 1960–4
Hirt, Peter 1952
Hobbs, David (GB) 1967
Howe, The Earl Francis (GB) 1935, 1937
Hulme, Denny (NZ) 1965–74
Hunt, James (GB) 1973–6
Hyde, A.B. (GB) 1937

Ickx, Jacky (B) 1968–74
Ireland, Innes (GB) 1960–5
Irwin, Chris (GB) 1966–7

James, John (GB] 1951
Jarier, Jean-Pierre (F) 1974–6
Johnson, Leslie (GB) 1948, 1950
Jones, Alan (AUS) 1975–6
Jones, Tom (US) 1968
Jucker, Philip F. (GB) 1936
    Killed, Isle of Man, 1937

Kautz, Christian (CH) 1936, 1938
  Killed, Swiss Grand Prix, 1948
Kelly, Joe (IRE) 1951
Kling, Karl (D) 1954–5

Laffite, Jacques (GB) 1975–6
Lanfranchi, Tony (GB) 1968
Lang, Hermann (D) 1937–8
Lauda, Niki (A) 1972–6
Lawrence, Chris [GB] 1966
Leitch, A. (GB) 1936
Leston, Les (GB) 1957
Lewis, The Hon. Brian (GB) 1935
Lewis-Evans, Stuart (GB) 1957–8
  Killed, Moroccan Grand Prix, 1958
Lewis, Jack (GB) 1961–2
Ligier, Guy (F) 1966–7
Lombardi, Signa. Lella (I) 1974–5
Lovely, Pete (US) 1970
Lunger, Brett (US), 1976

Macklin, Lance (GB) 1952–3, 1955
Maclure, Percy (GB) 1936–8
McAlpine, Kenneth (GB) 1952–3, 1955
McLaren, Bruce (NZ) 1959–69
  Killed, Goodwood, 1970
McRae, Graham (NZ) 1973
Maggs, Tony (SA) 1961–4
Maglioli, Umberto (I) 1956
Manzon, Robert 1951–2, 1954–6
Marimon, Onofre (ARG) 1953–4
  Killed, Nurburgring, 1954
Marr, Leslie (GB) 1954–5
Marsh, Tony (GB) 1961
Martin, Charlie (GB) 1935–7
Martin, Eugene (F) 1950
Mass, Jochen (D) 1973–6
Mathieson, T.A.S.O. (GB) 1949
Mays, Raymond (GB) 1937, 1948–9
Menditeguy, Carlos (ARG) 1957
Merzario, Arturo (I) 1972, 1974, 1976
Monkhouse, Peter (GB) 1938
  Killed, Mille Miglia, 1950
Morgan, David (GB) 1975
Moriceau, Jean (F) 1926
Moser, Silvio (CH) 1967–8
  Killed, Monza, 1974
Moss, Bill (GB) 1959
*Moss, Stirling (GB) 1952, 1954–9, 1961
Muller, H.P. (D) 1937–8
Munaron, Gino (I) 1960
Murray, David (GB) 1949–52
Musso, Luigi (I) 1955, 1957
  Killed, French Grand Prix, 1958
Mieres, Roberto (ARG) 1954–5
Miles, John (GB) 1969–70
Migault, Francois (F) 1973–4

Nasif, Estefano (ARG) 1963
Natili, Masimo (I) 1961
Naylor, Brian (GB) 1959–60
Nazzaro, Felice (I) 1927
Nicholson, John (GB) 1975
Nilsson, Gunnar (S), 1976
Nixon, George (GB) 1948–9
Nuckey, Rodney (GB) 1954
*Nuvolari, Tazio (I) 1938

Oliver, Jack (GB) 1968–73
Oliver, Mike (GB) 1956
Opel, Rikky von (L) 1973
d'Orey, Fritz (CH) 1959

Pace, Jose Carlos (BRA) 1972–6
Parker, R.F. (GB) 1948
Parkes, Mike (GB) 1959
Parnell, Reg (GB) 1936, 1948–52, 1954
Parnell, Tim (GB) 1959, 1961
Paul, Cyril (GB) 1935
Pescarolo, Henri (F) 1970–4, 1976
Peterson, Ronnie (S) 1970–6
Pilette, André (B) 1954
Piper, David (GB) 1959–60
Poore, Dennis (GB) 1952
Portago, Alfonse de (E) 1956
  Killed, Mille Miglia, 1957
Powys-Lybbe, Anthony (GB) 1936–7
Pryce, Tom (GB) 1974–6
Purdy, Harold (GB) 1927

Raby, Ian (GB) 1963–5
  Killed, Zandvoort, 1967
Ramos, Hernano da Silva 1955–6
'Raph, Georges' (F) 1938
Redman, Brian (GB) 1969–70
Rees, Alan (GB) 1967
Regazzoni, Gianclaudio (CH) 1970–1, 1973–6
Reutemann, Carlos (ARG) 1972–6
*Revson, Peter (US) 1964, 1972–3
  Killed, Kyalami, 1974
Rhodes, John (GB) 1965
Richardson, Geoffrey (GB) 1948–9
Richardson, Ken (GB) 1949
*Rindt, Jochen (A) 1965–70
  Killed, Monza, 1970
Rodriguez, Pedro (MEX) 1967–70
  Killed, Norisring, 1971
Rollinson, Alan (GB) 1965
Rolt, Tony (GB) 1948–50, 1953, 1955
Rose, Harry (GB) 1935
Rosier, Louis (F) 1948–54, 1956
  Killed, Montlhery, 1956
Rovere, Gino (I) 1935

Rosemeyer, Bernd (D) 1937
  Killed, record attempt, 1938
Riseley-Prichard, John (GB) 1954
*Ruesch, Hans (CH) 1936

Salamano, Carlo (I) 1927
Salvadori, Roy (GB) 1948–9, 1952–62
Sanesi, Consalvo (I) 1951
*Scheckter, Jody (ZA) 1973–6
Schell, Harry (F/US) 1949, 1952, 1954–9
  Killed, Silverstone, 1960
Schell, Laurie (F) 1936
Schenken, Tim (AUS) 1971–2, 1974
Scott-Brown, Archie (GB) 1956
  Killed, Spa, 1958
Scott, W.B. (GB) 1927
Scribbans, Dennis (GB) 1936
*Seaman, Dick (GB) 1936–8
  Killed, Belgian Grand Prix, 1939
Segrave, Henry O'N. de H. (GB) 1926
  Killed, record attempt, Windermere 1930
Seidel, Wolfgang (D) 1961–2
Selborne, A. (GB) 1936
*Senechal, Robert (F) 1926
Settember, Tony (US) 1962–3
Shelby, Carroll (US) 1958–9
Shelly, Tony (NZ) 1962
*Shuttleworth, Richard (GB) 1935
  Killed in action, 1940
*Siffert, Jo (CH) 1963–71
  Killed, Brands Hatch, 1971
Simon, André (F) 1951, 1955
Sommer, Raymond (F) 1935
  Killed, Cadours, 1950
Souders, George (US) 1927
Sparken, Mike (B) 1955
Spence, Mike (GB) 1964–7
  Killed, Indianapolis, 1968
Stacey, Alan (GB) 1958–9
  Killed, Belgian Grand Prix, 1960
Stewart, Ian (GB) 1953
*Stewart, Jackie (GB) 1965–73
Stewart, Jimmy (GB) 1953
Stommelen, Rolf (D) 1970–2
Stuck, Hans-Joachim (D) 1974–6

Surtees, John (GB) 1960–71
Swaters, Jacques (B) 1954
Shawe-Taylor, Brian (GB) 1948–51

Tapper, T.P. Cholmondeley- (NZ) 1936
Taruffi, Piero (I) 1952, 1955
Taylor, D. (GB) 1936
Taylor, Henry (GB) 1959–61
Taylor, John (GB) 1964, 1966
  Killed, German Grand Prix, 1966
Taylor, Mike (GB) 1959
Taylor, Trevor (GB) 1959? 1962–4, 1966
Thomas, J.G. Parry (GB) 1926
  Killed in record attempt, Pendine 1927
Thompson, Eric (GB) 1952
Thorne, Leslie (GB) 1954
Titterington, Desmond (GB) 1956
Tongue, Reggie (GB) 1936–7
Trintignant, Maurice (F) 1951–60, 1964
*Trips, Wolfgang G.B. von (D) 1958, 1960–1
  Killed, Italian Grand Prix, 1961

Villoresi, Luigi (I) 1948–9, 1951, 1953–4, 1956
Volonterio, Ottorino (CH) 1956

*Wagner**, Louis (F) 1926
Walker, Dave (AUS) 1972
Walker, Peter (GB) 1936, 1948–51, 1955
Watson, Gordon (GB) 1948
Watson, John (GB) 1973–6
Wharton, Ken (GB) 1952–5
  Killed, New Zealand, 1957
White, C. Mervyn (GB) 1936
  Killed, Cork, 1937
Whitehead, Graham (GB) 1952
Whitehead, Peter (GB) 1936–7, 1949, 1951–4
  Killed, Tour de France, 1958
Whitehouse, Bill (GB) 1954
  Killed, Reims, 1957
Widdows, Robin (GB) 1968
Wilkinson, 'Wilkie' 1938
Williamson, Roger (GB) 1973
  Killed, Dutch Grand Prix, 1973
Wisell, Reine (S) 1971

Index

144